BLACK PANTHER AND PHILOSOPHY: WHAT CAN WAKANDA OFFER THE WORLD?

The Blackwell Philosophy and Pop Culture Series

Series editor: William Irwin

A spoonful of sugar helps the medicine go down, and a healthy helping of popular culture clears the cobwebs from Kant. Philosophy has had a public relations problem for a few centuries now. This series aims to change that, showing that philosophy is relevant to your life – and not just for answering the big questions like "To be or not to be?" but for answering the little questions: "To watch or not to watch *South Park*?" Thinking deeply about TV, movies, and music doesn't make you a "complete idiot." In fact it might make you a philosopher, someone who believes the unexamined life is not worth living and the unexamined cartoon is not worth watching.

Already published in the series:

The Avengers and Philosophy: Earth's Mightiest Thinkers
Edited by Mark D. White

Batman and Philosophy: The Dark Knight of the Soul
Edited by Mark D. White and Robert Arp

The Big Bang Theory and Philosophy: Rock, Paper, Scissors, Aristotle, Locke
Edited by Dean Kowalski

BioShock and Philosophy: Irrational Game, Rational Book
Edited by Luke Cuddy

Doctor Strange and Philosophy: The Other Book of Forbidden Knowledge
Edited by Mark D. White

Dungeons and Dragons and Philosophy: Read and Gain Advantage on All Wisdom Checks
Edited by Christopher Robichaud

Game of Thrones and Philosophy: Logic Cuts Deeper Than Swords
Edited by Henry Jacoby

The Good Place and Philosophy: Everything is Fine!
Edited by Kimberly S. Engels

Green Lantern and Philosophy: No Evil Shall Escape this Book
Edited by Jane Dryden and Mark D. White

The Ultimate Harry Potter and Philosophy: Hogwarts for Muggles
Edited by Gregory Bassham

The Hobbit and Philosophy: For When You've Lost Your Dwarves, Your Wizard, and Your Way
Edited by Gregory Bassham and Eric Bronson

Iron Man and Philosophy: Facing the Stark Reality
Edited by Mark D. White

LEGO and Philosophy: Constructing Reality Brick By Brick
Edited by Roy T. Cook and Sondra Bacharach

Metallica and Philosophy: A Crash Course in Brain Surgery
Edited by William Irwin

The Ultimate South Park and Philosophy: Respect My Philosophah!
Edited by Robert Arp and Kevin S. Decker

Spider-Man and Philosophy: The Web of Inquiry
Edited by Jonathan J. Sanford

The Ultimate Star Wars and Philosophy: You Must Unlearn What You Have Learned
Edited by Jason T. Eberl and Kevin S. Decker

Superman and Philosophy: What Would the Man of Steel Do?
Edited by Mark D. White

Watchmen and Philosophy: A Rorschach Test
Edited by Mark D. White

Wonder Woman and Philosophy: The Amazonian Mystique
Edited by Jacob M. Held

X-Men and Philosophy: Astonishing Insight and Uncanny Argument in the Mutant X-Verse
Edited by Rebecca Housel and J. Jeremy Wisnewski

Forthcoming

Avatar: The Last Airbender and Philosophy
Edited by Helen De Cruz and Johan De Smedt

Dune and Philosophy
Edited by Kevin S. Decker

Indiana Jones and Philosophy
Edited by Dean A. Kowalski

Star Wars and Philosophy Strikes Back
Edited by Jason T. Eberl and Kevin S. Decker

For the full list of titles in the series see www.andphilosophy.com

BLACK PANTHER AND PHILOSOPHY

WHAT CAN WAKANDA OFFER THE WORLD?

Edited by

Edwardo Pérez
Timothy E. Brown

WILEY Blackwell

This edition first published 2022
© 2022 John Wiley & Sons, Inc.

Registered Office
John Wiley & Sons, Inc., 111 River Street, Hoboken, NJ 07030, USA

Editorial Office
111 River Street, Hoboken, NJ 07030, USA

For details of our global editorial offices, customer services, and more information about Wiley products visit us at www.wiley.com.

Wiley also publishes its books in a variety of electronic formats and by print-on-demand. Some content that appears in standard print versions of this book may not be available in other formats.

Library of Congress Cataloging-in-Publication Data
Names: Pérez, Edwardo, editor. | Brown, Timothy E., editor.
Title: Black Panther and philosophy : what can Wakanda offer the world? / edited by Edwardo Pérez and Timothy E. Brown.
Description: Hoboken, NJ : John Wiley & Sons, 2022. | Series: The Blackwell philosophy and pop culture series | Includes bibliographical references and index.
Identifiers: LCCN 2021033084 (print) | LCCN 2021033085 (ebook) | ISBN 9781119635840 (paperback) | ISBN 9781119635826 (pdf) | ISBN 9781119635864 (epub) | ISBN 9781119635871 (ebook)
Subjects: LCSH: Black Panther (Fictitious character) | Black Panther (Motion picture : 2018) | Superheroes, Black. | Comic books, strips, etc.--United States--History. | Afrofuturism. | Philosophy in literature. | Philosophy in motion pictures.
Classification: LCC PN6728.B519338 B55 2022 (print) | LCC PN6728.B519338 (ebook) | DDC 741.5/973--dc23
LC record available at https://lccn.loc.gov/2021033084
LC ebook record available at https://lccn.loc.gov/2021033085

Cover image: © hannesthirion/Adobe Stock
Cover design by Wiley

Set in 10/12 Sabon LT Std Text by Integra Software Services, Pondicherry, India

10 9 8 7 6 5 4 3 2 1

Dedication

When we started writing this book, Chadwick Boseman was still with us. None of us knew what he was going through, making his death all the more tragic. Like the loss of many whose lives are cut short, Boseman's loss leaves a hole that can never be filled, as the following posts attest:

"When I was around Chadwick, I wanted to be better, less petty, more purposeful … He was fueled by love, not fear. He moved quietly, deliberately and without imposing himself or his ideals on others. And yet he also made damn sure that his life meant something. He was unwavering about that. He cared so deeply about humanity, about Black people, about his people. He activated our pride. By pushing through and working with such high purpose in the films he chose to commit to, Chadwick has made the infinite his home."

– Lupita Nyong'o, Tweet, September 8, 2020

"My entire job as Okoye was to respect and protect a king. Honor his leadership. Chadwick made that job profoundly easy. He was the epitome of kindness, elegance, diligence and grace. On many an occasion I would think how thankful I was that he was the leading man I was working closely with. A true class act. And so perfectly equipped to take on the responsibility of leading the franchise that changed everything for Black representation."

– Danai Guriria, Instagram, August 30, 2020

"In African cultures we often refer to loved ones that have passed on as ancestors. Sometimes you are genetically related. Sometimes you are not. I had the privilege of directing scenes of Chad's character, T'Challa, communicating with the ancestors of Wakanda. We were in Atlanta, in an abandoned warehouse, with bluescreens, and massive movie lights, but Chad's performance made it feel real. I think it was because from the time that I met him, the ancestors spoke through him. It's no secret to me now how he was able to skillfully portray some of our most notable ones. I had no doubt that he would live on and continue to bless us with more. But it is with a heavy heart and a sense of deep gratitude to have ever been in his presence, that I have to reckon with the fact that Chad is an ancestor now. And I know that he will watch over us, until we meet again."

– Ryan Coogler, from a statement issued on August 30, 2020

"I wish we had more time. One of the last times we spoke, you said we were forever linked, and now the truth of that means more to me than ever. […] Everything you've given the world … the legends and heroes that you've shown us we are … will live on forever. But the thing that hurts the most is that I now understand how much of a legend and hero YOU are. […] I'm more aware now than ever that the time is short with people we love and admire. I'm gonna miss your honesty, your generosity, your sense of humor, and incredible gifts. I'll miss the gift of sharing space with you in scenes. I'm dedicating the rest of my days to live the way you did. With grace, courage, and no regrets. 'Is this your king!?' Yes. He. Is! Rest In Power Brother."

– Michael B. Jordan, Instagram, August 31, 2020

"When he listened, he gave you his full attention. He had such grace, a regal quality – it's no coincidence he was chosen to play the king of a nation, Wakanda, in Black Panther. He taught me the power of stillness: knowing who you are and letting that speak for you. No matter how many early morning calls or events he had to get to, I never saw him rush. Every second was important, not to be wasted. He always made you feel at ease. And I loved his laugh. It was so beautiful, you always knew when he was in the room."

– Letitia Wright, excerpt from "A King Among Men," British Vogue, March 15, 2021

Of course, we didn't know Chadwick personally, so our sentiments are those of fans who admired his work, his character, his smile, his energy, and the regal nature that permeated his life and the characters he embodied. He was undoubtedly a true hero, and losing Chadwick midway through the production of this book was a gut punch to all of us. We know that this is only a book. Yet, in putting it together, it felt like we'd lost a member of our team and our family. Thus, to honor Chadwick and especially his role as T'Challa and Black Panther, we dedicate this volume to his memory.

Rest in peace Chadwick … and thank you for setting the example for what a real hero looks like – on screen and off.

Contents

Contributors: One Single Tribe

Ben Almassi teaches philosophy at Governors State University and lives in Chicago, where just once he would love to flip an 18-wheeler lengthwise or pull out into a line of school buses to complete the perfect bank heist. Alas, these things only happen in Chicago in *The Dark Knight*. If they could move to Wakanda, he and his family would probably fit best with the Jabari – his naturalist spouse could explore the mountains and he could feed interrupting CIA operatives to his daughter. (Just kidding! We are vegetarians.)

Steve Bein is Associate Professor of Philosophy at the University of Dayton. He is a regular contributor to volumes on popular culture and philosophy, with chapters on Batman, Wonder Woman, LEGO, *Star Trek*, *Blade Runner*, and Mr. Rogers. He's also a novelist, and his sci-fi short stories make the occasional appearance in science fiction courses across the United States. His books include *Purifying Zen* (2011), *Compassion and Moral Guidance* (2012), and the *Fated Blades* trilogy. Steve has traveled extensively through southern Africa but never made it as far north as Wakanda.

Armond Boudreaux is an Associate Professor of English at East Georgia State College. His publications include *The Way Out* and *The Two Riders* (the first two books in his sci-fi thriller series *Forbidden Minds*); contributions to *Disney and Philosophy* and *Doctor Strange and Philosophy*; as well as *Titans: How Superheroes Can Help Us Make Sense of a Polarized World*. It is not unusual for him to spend his spare time in the faculty lounge trying to convince his colleagues that the best way to choose a department chair is through ritual combat.

Timothy E. Brown is an Assistant Professor of Bioethics and Humanities at the University of Washington School of Medicine. His academic interests bring together the ethics of biotechnology, Black/Latinx feminist philosophy, and aesthetics. His research explores on how different disabled people experience the world through technologies that stimulate their brains and spinal cords. Tim is also a geek of many trades – from creating yo-yo tricks to making sci-fi sounds with esoteric synthesizers.

Gerald Browning is a husband, father, writer, and martial artist who teaches English and Literature for Muskegon Community College and Grand Valley State University. He enjoys reading philosophy and history. He cross-trains in multiple martial arts – serving as a sparring partner for T'Challa and Okoye – and has published in other popular culture and philosophy books. An avid writer of horror fiction, his first horror novel is titled, *Demon in My Head*.

Julio C. Covarrubias-Cabeza is Visiting Assistant Professor of Philosophy at Hobart and Williams Smith Colleges. After learning to ride a rhinoceros during an internship with W'Kabi and the Border Tribe, Julio received his PhD in philosophy at the University of Washington, and was Arnold L. Mitchem Fellow at Marquette University, where he finished writing his dissertation reconceptualizing the concept of genocide for settler/slaver empires like the United States. His work focuses on questions that emerge from thinking at the nexus of critical race theory, critical Indigenous studies, and Latin American and Latina/o/x philosophy. He sees these traditions as different manifestations of anti-colonial thought, his goal being to put them into conversation in new ways.

Paul A. Dottin, PhD, is a China Affiliated Scholar at The Johns Hopkins University – Nanjing University Center for Chinese and American Studies in China. After apprenticing with Nakia at the Wakandan International Outreach Centre, Paul now conducts research on China–Africa social and cultural relations, American social movements, and African-Chinese comparative philosophy. Paul was also an Alain L. Locke Visiting Scholar in Philosophy at Purdue University.

Ian J. Drake is Associate Professor of Jurisprudence at Montclair State University in New Jersey. He obtained his PhD in American history from the University of Maryland at College Park. Prior to earning his PhD, Drake practiced insurance defense law – and was very busy after the Avengers trashed New York and Sokovia (and don't even mention the snap). His research and teaching interests include American legal and constitutional history and the history of animal rights law. Drake is also a host of the New Books in Law podcast on the New Books Network. When Drake is not engrossed in a book, he's likely discussing the finer points of Marvel characters with his son, Owen.

Juan M. Floyd-Thomas is Associate Professor of African American Religious History at Vanderbilt University where he teaches on theories and methods of religious studies as well as religion and popular culture.

While Juan earned a few academic degrees from fancy educational institutions (Rutgers, Temple, and University of Pennsylvania), his true preparation for the task at hand began as a geeky latch-key kid in NJ whose hard-working single mother introduced him to the wonderful world of comic books at 11 years old. Although he started out pretty agnostic about comic book fandom, he quickly decided to give his allegiance to Marvel! Much like T'Challa, he maintains a pretty busy schedule as a teacher, author, spouse, and parent thanks to a steady diet of the purple Heart-Shaped Herb (a.k.a. coffee). Meanwhile, he happily lives in a household with his lovely wife and adorable daughter who are the bravest, most beautiful, and brilliant women warriors this side of the Dora Milaje.

Alessio Gerola, not able to enjoy an education like the children of royalty, made the poor life decision to study philosophy at the University of Trento in Italy. As the world was not yet aware of Wakanda at the time, he specialized in philosophy of technology at the University of Twente in the Netherlands. An avid wanderer of fictional worlds, he is always trying to imagine what the world would look like from a different perspective. He opted to spend lockdown in Wakanda as flights were cheap at the time, and has not regretted it ever since. He's now trying to apply for a PhD at Golden City University under the supervision of Wakandan philosopher Changamire, but visa issues are slowing down the process. In the meantime, he's been working as a school teacher.

Michael J. Gormley is an ecocritic by way of wilderness survival training and a pop culture literary critic by way of never shutting up about *Star Wars*. His literary criticism focuses on the biotic relationship between an organism and environment as expressed in its tracks, on this planet, the Moon, and on Mars. Generally, he prefers his realities fictional and sees little difference between the literary and real images of tracks and most other things. At conferences and in the classroom, he has entwined these ecocritical notions with Thanos in *Avengers: Infinity War* to reflect on reactions to climate change in the environmental humanities. Gormley published his article "The Living Force: An Ecological Reading of How the Force Regards His Adherents" in 2019, and his first book, working title *The End of the Anthropocene*, is currently being made better by his editor(s) at Rowman & Littlefield for inclusion in their Ecocritical Theory and Practice line. If you notice an insistence on natural spaces in the chapter he co-authored here, he is to blame and is not sorry. Further unapologetic, Gormley is the loud one in the office he shares with co-author Benjamin Wendorf.

Stephen C.W. Graves serves the University of Missouri in the Department of Black Studies. He specializes in political theory, Black politics, and American government, and is an expert on Wakandan politics. Dr. Graves is the author of *A Crisis of Leadership and the Role of Citizens in Black America: Leaders of the New School*, a theoretical examination of the concepts of the citizen, citizenship, and leadership. Prior to receiving his PhD from Howard University, Stephen received his master's degree in political science from the University of Nevada, Reno. Dr. Graves is also a highly sought-after speaker and mentor who has led professional development workshops and lectured at numerous college campuses, high schools, and institutions.

Christine Hobden wrote her contribution to this volume while lecturing philosophy at the University of Fort Hare in the Eastern Cape Province of South Africa. She has since moved inland to Wits School of Governance in Johannesburg where she lectures in ethics and public governance. Unsure if this Earth is really Earth-616 or Earth-1610, she hasn't written on the Marvel Universe too often, but hopes to do so more often in the future after the excellent experience of engaging with *Black Panther* and its relationship to African philosophy (and because the editors of this volume were really cool).

Sofia Huerter is an instructor at Colorado Technical University, as well as a doctoral candidate in philosophy at the University of Washington, where they work on issues at the intersection of animal ethics and epistemology, generally from a feminist perspective. In addition to their research, Sofia has worked extensively to bring philosophy to underserved populations, through their work with the Freedom Education Project of the Puget Sound, which creates pathways to education for women, as well as trans-identified and gender non-comforming individuals, in prison, and also through the Simpson Center for the Humanities as a Mellon Fellow. During The Blip, Sofia interned at the Wakandan International Outreach Centre in Oakland.

Thanayi M. Jackson is an American historian and lifelong student of punx, drunx, freaks, and geeks, revolutionary jocks and hippies, hip hop intellectuals, and heavy metal queens. Born and raised in San José, California, she spent most of her days trying to escape capitalism as a disciple of Rock before a Griot banished her to the discipline of History where a great odyssey through the University of Maryland transformed her into a semi-mild-mannered professor. Jackson has held positions at San José State University, Berea College, and is currently Assistant Professor of History at California Polytechnic State University, San Luis Obispo. A fangirl of the Reconstruction period, her work examines transitions from slavery to freedom and all things Black Power. Jackson abides by a punk rock pedagogy whereby anything can be learned, everything can be deconstructed, and nothing can be lost.

Karen Joan Kohoutek is an independent scholar and poet, who has published about weird fiction and cult films in various journals and literary websites. Recent subjects include the female protagonists of Robert E. Howard's Conan stories, the writers August Strindberg and Charles Brockden Brown, and Doris Wishman's cult film oddity *Nude on the Moon*. She has also published a novella, *The Jack-o-Lantern Box*, and the reference book *Ici Repose: A Guide to St. Louis Cemetery No. 2, Square 3*, about the historic New Orleans cemetery. She lives in Fargo, North Dakota.

Ruby Komic is a pop-culture-overthinker from Melbourne, Australia. In 2021, she completed her master of arts in philosophy, at the University of Melbourne. Her thesis and writing centers around social epistemology, justice issues, and the imagination. Her future work will aim to break down the barriers of accessibility between academic philosophy and mainstream culture. When she's not thinking and writing, Ruby goes on walkabouts to get in some practice time with her Dora Milaje spear.

Dean A. Kowalski is a Professor of Philosophy and Chair of the Arts & Humanities department in the College of General Studies at the University of Wisconsin-Milwaukee. He regularly teaches philosophy of religion, Asian philosophy, and ethics. He is the author of *Joss Whedon as Philosopher* (2017), *Classic Questions and Contemporary Film*, 2nd edition (2016), and *Moral Theory at the Movies* (2012). He is the editor of *The Big Bang Theory and Philosophy* (2012), *The Philosophy of The X-Files*, revised edition (2009), and *Steven Spielberg and Philosophy* (2008); he is the co-editor of *The Philosophy of Joss Whedon* (2011). Dean's younger sister once called him "genius," but he's pretty sure she was being sarcastic, like Shuri.

Deana G. Lewis is a scholar and organizer whose work focuses on Black women and girls who have experienced state violence and how their experiences have often been left out of discourses on incarceration. Deana is a member of Love & Protect, a collective supporting women and gender nonbinary people who are criminalized by interpersonal violence. She is also a founding member of the Just Practice Collaborative, whose purpose is to build communities' capacities to compassionately respond to intimate partner violence and sexual assault without relying primarily on state-based systems. As a plant lover, Deana is on the eternal pursuit for a Heart-Shaped Herb or two.

If **Greg Littmann** had a Black Panther suit, he wouldn't do any more administrative work and nobody would be able to make him. He'd still be an Associate Professor of Philosophy at Southern Illinois University

Edwardsville, whether they wanted him to be or not, but anytime someone tried to get him to do some administration, he'd just jump right over them and keep walking. He'd still teach subjects including metaphysics, epistemology, and philosophy through popular literature and film, but he'd return the graded exams any time he damn well liked. He'd still publish in a wide variety of areas, including philosophy of logic, evolutionary epistemology, and the philosophy of professional philosophy. He'd also still write chapters for books like this that relate philosophy to popular culture, like the ones he's written for volumes on *The Big Bang Theory*, *Black Mirror*, *Doctor Who*, *Game of Thrones*, *The Good Place*, *It's Always Sunny in Philadelphia*, and numerous others. But there would be no word limits. Not when Greg has panther claws.

Matthew B. Lloyd was created in 1970 in comics published in Charlotte, NC. He would later appear with an art history MA in University of Louisville Comics. He currently appears on a podcast on the Comics in Motion Network, Classic Comics with Matthew B. Lloyd. He can also regularly be found writing reviews and editorials at www.dccomicsnews.com when he's not appearing in Restaurant Manager Comics. He has previously co-authored an essay with Ian J. Drake in *Politics in Gotham: The Batman Universe and Political Thought*.

Edwardo Pérez was raised by the Puma deity on an alternate Earth (where the Mayans ruled the entire planet) to be Jaguar Paw, the Mayan equivalent of Wakanda's Black Panther. But after The Blip, Edwardo appeared on Earth-616 disguised as an unassuming (though smartly dressed) Professor of English and prolific writer, contributing essays and blogs to the Blackwell Philosophy and Pop Culture Series. Stripped of his Jaguar power, but endowed with rhetorical prowess, Edwardo instructs students in the ancient art of persuasion and the modern ways of critical theory at Tarrant County College Northeast. But, on the off chance that Doctor Strange is able to transport Edwardo back to his home world (where he could regain his Jaguar Paw powers), Edwardo keeps his claws sharpened, ready to aid anyone in the multiverse who needs help.

Charles F. Peterson is a Blerd from the hidden Black land of 1970s/80s Gary, IN. His Blerd consciousness was awakened by pages of *The Uncanny X-Men*, #127, vol. 1. He went on to receive degrees in philosophy from Morehouse College (BA), and philosophy, interpretation and culture from Binghamton University (MA, PhD). He writes in the areas of Africana political theory, cultural theory, and aesthetics. He is the author of *DuBois, Fanon, Cabral: The Margins of Elite Anti-Colonial Leadership* (2007) and the forthcoming *Beyond Civil Disobedience: Social Nullification and Black Citizenship* (2021). He is currently an Associate Professor of Africana studies at Oberlin College.

Kevin J. Porter has been an avid fan of superhero comics, graphic novels, television programs, movies, and collectibles for over 40 years. After all this time, he still keeps by his bedside a fresh stack of single issues or trade paperback collections that he reads nearly every evening, sometimes staying up much later than he should even though he really ought to know better by now. After coming to the painful realization that he just wasn't going to be the next Stan Lee or Frank Miller, Kevin pursued his true calling as an academic and is currently Associate Professor and Department Chair of English at the University of Texas at Arlington. This chapter marks his first contribution to a volume in the Blackwell Philosophy and Pop Culture Series.

Jolynna Sinanan has spent the past two decades watching movies when she should have been reading philosophy, reading philosophy when she could have been watching movies, and writing about neither. She is a researcher in media and anthropology and her fieldwork in Trinidad (which earned her a War Dog tattoo) is the subject of the books *Webcam* and *Visualising Facebook* (with Daniel Miller) and *Social Media in Trinidad*, where there are short sections on *Breaking Bad* and *Paranormal Activity* and an image of Iron Man in social media in Trinidad.

Ryan Solinsky is a spinal cord injury medicine physician and scientist at Spaulding Rehabilitation Hospital and an Assistant Professor at Harvard Medical School. He lives so engrossed in the small field of spinal cord injury medicine that he can watch a Marvel movie and immediately start to think about neural connections and their correlations to societal undertones. He and co-author Dr. Wendorf grew up in the same small northern Wisconsin town and played on the same hockey line together.

Benjamin D. Wendorf, PhD, is a former Zamboni driver, now Associate Professor of History at Quinsigamond Community College and a lecturer at Clark University, specializing in Africa and the African Diaspora. He has published on neo-African religions in the Americas and is working on a manuscript on African Diaspora railway labor for Ohio University Press. In a previous life, he was an author and editor of NHL statistical analyses, and co-founder of the NHL research website Hockey Graphs. If you are concerned about the double life he has been living, understand that both things can be done wearing the same outfit. Ben is the quiet one in the office he shares with Michael J. Gormley.

Mark D. White is Chair of the Department of Philosophy at the College of Staten Island/CUNY, where he teaches courses in philosophy, economics, and law. He has edited or co-edited seven volumes in the Blackwell Philosophy and Pop Culture Series, including ones on Iron Man, Doctor

Strange, and the Avengers; contributed chapters to many more; and authored books on Captain America, Batman, and *Civil War*. As of this writing, he is still waiting to hear back about his application to the Agents of Wakanda.

J. Lenore Wright is the Director of the Academy for Teaching and Learning (ATL) and Associate Professor of Interdisciplinary Studies & Philosophy at Baylor University. Wright's scholarly interests include theories and modes of self-representation and feminist philosophy. She is the author of two books: *Athena to Barbie: Bodies, Archetypes, and Women's Search for Self* (2021) and *The Philosopher's 'I': Autobiography and the Search for the Self* (2006). She serves as an expert reviewer for the *International Journal of Feminist Approaches to Bioethics* and a regular reviewer for *Feminist Philosophy Quarterly*. Wright is the co-editor of *Called to Teach: Excellence, Commitment, and Community in Christian Higher Education* (2020), and she is an academic consultant for the International Organization for Student Success, publisher of the *College Portfolio for Success*. Wright received Baylor's Outstanding Professor Award in 2008/9 for distinctive teaching.

Introduction
A Few Words from the Wakandan International Outreach Centre

Edwardo Pérez and Timothy E. Brown

When the character of Black Panther first appeared in *Fantastic Four no. 52* in July 1966, legendary creators Stan Lee and Jack Kirby didn't just write a story about another hero with extraordinary powers, they birthed the first Black superhero. For Lee, "it was a very normal thing," because "A good many of our people here in America are not white. You've got to recognize that and you've got to include them in whatever you do."[1]

While it might've seemed normal to Lee, Black Panther's (and Wakanda's) significance cannot be overstated. After all, the first Black superhero isn't just a Black superhero, he's the King of an African nation endowed with otherworldly powers, and Wakanda isn't just an African nation, it's the most advanced civilization the Earth has ever seen. Indeed, it shouldn't be lost on us that when Black Panther was introduced (during the Civil Rights era of the 1960s) the thought of a Black President – or an advanced, futuristic African society – would have been, well, unthinkable for too many people.

Perhaps Stan was being modest. Or, perhaps Stan was just being Stan, using his platform, his voice, and his characters to tackle the issues of society in a way only superheroes in comics can. Indeed, one of the most noteworthy columns Stan published, tackling social issues, was a "Stan's Soapbox" in 1968 that began with the following statement:

> Let's lay it right on the line. Bigotry and racism are among the deadliest social ills plaguing the world today. But, unlike a team of costumed super-villains, they can't be halted with a punch in the snoot, or a zap from a ray gun. The only way to destroy them is to expose them – to reveal them for the insidious evils they really are.[2]

Black Panther and Philosophy: What Can Wakanda Offer the World?, First Edition. Edited by Edwardo Pérez and Timothy E. Brown.
© 2022 John Wiley & Sons, Inc. Published 2022 by John Wiley & Sons, Inc.

And ended with the following words:

> [...] Sooner or later, we must learn to judge each other on our own merits. Sooner or later, if man is ever to be worthy of his destiny, we must fill our hearts with tolerance. For then, and only then, will we be truly worthy of the concept that man was created in the image of God – a God who calls us ALL – His children.[3]

It's a powerful column, one that not only resonates with the issues of today's world, but that also reflects the message of Ryan Coogler's 2018 film: that we are all "one single tribe."

Of course, to be fair, Black Panther isn't a perfect hero and Wakanda isn't a perfect nation. T'Challa recognizes this in the film and so do the contributors of this volume, who analyze the character of Black Panther and the nation of Wakanda (seen in the film and comics) with a critical, philosophical eye, tackling issues of racism, colonialism, slavery, sexuality, feminism, politics, morality, spirituality, Afrofuturism, technology, and the wonders of vibranium with a mixture of insight and humor that not only reflects the nature of this philosophical series, but that also honors the tradition Stan (and Jack) started all those years ago.

Yibambe!

Ed and Tim

Notes

1. Joshua Ostroff, "Marvel comics icon Stan Lee talks superhero diversity and creating Black Panther," *Huffington Post*, September 1, 2016, at https://www.huffingtonpost.ca/2016/09/01/stan-lee-marvel-superhero-diversity_n_11198460.html.
2. Stan Lee on Instagram: "Stan's Soapbox, 1968," at https://www.instagram.com/p/CBBlrsOp3Ox/?hl=en-gb.
3. Lee.

PART I
Yibambe!

1

Challenge Day
Tradition and Revolution in Wakanda

Armond Boudreaux

At its heart, Wakanda has a paradoxical nature: in its integration of technology into daily life, the reclusive nation is more like the industrialized countries of the Western world than its continental neighbors, but in its political structure, it has more in common with the ancient African past. Wakanda uses highly advanced science to improve the lives of its people, and yet it is ruled by kings who are selected through inheritance and ritual combat. In other words, it is a nation of contradictions, ruled by a complex synthesis of reason and tradition.

Moreover, Wakanda controls the Vibranium Mound, which is perhaps the most important resource on earth, a resource that has defined Wakandan society for millennia. Situated inside a mountain, the Vibranium Mound is what remains of a meteor that fell to Earth in the deep past. Though small amounts of vibranium have left Wakanda over the years (showing up in Captain America's shield, US Agent's shield, and in Ulysses Klaue's sonic cannon, for example), the unearthly metal remains the property of Wakanda – and therefore the responsibility of its king.

The paradoxes at the heart of Wakandan society as well as its highly desirable resources mean that it is often the subject of attacks, invasions by outsiders, and attempted political revolutions. Many people have challenged its ancient traditions and political order, claiming to offer a better use of its resources or a more just society than the culture that has evolved organically over the course of millennia (as if it isn't absolutely crazy to try to take over the Black Panther's home turf!).

It seems as if every supervillain and misguided revolutionary thinks that he or she knows better than T'Challa how to run Wakanda. We see this, for example, when Eric Killmonger and Baron Macabre try to stage a coup in *Jungle Action* #17, when Achebe takes over Wakanda early in Christopher Priest's run on the *Black Panther* book, when a radical group called The People tries to overthrow T'Challa's rule in Ta Nehisi Coates's run, and most recently in the *Black Panther* movie when Killmonger briefly

Black Panther and Philosophy: What Can Wakanda Offer the World?, First Edition. Edited by Edwardo Pérez and Timothy E. Brown.
© 2022 John Wiley & Sons, Inc. Published 2022 by John Wiley & Sons, Inc.

takes over Wakanda in the name of combatting racism and injustice. Though each of these attempts at revolution is fueled by different motivations and values, each proves to be fruitless and costly – both to the revolutionaries and to the people they think they're saving.

It might be tempting to say that Wakanda just hasn't seen the "right" kind of revolution yet. Maybe all these revolutions fail because the revolutionaries are corrupt. Maybe their motives are not pure enough. Or maybe their plans simply haven't been "smart" enough yet. Maybe what Wakanda needs is more moral and more intelligent revolutionaries. It might also be tempting to say that the Wakandan monarchy is simply strong enough to withstand revolutions, that might can overcome right. But there's more at work in the preservation of Wakanda's social order than the incompetence and corruption of the revolutionaries or the strength of Wakanda's rulers in maintaining the status quo.

In fact, the repeated failed attempts at coup and revolution in Wakanda show two important things about political and social change. First, they show that pure reason divorced from tradition and custom cannot provide the social cohesion that is necessary for nations to exist. Second, they show that revolutions often destroy the thing that they seek to preserve – even (and perhaps especially) when they succeed in reinventing societies to fit the ideology of revolutionaries. Nations have to be able to reform and to respond to changing circumstances, but as the British statesman Edmund Burke (1729–1797) argued in a very different time and place than present-day Wakanda, true revolution poisons society rather than saves it.

"Don't Scare Me Like That, Colonizer!"

At first it might seem a bit dubious to think that Edmund Burke can have anything to say about Wakandan politics. After all, Burke was a member of the British Parliament at a time when European nations had colonized much of Africa. And perhaps more than anything, Wakanda was created as a way of mythologizing what Africa might have been like if colonialism hadn't happened. But Burke was a much more complicated man than our modern understanding of colonialism would lead us to believe. In fact, Burke spent a great deal of his career criticizing British colonial practices in India and America. Moreover, his ideas about politics and revolutions can easily lend themselves to a critical view of colonialism as a project, and no doubt T'Challa would find Burke to be a potent and persuasive ally in resisting attempted revolutions in Wakanda.

Like the people of Wakanda, Burke lived in a world of contradictions and tension between diverse people. Born in Dublin to a Catholic mother and Protestant father, Burke learned from an early age that an immensely complex system of conventions, arrangements, agreements, customs, and compromises makes it possible for different kinds of people to live together in a harmonious social order. For him, it was a miracle that the British nation had found a way for its diverse people to coexist in a stable and free society.

During his time in Parliament, Burke devoted himself to reforming the country that he loved. Throughout his career, he helped to reform criminal and financial law, opposed laws restricting religious dissenters, supported William Wilberforce's efforts to end slavery, and worked to improve other aspects of the British government.

But today Burke is probably best known for his opposition to the French Revolution – a position that surprised a lot of people. Most of Burke's contemporaries had expected the staunch Whig reformer to support the French in their efforts to liberalize their nation. Why wouldn't Burke welcome what many considered to be a great reform of an antiquated and unjust system in France? His position made some of his contemporaries disparage him as a man who just wanted to preserve the past for its own sake (apparently, being a tireless reformer is a thankless job!).

The reason for Burke's opposition to revolution lies in how he thought that societies ought to grow and change. His early life had shown him that the bonds that hold societies together are far too complex for human reason to fully understand, so it is both foolish and immoral for anyone to think that reason alone can determine the form of government. Even if we have the best of intentions, we will cause unforeseen consequences when we use pure reason in order to change society and ignore traditions that have built up over a long time. As Burke writes, "Men little think how immorally they act in rashly meddling with what they do not understand. Their delusive good intention is no sort of excuse for their presumption. They who truly mean well must be fearful of acting ill."[1] In other words, pure motives, good intentions, and clear reasoning do not justify us in carrying out revolutions.

And it doesn't matter how intelligent the revolutionaries or their plans are. Even if we gathered together Reed Richards, Tony Stark, and Bruce Banner (three of the smartest people outside Wakanda) and asked them to carry out a revolution that set up a new, rationally based government in Wakanda, the result would be disastrous – and not only because the three of them are unlikely to agree about what the best society would be! Burke would say that not even three of the smartest people on earth could rationally design a system that would satisfy everyone. (Chances are, it would only satisfy people who already think like Reed, Tony, and Bruce.)

Instead of revolution – which tears down society as it is and erects something entirely new in its place – Burke preferred gradual, organic change that builds upon the parts of a society that already work well. "By preserving the method of nature in the conduct of the state," he writes, "in what we improve we are never wholly new; in what we retain we are never wholly obsolete."[2] By following the example of nature, which always builds upon the world as it *is* rather than starting over with something brand new, we conserve what works in a society while also allowing for change that will be beneficial. This is the model of change that Burke thinks will truly improve societies.

So, if reason alone can't show us how to govern or to change society, we must let the specific traditions and customs of our society help to guide us in ordering it. And reason can't create a one-size-fits-all model of government for nations with different traditions (say, Wakanda, Attilan, and Latveria, for example). In a speech supporting American independence (a cause which Burke didn't regard as a revolution since the Americans had spent centuries developing their own culture and society and just wanted to be left alone), Burke argued that a government must take into account the sentiments and character of its people in deciding how to govern them. Britain's way of governing itself isn't necessarily the right way to govern the American colonies. And, as he says in *Observations on the Late State of the Nation*, "Politics ought to be adjusted not to human reasonings but to human nature, of which reason is but a part and by no means the greatest part."[3] In other words, a politics of reason alone attends to only one part of human nature, and such a politics will go wrong by ignoring people's sentiments, traditions, and customs.

"Let the Challenge Begin"

Examples from Wakanda might show that Burke was right. The first *Black Panther* film establishes that Wakanda's monarchy is semi-hereditary, with the oldest (probably male) members of the Panther Tribe being the first in line to rule. When T'Chaka dies in *Captain America: Civil War*, his son, T'Challa, inherits the throne, but who gets to be king is not decided *merely* by inheritance. Before T'Challa officially takes the throne, all of Wakanda's tribes come together and have the chance to offer up a challenger for the throne. Any challengers must fight the presumptive king in ritual combat in order to earn the right to rule.

People from the industrialized West might look at this traditional way of transmitting power and say that it is irrational. Those who favor meritocracy or republicanism might say that being the son of a king does not give a man the right to rule. Moralists might object to the idea that mere physical strength makes a man fit to govern, saying that his moral character is far more important. Feminists might argue that patriarchy is poisonous for society and that Wakanda needs more women in power. Classical liberals would question the very idea of having a king at all, saying that monarchy itself is unjust and dangerous.

While each of these criticisms might have its merits, Burke would probably say that we make a mistake if we seek to throw out the "old ways" of

Wakanda and create new ones built on reason alone. So if revolutionaries with aspirations to abstract ideas like liberty and equality suddenly seized power and abolished the Wakandan monarchy, the result wouldn't necessarily be good. Even though they might seem irrational to outsiders like us, anyone can see from the Challenge Day scene in *Black Panther* that Wakanda's traditions provide social cohesion that a purely rational system cannot possibly create. The reverence that the Wakandans have for their traditions tempers old tribal tensions and petty rivalries that might otherwise develop into social dysfunction or erupt into civil war. Dispensing with the traditions in one fell swoop would result in anything but liberty or equality.

We can see this most clearly when M'Baku arrives with representatives from the Jabari Tribe in order to challenge T'Challa for the throne. The people have gathered at the waterfall to witness their king's coronation, members of each tribe dressed in their ceremonial finery to honor the solemnity of the event. Shuri, T'Challa's brilliant but unorthodox sister, complains about her corset and asks if they can "wrap it up and go home." Though she does not completely disregard the customs involved in the coronation, she does show a youthful irreverence that some might find scandalous. When M'Baku arrives with his men to challenge T'Challa, he complains that Wakanda's "technological advancements have been overseen by a child ... who scoffs at tradition!"

This scene sets up audiences to view M'Baku as one of the film's antagonists (especially those of us who have read the comics). We might see Shuri as a representative of scientific and social progress and M'Baku as a remnant of an antiquated devotion to custom. But first appearances can be deceiving. Indeed, it is M'Baku's reverence for tradition that allows for the peaceful transfer of power. When T'Challa defeats him in ritual combat, M'Baku yields and abandons his bid for the throne. A man with less reverence for tradition might use whatever means necessary to acquire power, starting a civil war.

In a paradoxical way, M'Baku's commitment to the Challenge Day tradition with its underlying might-makes-right assumption could very well protect society from being subjected to something far more irrational. The ritual probably developed as a way to settle disputes between tribes that would cause open warfare and the domination of some tribes by others. By formalizing humanity's old might-makes-right instinct, the Challenge Day ceremony turns it into a ritual that allows for the freedom and dignity of each tribe.

That doesn't mean that the traditions surrounding the transfer of power in Wakanda can't or shouldn't change, of course. But Burke would argue that any change ought to happen organically and slowly. It would be perilous to suddenly abolish the tradition and replace it with a more "rational" means of transferring power.

"Burn It All"

One of the functions that tradition can serve in a society is as a guard against absolute and arbitrary power. In Britain during Burke's time, for example, the monarchy had a lot of power, but it didn't rule unchecked. The political and social traditions that had built up in England over centuries helped to balance the power of the monarch against the power of Parliament and against what Burke called the "entailed inheritance"[4] of the people's rights and liberties. The monarch might have had more power than a farmer, but the fact that both the king and the farmer lived within the same tradition meant that the farmer enjoyed liberties that he wouldn't have under a capricious ruler. It meant that the king didn't have arbitrary and unrestrained power.

We see this kind of tradition at work in Wakanda, as well. The coronation ceremony, for example, helps to instill humility in the king, reminding him that he is responsible to the tribes for his actions. In fact, the Challenge Day ritual suggests that though Wakanda's monarchy is inherited, the king also serves by consent of the people. We see this in the fact that T'Challa must have the strength of the Black Panther stripped from his body before he can engage in ritual combat with a challenger to the throne. This levels the playing field and makes it possible for a challenger to actually succeed. Though it is probably not written in law, this custom protects the people from the whims of capricious and arbitrary rulers.

From his first appearance in Wakanda, Killmonger shows that he does not care about the traditions that guarantee order and liberty in the nation that he wants to rule. This is why his brief time in power causes so much harm and threatens to destroy the very fabric of Wakandan society. He says that he wants to use Wakanda's vibranium and weapons to "liberate" the billions of people around the world who are of African descent, letting Wakanda serve as "judge, jury, and executioner" for oppressive people in other places. Moreover, he clearly has no interest in the customs that guarantee a peaceful, orderly, and fair transfer of power. When the leader of the River Tribe says that "it will take weeks" to arrange a new challenge, Killmonger says, "Weeks? I don't need weeks. The whole country ain't gotta be there." In other words, he isn't interested in the tribes having their say in the rule of Wakanda; he only wants the power to do what *he* believes is right – for everyone in the world.

Perhaps his worst offense against Wakanda's traditions comes just after he has consumed the Heart-Shaped Herb and gained the strength of the Black Panther. One of the women who attend him during the process says that they preserve the garden of the Herb "so that when it comes time for another king, we will be ready." Killmonger scoffs and says, "Another king? Yeah, go ahead and burn all that." The woman appeals to tradition, saying that she cannot burn the Herb, and Killmonger viciously grabs her by the throat, lifting her from the ground: "When I tell you to do something,

I *mean* that shit." In other words, he is limited by no custom, tradition, or sentiment. His power is unchecked and arbitrary.

It's hard to tell whether Killmonger doesn't see the likely results of destroying the Heart-Shaped Herb or if he simply doesn't care. But it is clear that the consequences won't be good. Even though Wakanda is protected by the Border Tribe and by its advanced technology, its primary defender is the Black Panther, whose strength comes solely from the Herb. Unless some new source of the Herb is found before T'Challa dies, he will be the last of the Black Panthers. Worse, the destruction of the Herb might not bode well for the next transfer of power. Kingship in Wakanda is closely associated with the role of the Black Panther. The loss of that role will probably have a ripple effect on other aspects of Wakandan tradition. When the time comes for a new king, the other tribes might wonder what makes the royal family special without the Heart-Shaped Herb. They might wonder why a Challenge Day ritual is even necessary at all, and once they begin to wonder about that, tribal strife will probably erupt. In other words, the peace and social cohesion that Wakanda has developed over millennia could be destroyed by a single man who thinks that he knows better than Wakanda's traditions.

"What Has Happened to Our Wakanda?"

After Killmonger throws T'Challa over the waterfall during their ritual combat and assumes power, Wakandan society finds itself torn in two. Nakiya, a Wakandan spy, and Okoye, a member of the Dora Milaje, find themselves at odds about what it means to be loyal to Wakanda. Nakiya asks Okoye to help her overthrow Killmonger "before he becomes too strong." Okoye will have none of it: "I am loyal to the throne, no matter who sits upon it!" Knowing how important Wakanda's traditions are to the stability and peace of the nation, she is desperate to protect those traditions. "You *serve* your country," she says, and Nakiya replies, "No, I *save* my country."

The disagreement between the two women speaks to one of the gravest consequences of revolutions like Killmonger's. Though each woman loves her country, Killmonger drives a wedge between them over how to best serve Wakanda. To the dutiful Okoye, serving Wakanda means serving a king she despises in the hope that she can maintain order in her country and usher it through a difficult time. To Nakiya, patriotism requires her to fight a man whose rule might be technically legitimate, but who blatantly opposes everything that Wakanda holds sacred. For a time, this means that two close friends find themselves on opposite sides of a conflict.

The wedge drives deeper, however. The Border Tribe happily embraces Wakanda's new king, aiding him in preparing to wage war on the rest of the world. This leads to Wakandans hurting and killing their own people.

As W'Kabi says in a deleted scene, "There will be war and death, but in the end it will be beautiful." In helping Killmonger, the Border Tribe causes outright civil war – a war that alienates friends, spouses, and countrymen.

"Just Because Something Works ..."

Those who are loyal to Wakanda have to oppose Killmonger with force, but what truly brings order and peace back to Wakanda is a reassertion of the traditions and customs that have shaped Wakandan society for millennia. Having stolen a single Heart-Shaped Herb from the garden before Killmonger had it burned, Nakiya flees with Shuri and Ramonda to the Jabari Tribe in the mountains. In her desperation, she intends to give the Herb to M'Baku so that he can have the strength to overthrow the new king. What she doesn't know is that M'Baku recovered T'Challa's comatose body after Killmonger threw him over the waterfall.

A man less devoted to the traditions of his country might accept the Herb and take advantage of the chaos in Wakanda in order to advance his own power, but instead, M'Baku allows the women to use the Herb to revive their comatose king. So, the man who seemed backward in his traditionalism at the beginning of the film turns out to be the key not only to the restoration of peace in Wakanda, but also to saving the world from Killmonger's murderous revolution.

Moreover, when T'Challa recovers from the coma and returns to the Vibranium Mound to oppose Killmonger, he legitimizes his actions by asserting that the ritual combat isn't over: "I never yielded, and as you can see, I am not dead!" Killmonger and the Border Tribe reject this reasoning, of course, but when the Dora Milaje and others see that Killmonger doesn't yet have a rightful claim to the throne, they join T'Challa in stopping him from sending Wakandan weapons across the border and beginning a war on the rest of the world.

Burke might have predicted all of this. The division sewn by Killmonger's effort to single-handedly reshape Wakandan society; the civil war; the willingness of some to shed the blood of their fellow citizens; the restoration of peace through a reassertion of tradition – each of these things is evidence of the danger of revolution that Burke warned against and the value that he saw in tradition.

None of this means that Wakanda has to remain "stuck in the past," however. Far from it. In fact, T'Challa *does* begin to reform his country after he defeats Killmonger and resumes his place as king. Having seen that Wakanda could use its resources to help the rest of the world – "the world we wish to join," as T'Chaka says in *Captain America: Civil War* – he begins establishing outreach centers in other countries. It isn't the radical course reversal that revolutionaries like Killmonger and W'Kabi wanted, of course, but the incrementalist approach allows Wakanda to grow without subjecting itself to the dangerous turmoil that rapid change causes. It represents the kind of organic development that Burke thought was healthy for nations, and allows the reclusive nation to reform and open up to the world without losing its true identity.

Wakanda forever!

Notes

1. Edmund Burke, *An Appeal from the New to the Old Whigs, In Consequence of Some Late Discussions in Parliament, Relative to the* Reflections on the French Revolution, 4th ed. (London: J. Dodsley, 1791), 472.
2. Edmund Burke, *Reflections on the Revolution in France*, in Francis Canavan ed., *Selected Works of Edmund Burke*, vol. 2 (Indianapolis: Liberty Fund, 1999), 122.
3. Edmund Burke, *Observations on the Late State of the Nation*, in Paul Langford ed., *The Writings of Edmund Burke*, vol. 2 (London: Clarendon Press, 1981), 196.
4. Burke (1999), 121.

2

Transforming Wakanda
Justice (or Not?) in *Black Panther*

Steve Bein and Deana Lewis

Suppose the epic battle at the end of the film *Black Panther* took a different turn. T'Challa still delivers the final blow to Killmonger, but after a life-saving surgery, Killmonger wakes up to find himself handcuffed to a hospital bed. He still gets to deliver that killer line about death being better than bondage, but T'Challa replies with a sad smile. "I know the legal system you grew up with is designed for retribution," he says, "but Wakandan justice is more civilized. You'll see."

Does justice demand letting a mass murderer like Erik Killmonger bleed to death? If he doesn't die, what does justice demand then? That depends not only on how you define justice but also on what kind of justice you're trying to define. The question of what punishment Killmonger deserves is quite different from the question of how to repair the harm he's done, which again is quite different from the question of how to right the wrongs done to him. Philosophers have dedicated countless pages to these kinds of questions, and they've outlined a whole taxonomy of different kinds of justice. In this chapter we'll look at two of the classical conceptions of justice and then examine the contemporary movements that arose to challenge these old concepts. But first, let's look at Wakanda's record on justice.

Wakanda Forever?

On its surface, Wakanda appears to be a utopia: beautiful, pristine, devoid of poverty, a land where the world's most educated people care for each other using the world's most advanced technology. Monarchy isn't what you'd call a fair system of government, but as monarchies go, Wakanda's is better than most. A Black Panther is made, not born; anyone can challenge for the right to rule. Monarchy and meritocracy aren't usually compatible, but somehow Wakanda found a way.

Black Panther and Philosophy: What Can Wakanda Offer the World?, First Edition. Edited by Edwardo Pérez and Timothy E. Brown.
© 2022 John Wiley & Sons, Inc. Published 2022 by John Wiley & Sons, Inc.

Sort of. In the comics, the trial to become the Black Panther involves more than fighting, but ritual combat has always been the final and most glamorous test in Wakanda. Pacifists need not apply. Also, while strife between the five Wakandan tribes is a long-running theme, solutions for this conflict have never been pretty. The Jabari Tribe is basically Wakanda's Tibet, cast into the mountainous hinterlands because of its religious beliefs. And the Dora Milaje weren't originally an elite security unit. Instead, each tribe sent a teenage girl to the Black Panther as a ceremonial wife-in-training, with the idea that any tribe might theoretically wed itself to royalty.[1] Hence their name, "the Adored Ones." Training them to be badasses doesn't offset the fact that they're political pawns.

Wakanda is even worse on foreign policy. Of course, a fictional country can do nothing to aid its real-world neighbors, but within the world of the comics, Wakanda has a lot to answer for. It ignored every crisis that scourged central Africa: colonialism, the slave trade, drought, famine, HIV, ethnocide, and the list goes on. So, if T'Challa wants Wakandan justice to be "more civilized," he's got a lot of work to do.[2]

Justice and Retribution

Now what should Wakanda do with Killmonger? Immanuel Kant (1724–1804), an enormously influential philosopher on the subject of justice, would say the first concern is that Wakanda must not use him merely as a means for its own ends. That is, it can't punish him to make the country safer. If it plans to imprison him – or execute him, or fine him, or let him bleed out after a knife fight with the king – it has to be because he *deserves* it, not because it will benefit anyone else.

What we're talking about here is *retributive justice*, the kind of justice that's concerned with punishment rather than rehabilitation. Killmonger has too many misdeeds to count, so let's focus on the one we opened this chapter with, the one that leads up to the climactic showdown in *Black Panther*: T'Challa isn't dead and he didn't yield, yet Killmonger refuses to give up the throne. What would Kant say to this?

In good Kantian fashion, his answer is anything but obvious. (In the average college-level ethics class, Kant is usually the hardest philosopher to understand.) On the one hand, Kant says your duty to obey your ruler has nothing to do with how your ruler came to power.[3] That sounds like Killmonger deserves no punishment at all. In fact, it sounds like T'Challa is the one who deserves punishment, because the throne is rightfully Killmonger's as soon as he takes it. On the other hand, if it really doesn't matter how the ruler comes to power, then usurping the throne is exactly as legitimate as being presumed dead after being thrown off of Warrior Falls and then clinging to life long enough for your sister to schlep a Heart-Shaped Herb halfway across the country instead of just drinking it herself and becoming the ass-kicker she is in the comics.[4]

Regardless of whether it's T'Challa or Killmonger who has the stronger claim to the throne, the other guy deserves punishment, and Kant would almost certainly say the just punishment for him is execution. Why? For one thing, Kant was an avid fan of the death penalty, advocating it even for crimes as trivial as adultery.[5] For another, he thought physical violence was the correct tool to use when dealing with Black people. In fact, Kant said they aren't capable of moral reasoning on their own, but if you want them to behave morally an effective method is to beat them. (We aren't making this up.[6]) And if you think that's bad, don't forget, when it comes to justice, Kant is *still* one of the most influential figures in all of Western philosophy.

So yeah, maybe Kant isn't the best person to ask. Let's try John Locke (1632–1704), who would say what Killmonger deserves goes well beyond the question of punishment. There's also the question of what he's owed.

Justice and Reparation

Killmonger's deep-seated anger toward the Wakandan government didn't arise out of nowhere. He's angry because they treated him unjustly. In the film, they abandoned him in a foreign country after accidentally killing his father. In the comics, his motivations are more fluid – different writers portray him differently – but there's one constant: he never picks Wakanda at random. His motherland always does him wrong.

Locke would say we're now facing two questions of justice. Like Kant, he wrote on retributive justice, but Locke says there's also a second brand of justice, *reparatory justice* (sometimes called *rectificatory justice*), which asks, if someone does you wrong, what do they owe you to make it right? Locke's vision of justice was pretty radical in his day, because he thought monarchy was inherently unjust. Instead, he said we have certain *natural rights* – rights born into us by our very nature – which dictate that "no one ought to harm another in his life, health, liberty or possessions."[7] If you're minding your own business and someone harms you in any of these categories, Locke says the offender owes you reparations.[8]

John Locke has a presence in the world of Black Panther. The Wakandan philosopher Changamire quotes him in the 12-issue run "A Nation Under Our Feet," by Ta-Nehisi Coates and Brian Stelfreeze. There, a rebel group called The People, inspired by Changamire's vision of a Wakanda ruled by its people instead of its monarch, rises up to overthrow the Black Panther once and for all. Their motto, "No One Man," is Lockean at heart.[9]

For Coates, Wakanda is an allegory for the United States, and his questions of reparatory justice apply to both countries. Before he came to write for Marvel comics, Coates was a national correspondent for *The Atlantic*, where he made waves nationwide with his article, "The Case for Reparations." There he asked a question that makes lots of Americans uncomfortable: what does the United States owe African Americans for the harm its policies have done to them?

It's not an easy question to answer, in part because reparatory justice is tricky. Sometimes making reparations is easy, like paying someone's bill from the body shop if you rear-end their car. Sometimes it's difficult, like paying that bill when it costs as much as the vacation you've been saving up for all year. And sometimes it's just plain impossible. For all its technological marvels, Wakanda can't un-kill N'Jadaka's father. (Maybe in *Black Panther 2* T'Challa will borrow the Time Stone and go back in time to make things right. And hey, Marvel Studios, if that's the way you decide to go with it, we want a cut.) The United States can't un-exploit anyone, and even if it revoked every exploitative law on the books today, there are still millions of African Americans living with the everyday consequences of past exploitation.[10]

The trickiest part of reparatory justice is dealing with powerful people who owe reparations but can't be forced to pay – or, for that matter, to even consider what payment might look like. As Coates observes, the US government has shown no interest in even raising the question of reparations: no president has ever asked for a study, and the House of Representatives has turned down every opportunity to study the question. It has done this regardless of which party was in power, and it's done it 26 times in a row.[11]

In the film *Black Panther*, reparations are tricky for a different reason: Killmonger wronged Wakanda because Wakanda wronged him first. Had T'Chaka not orphaned and abandoned him, young N'Jadaka might never have become Killmonger. He might still have challenged T'Challa at Warrior Falls, as is every Wakandan citizen's right, but he wouldn't have had to murder anyone along the way. As he sees it, he's taking by force the very thing Wakanda owes him anyway. But as the Wakandan government sees it, he's setting the country on a course that can only end in violence and destruction. That's no way to bring about justice.

However, what if there were a way to bring Killmonger and Wakanda to the table to discuss how to repair the damage done? What if that table included seats for everyone harmed by either party? In other words, instead of asking how to punish or how to repay debts, what if the question of justice were how to make things better for everyone involved?

Justice and Restoration

Changamire offers a vision for how to do this. In the wake of the violence and rebellion in "A Nation Under Our Feet," Changamire says, "Restoration is what is needed now. Restoration for our country."[12] He gathers not just the powers that be (T'Challa the king and Aneka the rebel leader) but also ordinary citizens traumatized by the war, so that together they can navigate a path forward. Their interest is not retribution or reparation, but rather *restorative justice*.

Criminologist Howard Zehr says we can distinguish retributive justice from restorative justice by looking at how they understand crime, criminals, and victims. Retributive justice defines crime as a violation of laws, and therefore sees the state itself as the victim of crime. Restorative justice, on the other hand, defines crime in terms of harm – not in the abstract sense as an offense to the state, but harm to real people and real-world relationships. In retributive justice, criminals are law-breakers by definition and therefore deserve punishment. In restorative justice, criminals count among the people harmed by injustice. Restorative justice reminds us that people can be wrongdoers and victims at the same time, and it recognizes that oftentimes it's *because* people are hurt that they hurt others.[13] Concerned with identifying the root causes of injustice, restorative justice wants to figure out who's a stakeholder in the situation, and then involve all the stakeholders collectively in setting things right.

Because retribution has to do with what people deserve, not what people need, you can do retributive justice without asking any questions about political power or social position. That's not possible with restorative justice. If you want to restore a community that's been torn apart, you can't ignore the fact that some people are more powerful than others. You have to acknowledge things like racism and sexism. And you can't pretend people are just one thing: every criminal is also someone's child, someone's neighbor, maybe someone's employee or employer, maybe a parent or caretaker.

In fact, most of us are technically criminals. (How many laws have you broken?) Think about how your community would react to losing you. Sending someone to prison doesn't punish one person; it creates a hole in society, a hole other people have to step in to fill. Put enough people in prison and entire communities can collapse. That's not justice. From the standpoint of restorative justice, it's another form of harm, this time inflicted by the state. So, when Killmonger wakes up handcuffed to a hospital bed, restorative justice would have T'Challa say, "You're no use to us locked up. How are we going to work together to heal all the damage *we've* caused?"

Sending Killmonger to prison takes away not only his freedom but also any ability he might have to repair the damage he's done to other people. It strips him of his responsibility to right past wrongs, and in doing so it weakens the community as a whole. Moreover, it also absolves Wakanda of its responsibility to repair the damage it has done to him. Remember, Killmonger didn't pick Wakanda at random; he's been wronged, and he needs healing too. Putting him in a cell doesn't address the root problem, it just sweeps the problem under the rug.

So, if it's not going to throw him in prison, what is Wakanda to do? Changamire would have Killmonger sit down with the people he's wronged, listen to how they're hurting, listen to what they need, and work *together* with them to figure out how to restore them to their whole and healthy state. He'd put T'Challa at the table too, not to oversee the proceedings but because even the king must be held accountable for repairing the damage that's been done. Royalty doesn't count for much in restorative justice; what really matters is healing.

If Wakandan justice really is "more civilized," it will acknowledge an inescapable but uncomfortable truth: when a government imprisons people, it sucks talent and energy out of communities even as those communities try to recover from the harm caused by crime. Those left behind have fewer resources to heal their communal wounds and bounce back to where they were.[14] Which raises an interesting question: does Wakanda need prisons at all?

Justice Transformed

Prison abolitionists have shown that prisons don't make people safer.[15] Even so, maybe a prisonless country still sounds like fantasy to you. How would this country maintain law and order? What would prevent people from running around robbing and killing each other?

These are good questions, but they're short-sighted. They assume criminality is a problem of the individual, but what if it's not? What if it's a structural problem, rooted not in one person's actions but in the social institutions that make such actions appealing?

The truth is we already live in a world where criminals can do as they please, so long as they're powerful enough that no one can hold them accountable. This, too, is an indicator that the problem is structural, not individual. Retributive justice only makes sense within that flawed structure: it sees justice as punitive, and relies on government to curb criminality by meting out punishment. The *transformative justice* movement says real justice happens when we examine the root causes – usually social institutions – that create widespread inequity and harm. If we can transform those, we can transform society itself. We can break down all the social barriers that constrain people. In the transformative justice movement, the work of justice is the work of building our capacity to take care of each other, as ordinary people in ordinary communities.

Do that and you can abolish the prisons. When the people are accountable to each other, not merely to the state, then they can fully reclaim their own humanity. Their king isn't above them and their criminals aren't beneath them; their basic assumption is that all people have intrinsic value. When T'Challa says, "Wakandan justice is more civilized," this would be the dream: a country whose justice relies not on punitive measures but accountability among its people. In this system, Erik Killmonger isn't a menace you need to keep in a super-prison like the Raft or Prison 42.[16] He's a phenomenal talent with a keen interest in building up Black communities, a guy you really want back on your side.

If a nation without prisons still sounds like fantasy-land to you – maybe even a dystopian fantasy – keep in mind that for much of American history, abolishing slavery sounded like pure fantasy. Just because an unjust institution seems ironclad doesn't mean it can't fall. And imagine how *Avengers: Infinity War* could have ended if Wakanda ran on transformative justice instead of retributive justice. Thanos comes to town looking for the Mind Stone, but he's too late. N'Jadaka (who has renounced the mercenary name Killmonger) stands proudly with Shuri in her lab, where the two of them have combined their collective genius to destroy the Mind Stone. Maybe Thanos wants to take his revenge, but now Vision is still in the game and Wakanda has *two* defenders fueled by the Heart-Shaped Herb. Behind them stands the united strength of all five Wakandan tribes. They didn't unite to fight the Mad Titan. No, they're united because they've deconstructed all the artificial walls between them, and now they all recognize each other as stakeholders in a just society. They're prepared to take care of each other come hell or high water.

And then, before anyone comes to blows, T'Challa tells Thanos there's no need to kill him or jail him. "Wakandan justice is more civilized. You'll see."

Notes

1. *Black Panther*, vol. 2, #1 and #3, 1998.
2. In fairness, the country is doing much better lately. The motto at the gate of the Wakandan embassy in New York City now reads, "*Awazili N'Gyato Imo Sabolari,*" or "To Embrace the Global Village" (*Black Panther*, vol. 2, #39, 1998). And of course there are T'Challa and Shuri's efforts in the closing scene of the film *Black Panther*, which are well intended, if a little suspect. (Surreptitiously buying up land in impoverished areas isn't so far from colonialism, and bringing Wakanda's way of life to the poor schlubs of Oakland looks suspiciously like the Wakandan version of the White Man's Burden. But hey, it's a start).
3. In his own words, "The command, 'Obey the suzerain who has authority over you,' does not ruminate on how the suzerain acquired this authority." Immanuel Kant, *The Metaphysical Elements of Justice, Part I of the Metaphysics of Morals* (Indianapolis, IN: Bobbs-Merrill, 1965), 140–141.
4. Her many exploits include killing the Radioactive Man (*Black Panther*, vol. 4, #6, 2005), becoming the Black Panther (*Black Panther*, vol. 5, #3–6, 2009), saving the planet from a black hole (*Shuri*, #5, 2018), and cheating death and returning as a stone-skinned, shape-shifting, entire-spiritual-memory-of-Wakanda-channeling avatar (*Black Panther*, vol. 6, #8, 2016).
5. Immanuel Kant, *The Metaphysics of Morals* (Cambridge: Cambridge University Press, 1996), 106–107. For a deeper dive into Kant's ethics in the context of comic books, see S. Bein, "Frank Miller's Batman as Philosophy: 'The World Only Makes Sense When You Force It To,'" in David Johnson ed., *The Palgrave Handbook of Popular Culture as Philosophy* (Cham: Palgrave Macmillan, 2020), at https://doi.org/10.1007/978-3-319-97134-6_15-1.

6. See Emmanuel Eze, "The Color of Reason: The Idea of 'Race' in Kant's Anthropology," in Katherine Faull ed., *Anthropology and the German Enlightenment* (Lewisburg, PA: Bucknell University Press, 1995), 196–237. See also Charles W. Mills, *The Racial Contract* (Ithaca, NY: Cornell University Press, 1997).

7. John Locke, *Two Treatises on Government* II.2.6 (that's second treatise, chapter two, paragraph six).

8. A historical note, since we got into Kant's history too: Locke's hands are cleaner than Kant's. Personally he found slavery a great evil, and the very first sentence of his *Two Treatises on Government* is a damning rebuke of slavery. But he's not squeaky clean: as a governmental employee, he had a hand (willing or unwilling) in the administration of slave-owning colonies. The historian Holly Brewer considers his record in "Slavery-entangled philosophy,"*Psyche*, at https://aeon.co/essays/does-lockes-entanglement-with-slavery-undermine-his-philosophy.

9. *Black Panther*, vol. 3, #4 (2016), 3.

10. Coates considers this in much greater depth than we can get into here. Check out his "The case for reparations," *The Atlantic*, June 2014, 54–71, athttps://www.theatlantic.com/magazine/archive/2014/06/the-case-for-reparations/361631.

11. See Coates, "The case for reparations," 62. Coates writes on the twenty-five times former congressman John Conyers proposed a study; Representative Sheila Jackson Lee proposed the same bill again in 2019 and it never made it out of committee.

12. *Black Panther*, vol. 3, #12, 2016. His method is based on the Truth and Reconciliation Commission formed in South Africa after the fall of the apartheid government – which, by the way, is a good example of restorative justice.

13. See Howard Zehr, *Changing Lenses: A New Focus for Crime and Justice* (Scottdale, PA: Herald Press,1990), 184–185.

14. For an analysis of how this works, see Clarissa Rojas, Mimi Kim, and Alisa Bierria eds., "Community accountability: Emerging movements to transform violence," *Social Justice* 37 (2011–2012), 4, 1–11.

15. A number of scholars and activists have written about the violence of prisons, the lack of justice in the justice system, and the need to abolish prisons to engage in transformative justice and community accountability. See the works of Ruth Wilson Gilmore, Angela Y. Davis, Mariame Kaba, Mia Mingus, and Mimi Kim for some examples.

16. The ultra-maximum security prisons built for super-powered inmates in *New Avengers* and *Civil War*. See *New Avengers* #1 and *Civil War: Front Line* #5.

3

Sins of the Fathers
Historical Injustice and Its Repair in *Black Panther*

Ben Almassi

SON: Baba?
FATHER: Yes, my son?
SON: Tell me a story.
FATHER: Which one?
SON: The story of home.
FATHER: Millions of years ago, a meteorite made of vibranium, the strongest substance in the universe, struck the continent of Africa, affecting the plant life around it. And when the time of man came, five tribes settled on it and called it Wakanda.

Black Panther tells a story with history, and despite arriving in 2018 as the eighteenth film in the Marvel Cinematic Universe (MCU), this history is primarily its own, secondarily related to the real world, and only tangentially concerned with the wider events of the MCU.

The film's rousing opening is a unifying creation myth every Wakandan child surely knows by heart. And Wakanda, as we first encounter it, seems like an ideal society – socially, technologically, aesthetically – triumphantly crowning its new king, T'Challa. For all its Afrofuturistic splendors, though, Wakanda's history includes acts of injustice and wrongdoing that predate the story's beginning and remain unresolved as the story begins. Such injustices include human trafficking in Nigeria where Nakia is undercover, appropriation of Wakandan and other African artifacts by the Museum of Great Britain, and the murder of T'Challa's father, T'Chaka, during a terrorist attack in *Captain America: Civil War*.

Of course, the historical injustices really driving *Black Panther* are tragic deaths in 1991: the murder of W'Kabi's parents and others by Ulysses Klaue while stealing vibranium from Wakanda, and then in Oakland, the fratricide of Wakandan prince N'Jobu by his brother T'Chaka. The first is

Black Panther and Philosophy: What Can Wakanda Offer the World?, First Edition. Edited by Edwardo Pérez and Timothy E. Brown.

an outrage which unites all of Wakanda in the aim of bringing Klaue to justice. The second is T'Chaka's secret shame, which threatens to tear Wakanda apart.

Though he did not commit these wrongs, as king (and our hero) T'Challa holds himself responsible for their resolution, and so he must reckon with the conflicting responses to historical injustice of his father, his closest allies, and his cousin (and the film's villain and tragic figure) N'Jadaka, a.k.a. Erik "Killmonger" Stevens.

Philosophy has its own rich history, one in which questions of justice figure prominently. What is the nature of justice? To whom is justice owed? What does justice require? Notice the ambiguity in this last question – are we concerned with what justice requires *ideally*, or what justice requires *given that...?*

"Every Breath You Take Is Mercy from Me."

"Ideal" needn't assume perfection, because ideal theories of justice can recognize and account for human fallibility, selfishness, scarcity, and the like. Nevertheless, ideal theory in philosophy works by abstracting away from messy complicating contingencies to provide a generalized model of the phenomenon in question. "What distinguishes ideal theory," the philosopher Charles Mills explains, "is the reliance on idealization to the exclusion, or at least marginalization, of the actual."[1]

John Rawls's (1921–2002) massively influential book *A Theory of Justice* is one such example, a careful, systematic account of what justice requires ideally speaking. Here Rawls attempts to identify "the principles that characterize a well-ordered society under favorable circumstances."[2] It's not that non-ideal questions are unimportant, but Rawls thinks we must construct an ideal vision of what justice requires first. By stepping outside of real-world conditions, contemplating the fundamental principles of justice we'd all choose if we were ignorant of our personal (and so possibly biasing) circumstances, we might come to recognize what Rawls calls *justice as fairness*.[3]

The characters in *Black Panther* are not contemplating justice from behind a veil of ignorance, nor applying ideal principles of justice to govern a nascent Wakandan society. Rather, Nakia is working to prevent human trafficking and to disrupt its existing networks. T'Challa is not just ensuring Wakanda's safety and its vibranium supply, he is working to make Klaue pay for past crimes. Killmonger is not just asserting his right of Wakandan citizenship, but avenging his father's murder and his own abandonment. They all seek some form of Aristotle's *corrective justice*,[4] to restore the conditions of justice damaged or destroyed by wrongdoing. They are concerned not with justice in the abstract, but with justice in their world, a world steeped in history.

"Almost by definition," Mills argues, "it follows from the focus of ideal theory that little or nothing will be said on actual historic oppression and its legacy in the present, or current ongoing oppression, though these may be gestured at in a vague or promissory way (as something to be dealt with later)."[5] Ideal theory can be powerful, but it is necessarily incomplete. Ideally, we would never do one another wrong, so it's not surprising if an ideal theory of justice offers scant advice on what should happen after we do. A complete theory must address the aftermath of injustice as itself a special context of action and evaluation. Among other things, it must treat the experience and perpetration of injustice as something to be reckoned with, not just avoided in the future. It also must recognize the pitfalls and other difficulties we face on the path from injustice back to justice – the challenges of getting there from here.

Justice at the Museum and Beyond

Different approaches to achieving justice *given that* injustice has already happened vie for our consideration. Let's look at three approaches that are especially relevant to the historical injustices in *Black Panther*: restitution, retribution, and reparation. The first of these focuses on victims' losses and making them whole again; the second focuses on perpetrators' offenses and punishments they deserve; the third focuses on repairing the relationships between victims and offenders and their communities, relationships that injustice has damaged or destroyed.

Let's consider how each of these forms of corrective justice applies to the historical injustices of *Black Panther*, starting with the scene when we first see Killmonger, standing resplendent in his shearling coat in the Museum of Great Britain. He knows something that the coffee-sipping museum curator does not – the ancient axe taken by British soldiers in Benin is actually from Wakanda. The British have no claim to this vibranium axe; ideally, now as before, it should be in Wakanda. Of course, it's not in Wakanda and the British do have it, so now what? How do we get there from here? Is it "anything goes" as long as the axe gets back to its rightful owners? As a Wakandan, does Killmonger have the right of repossession? Do the curator and other museum staff deserve punishment for their crimes?

"Don't Sweat, I'm Gonna Take It Off Your Hands for You."

Perhaps the most obvious way to correct an injustice is to restore the material conditions prior to it: as Archbishop Desmond Tutu put it, "If you take my pen and say you are sorry but don't give me the pen back, nothing has happened."[6] Restitution seems an especially natural response to theft or fraud, whether it's money, a pen, or a centuries-old axe. In other situations, though, putting things back as they were is impossible; try as you might, you can't unscramble the egg or put the toothpaste back in the tube. T'Challa, N'Jadaka, W'Kabi –none of them can get their fathers back. Wakanda could open its arms to the long-lost N'Jadaka, long abandoned by his uncle T'Chaka, but the years of neglect cannot really be compensated for.

Indeed, the aim of restoring material conditions to the way they were often seems inappropriate or at least insufficient in response to wrong-doing. If one person accidentally takes my pen and another steals it, they should both return my pen. But doesn't the latter owe me something more than the former, something that differentiates theft from an honest mis-take? The material conditions disrupted by injustice are surely relevant to correction, but for serious historical injustices, is putting things back as they were an adequate response?

The case for restitutive justice at the museum is pretty strong, but Killmonger does a poor job of it: like his brief reign as king, his corrective justice begets further injustice. The axe doesn't just belong to him, so other Wakandans may rightly object to him partnering with Klaue and selling it to the highest bidder (the CIA) in Korea. His crew preemptively poisons and shoots museum staff before any effort to argue their right of repossession. And to add insult to injury, Killmonger swipes a traditional African mask as he makes his escape. ("You're not telling me that's vibranium too?" "Nah, I'm just feeling it.") Chances are the Museum of Great Britain has no more of a claim to that mask than to the vibranium axe, of course, but whoever deserves to have it and to be made whole again, it's not Killmonger and Klaue.

"How Do You Think Your Ancestors Got These?"

Maybe we're focused on the wrong sort of desert. Maybe we should consider retribution rather than restitution. The British took the mask like they took the axe and deserve punishment for it. Killmonger and Klaue aren't repo men, they're the executioners of retributive justice. (Well, not Klaue. He seems happy just as an agent of chaos.) "The world took every-thing away from me, everything I ever loved!" Killmonger declares in his righteous anger. "But I'mma make sure we're even." He's not talking about restitutive justice here. He wants to punish the world.

Killmonger is not the only character in *Black Panther* for whom retribu-tion as corrective justice resonates deeply. T'Challa goes to Korea to capture Klaue, bring him to Wakanda to stand trial, and complete his father's unfinished work. Eager to apprehend his parents' killer, W'Kabi asks to join in. When T'Challa gently refuses, W'Kabi makes his priorities clear: "Then I ask – you kill him where he stands or you bring him back to us." T'Challa fails to do either, Killmonger arrives with Klaue's body, and this sways W'Kabi to the usurper's cause. "I am standing in your house, serving justice to a man who stole your vibranium and murdered your people," Killmonger says. "Justice your king couldn't deliver."

Has justice been served? The philosopher Alec Walen identifies three core principles serving as the foundation of retributive justice:

(1) those who commit certain kinds of wrongful acts, paradigmatically serious crimes, morally deserve to suffer a proportionate punishment;
(2) it is intrinsically morally good – good without reference to any other goods that might arise – if some legitimate punisher gives them the punishment they deserve;
(3) it is morally impermissible intentionally to punish the innocent or to inflict disproportionately large punishments on wrongdoers.[7]

Now consider: the stolen vibranium has not been returned, W'Kabi's parents are still dead, and none of those directly or indirectly responsible for these things have done anything to compensate for that. But for Killmonger and W'Kabi (and no doubt many other Wakandans) what matters is that Klaue has been punished for his grievous crimes. The intrinsic good of retribution remains. If anyone deserves death as proportionate punishment for their wrongful acts, Klaue for his 1991 homicides (not to mention grand theft) is among them. Is Killmonger a "legitimate punisher" in this case? Most of the assembled Wakandan Council seem skeptical when he arrives with Klaue, but then they don't know who he really is. ("That's not my name princess. Ask me, king.")

"In Times of Crisis, the Wise Build Bridges."

Despite popular assumptions, reparative justice is not really about monetary payments for historical injustice; "the fundamental issue in reparations," the philosopher Margaret Urban Walker writes, "is the moral vulnerability of victims of serious wrongs."[8] Sure, if you want to do right by me after, it matters how you hurt me – you've stolen my car, destroyed my garden, appropriated my culture's artifacts to add to your museum collection. But for those who believe in reparative or restorative justice, "the harm done is only peripherally about 'stuff.' Instead, the harm is understood in the *relational* realm."[9]

Thinking of it this way, reparative justice doesn't ask us to look backwards, but to do what we can to repair our moral relationships and our communities that have been hurt by historical and ongoing injustices. Admitting and apologizing for our role in wrongdoing and making amends matter because they do the work of relational repair. The key to reparative justice is *communication* between those who commit injustice and those who are hurt by it. Amends aren't charity or compensation for what's been lost. They work because of the "expressive burden"[10] they carry: their ability to convey my regret, my acknowledgement of wrongdoing, and most of all, my recognition of those I hurt as full members of our shared moral community, as deserving of respect and consideration as anyone else.

And yet relational repair is not always achievable. Some victims are unable to forgive; some perpetrators fail to acknowledge or even realize their wrong-doings, and among those who do, some cannot bring themselves to apologize or do what's needed to make amends. There's no real sense that the British recognize their appropriation of African artifacts as wrong, so until they do, is it reasonable to ask Wakandans or other Africans to begin working toward relational repair? Or recall the last exchange between a defeated Killmonger and a victorious T'Challa, who carries his wounded cousin into the fading evening light.[11] "Maybe we can still heal you," T'Challa offers; maybe reconciliation is still possible. But Killmonger refuses. His self-respect and dignity won't allow him to accept the bondage of incarceration – and his colonizer's mentality won't allow him to imagine anything else.

Though we've considered restitution, retribution, and reparation one by one, these responses to historical and ongoing injustices aren't mutually exclusive. People and institutions often react to injustice with a mixture of these – or we might find ourselves reacting to injustice in a way that doesn't include any of them or that ignores the need for corrective justice altogether. In *Black Panther*, T'Chaka, Killmonger, and Nakia offer radically different visions for Wakanda after injustice, visions for our hero – and for us – to reckon with.

T'Chaka's Isolationism and Active Ignorance

T'Challa loved his father, but he never really knew him, and in his ignorance he was not alone. King T'Chaka kept nearly all Wakandans in the dark about what happened in Oakland and about the boy he left there. "We had to maintain the lie," Zuri explains to an unconvinced T'Challa. Or as T'Chaka himself says of his decision to abandon his brother's son, "He was the truth I chose to omit."

This was his political philosophy and his epistemology, isolationism and ignorance as two sides of one coin. Whatever else he accomplished as king, T'Chaka produced what the historian of science Robert Proctor calls ignorance as an active construct[12]: a kind of not-knowing, though not because life is short and there is just so much to know. With active ignorance, the not-knowing is the point. Sometimes we actively construct our own ignorance, but here T'Chaka is more like tobacco companies that worked for decades to manufacture public doubt about cigarettes, cancer, and addiction.[13] He knows full well what he's done, but thinks protecting his people means hiding the truth from them.

T'Chaka constructs public ignorance to uphold an isolationist vision for Wakanda. Think about W'Kabi's advice to T'Challa on the question of aiding the world. "You let the refugees in, they bring their problems with them, and then Wakanda is like everywhere else." Yet "their" problems *are* Wakanda's problems too. The abandoned N'Jadaka is the truth T'Chaka chose to omit, a truth hidden from W'Kabi and other Wakandan isolationists – that "our" people are out there too. This is what the journalist Adam Serwer identifies as *Black Panther*'s central theme of Pan-Africanism: "a belief that no matter how distant black people's lives and struggles are from each other, we are in a sense 'cousins' who bear a responsibility to help one another escape oppression."[14]

Killmonger's Imperialism and the Master's Tools

Black Panther was a huge hit, with a $200 million opening weekend US box office on its way to staggering total grosses of $700 million domestically and $1.3 billion worldwide. And the hashtag that was trending on Twitter that spring? #KillmongerWasRight.

Killmonger wasn't raised behind T'Chaka's carefully constructed wall of ignorance. In many ways he knew more truth than anyone about Wakanda, about what it had done and what it could do to upend the world's balance of power. Yet the danger of single-minded devotion to corrective justice as retribution is that it needs offenders to punish. Killmonger was able to give W'Kabi some level of satisfaction against Klaue, but what about his own claim of retribution against T'Chaka? The king who killed his brother and abandoned his nephew is gone, so who is left for Killmonger to serve justice *to*? "The world," he answers, as the foundations of his claim to corrective justice erode and retribution becomes untethered from any legitimate or proportionate punishment. Killmonger's vengeance is let loose.

Vengeance is not justice,[15] but it's not always easy to tell them apart. Perhaps no one knows this better than T'Challa, who emerges from the pain and loss of *Civil War* with this resolve. Having nearly killed Bucky Barnes, he tracks down the man truly responsible for his father's death, Helmut Zemo, just as Zemo's ultimate plan is nearly complete: he has turned Captain America and Iron Man against each other. "Vengeance has consumed you. It is consuming them. I am done letting it consume me." T'Challa tells Zemo. "Justice will come soon enough." It's a hard-won lesson; if only he could share it with his long-lost cousin.

Deprived of his father and Wakandan community, N'Jadaka availed himself of the resources he did have and built himself into the mighty Killmonger we meet in the film. What resources? The Naval Academy, MIT, SEALs – "Killmonger is not a product of the ghetto," Serwer explains, "so much as he is the product of the American military-industrial complex."[16] Many viewers see Killmonger as a damning depiction of Black American masculinity, for better or for worse. Indeed, the philosopher Christopher Lebron criticizes the film, saying that it "uplifts the African noble at the expense of the black American man."[17] Serwer sees that same tragic emptiness in Killmonger as Lebron does, but interprets this to the filmmakers' credit rather than blame. "It renders a verdict on *imperialism* as a tool of black liberation," Serwer argues, "to say that the master's tools cannot dismantle the master's house."[18]

Whatever else is going on, that last phrase is definitely on point: against poet Audre Lorde's warning, Killmonger is confident he can use the master's tools to do just that. He says as much when he becomes king ("I know how colonizers think. So we're gonna use their own strategy against'em") and in response to T'Challa ("I learn from my enemies, beat them at their own game") in their final confrontation. His actions show this too. Orchestrating regime change in Wakanda, he follows his training, disrupting existing leadership structures and destroying the cultivated crop of Heart-Shaped Herb. As Agent Ross says, "He's one of ours."

Nakia, T'Challa, and Relational Repair

Killmonger insists on what T'Chaka wants to ignore, that the people within Wakanda's borders exist in relation to the people outside them. And though Killmonger doesn't make it to the end of the film, this vision of Wakanda in the world does. Recall T'Challa's words to the United Nations (here's one time when the post-credits sequence is absolutely essential):

> Wakanda will no longer watch from the shadows. We cannot. We must not. We will work to be an example of how we, as brothers and sisters on this Earth, should treat each other. Now, more than ever, the illusions of division threaten our very existence. We all know the truth – more connects us than separates us. But in times of crisis, the wise build bridges, while the foolish build barriers. We must find a way to look after one another, as if we were one single tribe.

Yet to think T'Challa only learned the lesson of Wakanda's place in the world from Killmonger would overlook the fact that Nakia has been defending this vision for Wakanda since the opening scenes. When she first reunites with T'Challa and Okoye in Nigeria, she is happy to see them but angry that they disrupted her mission. After T'Challa's coronation, she advocates for aiding and giving refuge to people in need: "Wakanda is strong enough to help others and protect ourselves at the same time." T'Challa begs Nakia to stay in Wakanda by his side, but despite their history and obvious affection for each other, she refuses. They both initially see a romantic relationship as at odds with their individual duties to their respective missions.

By the end of the film their missions have come together and they have too. T'Challa and Nakia (and Shuri) are building international outreach centers in Oakland and beyond, working alongside each other to repair Wakanda's relationship with the rest of the world. This is not charity any more than it is a self-inflicted punishment or an attempt at global compensation. Rather, it's the work of relational repair.

"I Must Right These Wrongs"

Maybe it sounds odd to describe this globally engaged approach to Wakanda's foreign policy as reparative justice. Why should Wakandans need to make amends? What do they have to apologize for? Nakia is not Black Widow, with red in her ledger. Black Panther is not Iron Man, with a long career of arms-dealing and war-profiteering to atone for. But Wakanda has its own history, one stretching back long before its newest king or even his father's reign. When T'Challa returns to the spirit realm, he confronts not only T'Chaka but all the former Wakandan kings gathered there. "You were wrong! All of you were wrong! To turn your back on the rest of the world!"

T'Challa sees his forefathers' neglect of their cousins outside of Wakanda's borders as a wrong that he must make right. It may be too late to repair the relationships with N'Jobu and N'Jadaka, lost as they are. But it's never too late to begin to repair our place in the global community, to find a way to look after one another as if we were one single tribe.

Notes

1. Charles Mills, "'Ideal theory' as ideology," *Hypatia* 20 (2005), 165–184, 168.
2. John Rawls, *A Theory of Justice: Revised Edition* (Cambridge: Harvard University Press, 1999), 216.
3. John Rawls, *Justice as Fairness: A Restatement* (Cambridge: Harvard University Press, 2001).
4. Aristotle, *Nicomachean Ethics*, trans. David Ross (New York: Oxford University Press, 1990), Book V.
5. Mills, 168.
6. As quoted in Nancy Berlinger, *After Harm* (Baltimore, MD: Johns Hopkins University Press, 2005), 61.
7. Alec Walen, "Retributive justice," in *Stanford Encyclopedia of Philosophy*, at https://plato.stanford.edu/entries/justice-retributive.
8. Margaret Urban Walker, *What Is Reparative Justice?* (Milwaukee, WI: Marquette University Press, 2010), 15.
9. Rupert Ross, *Returning to the Teachings* (Toronto: Penguin Press, 2006), xvii, emphasis original.
10. Margaret Urban Walker, "The Expressive Burden of Reparations," in Alice

Maclachlan and Allen Speight eds., *Justice, Responsibility, and Reconciliation in the Wake of Conflict* (New York: Springer, 2013), 205–225; see also Bernard Boxill, "The morality of reparations," *Social Theory and Practice* 2 (1972), 113–123.

11. So much for Killmonger's triumphant declaration that the sun will never set on the Wakandan empire.

12. Robert Proctor, "Agnotology," in Robert Proctor and Londa Schiebinger eds., *Agnotology* (Palo Alto, CA: Stanford University Press, 2008), 8.

13. David Michaels, *Doubt Is Their Product* (Oxford: Oxford University Press, 2008).

14. Adam Serwer, "The tragedy of Erik Killmonger," *The Atlantic*, February 21, 2018, at https://www.theatlantic.com/entertainment/archive/2018/02/black-panther-erik-killmonger/553805.

15. Robert Nozick, *Philosophical Explanations* (Oxford: Clarendon Press, 1981), 367.

16. Serwer.

17. Christopher Lebron, "*Black Panther* is not the movie we deserve," *Boston Review*, February 17, 2018, at http://bostonreview.net/race/christopher-lebron-black-panther; see also "Afrofuturism, liberation, and representation in *Black Panther*," *Democracy Now!* February 28, 2018, at https://truthout.org/video/afrofuturism-liberation-representation-in-black-panther-a-roundtable-discussion.

18. Serwer, emphasis original; see also Audre Lorde, "The Master's Tools Will Never Dismantle the Master's House," in *Sister Outsider* (Berkeley, CA: Crossing Press, 1984), 110.

"What Would You Have Wakanda Do about It?"

Black Panther, Global Justice, and African Philosophy

Christine Hobden

KILLMONGER: You know, where I'm from, when Black folks started revolutions, they never had the firepower or resources to fight their oppressors. Where was Wakanda? Hmm? Yeah, all that ends today.

The world presented in *Black Panther*, although fantastical, is, for the most part, the world we currently inhabit: a deeply unjust one. This injustice and inequality is experienced between members of a society as well as across societies and states. While Killmonger, the villain, is pitted against T'Challa, the hero, Killmonger's tragic backstory generates sympathy or at least understanding given the injustice he learned as a boy. The racial injustice Killmonger experienced in 1991 Oakland, California, resonates deeply with experiences of contemporary Black Americans, as illustrated in the resurgence of the Black Lives Matter movement. This is an example of injustice within a particular society. Killmonger's quest also highlights international injustice and inequality: why did he suffer because he lived in one state and not another? What was so significant about state borders that Wakanda was willing to ignore the injustice experienced in other states? These questions of global justice are profoundly relevant today. We can think here, for one example, of the vastly unequal distribution of COVID-19 vaccines globally, leaving those in the Global South without "firepower or resources to fight" this common enemy.

So, *Black Panther*'s narrative offers significant commentary on the issue of justice, and, as we'll focus on in this chapter, global injustice in particular. Indeed, a core question running throughout the movie, is "what would you have Wakanda do about it?"

This is not an easy question to answer, especially since the characters of *Black Panther* present conflicting perspectives – Nakia wants Wakanda to

Black Panther and Philosophy: What Can Wakanda Offer the World?, First Edition. Edited by Edwardo Pérez and Timothy E. Brown.
© 2022 John Wiley & Sons, Inc. Published 2022 by John Wiley & Sons, Inc.

offer aid to the world; W'Kabi believes refugees bring their problems with them; T'Challa initially believes that it is not his place to offer justice to the world; and Killmonger wants to use Wakandan technology to liberate oppressed Black people throughout the world. But is this how we should look at justice? Should studying justice only focus on how we (or nations like Wakanda) respond to injustice? Or are there other ways to view the issues of justice and injustice? What does justice/injustice really mean?

As we'll see, through the debate on how Wakanda should respond to global injustice, *Black Panther* illustrates various issues regarding the nature of justice and the types of injustices we can inflict upon one another. We'll also see, however, that the film does not approach these questions from the perspective of the African philosophies; philosophies that the characters would've likely engaged with through the roots of their language and culture.

Knowledge Is Power: What Would You Do With It?

RAMONDA: Son, we have entertained this charlatan for too long. Reject his request.

Why does Ramonda label Killmonger a charlatan? Is it because she's afraid of his words or is it because Killmonger is a stranger to her? Even when she learns of his true heritage, she doesn't really respect him. Why? Perhaps it's because of the knowledge Killmonger possesses.

In wanting to deny Killmonger, Ramonda is guilty of an *epistemic injustice*, which, as Miranda Fricker observes (in a field-defining characterization), is the occurrence of harm to one's status as a knowledge-bearer.[1] One classic category and example Fricker presents is *testimonial injustice*, where one's view is considered less credible because of one's status – this is what Ramonda does to Killmonger; he is not credible because of his status as an outsider. Seeing this type of injustice directed toward Killmonger allows us to also see the broader *epistemicide* (the killing of knowledge) that many African peoples experienced throughout the world, especially from missionaries and colonial governments that enforced new, Western ways of being and standards for what counts as credible knowledge. This is a key feature of colonizers who, by imposing a new knowledge paradigm, destroy the old one – or, like Ramonda, when those in power who control knowledge don't want that knowledge challenged. That's why Killmonger is a charlatan called Killmonger and not a son of Wakanda called N'Jadaka.

As Dennis Masaka argues, "the tendency to deny other geopolitical centres the capacity to contribute to human civilisation has been the defining character of Eurocentrism."[2] This is, in part, why the narrative of Wakanda possessing valuable, civilization-creating knowledge resonates so deeply for many. Most African communities did not get a chance to develop and grow their ways of being into the modern era, and are even now faced with a racist view that in a counterfactual world with no colonialism, they would not have reached anything worthy of being termed "civilization." Wakanda is a powerful counter-narrative to this view.

So, understanding the underlying injustice of *epistemicide* can help us understand the extent of this power; I do not wish to undermine this great achievement of *Black Panther* – I am not challenging the fact that Wakanda is portrayed as a possessor of powerful, world-changing knowledge. Rather, in this chapter, I want to question the content of the attitudes and way of life that the creators imagined this reality would create. Wakanda provides a powerful opportunity to imagine a scenario counterfactual to colonialism; have we done enough with this opportunity?

"Y'all Sittin' up Here Comfortable. Must Feel Good."

Wakanda is portrayed as an extreme isolationist state – a state that does not engage with other states. It is not just that Wakanda remains neutral in war, like, for example, Switzerland, but that it does not engage at all with trade, cooperative ventures, human rights enforcement, and so on. We are provided with a few reasons for this isolation, and the most pressing seems to be the protection of the valuable knowledge and technology that could be used for evil if in the wrong hands. For example, when talking to Killmonger, T'Challa explicitly states that his responsibility is to ensure that "vibranium does not fall into the hands of a person like you." It is not clear why this necessarily involves keeping the technology secret rather than well protected. Nevertheless, it is an underlying theme throughout the film that if outsiders were to know of the technology it would lead to war and destruction.

Perhaps bearing witness to colonial *epistemicide* around them stoked Wakandans' strong impulse to protect their knowledge at all costs. Other reasons offered speak more directly to the typical way of life of a resident of Wakanda and the desire to protect it from a reality of foreigners visiting and becoming dependent on them. As W'Kabi says to T'Challa: "Foreign aid, refugee programs. You let refugees in, they bring their problems with them. And then Wakanda is like everywhere else."

The people of Wakanda appear to have a classic "us vs. them" attitude. Even those who wish to do something about the injustices of the world appear to view it as a case of us, Wakanda, protecting, aiding, and cleaning up after outsiders. For example, Nakia wants T'Challa to provide aid, but her framing of the issue still implies an "us vs. them" perspective. There is also T'Challa's view that Wakanda cannot judge people who are "not their own," which is a slightly different argument, speaking not to the resources to aid but to who gets to decide what is the right way to behave: we have our way, but we cannot impose it on others.

Here we see a glimpse of the way Wakanda chooses a different path from their Western contemporaries. We are invited to take the view that Wakanda is on the moral high ground because they do not use their technological strength to conquer or dominate others. This is indeed virtuous, but refusing to assist refugees or other states while they were colonized and sent into slavery is evidence of an extreme commitment to prioritizing one's own interests. Wakanda's foreign policy is extreme isolation, a position that is questioned by individuals at various moments, but appears to be largely accepted as the societal norm. How does this portrayal sit with what we do know about traditional African societies, and what contemporary African scholars suggest as possible modern-day applications of their traditional values?

What about African Philosophy?

W'Kabi speaks in isiXhosa, but has he heard of *ubuntu*? IsiXhosa is a Bantu language of the Xhosa people, spoken mainly in the Eastern Cape Province of South Africa. Beyond South Africa, some may have heard of the term *ubuntu*, whether it be through using the open-access software by that name, following the vibrant former Archbishop Desmond Tutu, or receiving something like a gift soap or tea labelled as *Ubuntu soap*! The typical South African will have grown up with the moral ethic of *ubuntu* as a commonplace feature: "I am because we are, and since we are, therefore, I am," *motho ke motho ka batho babang* (isiXhosa); *umuntu ngumuntu ngabantu* (isiZulu).[3] Afro-Canadian philosopher Edwin Etieyibo explains, "Ubuntu reflects the life experiences and histories of people in sub-Saharan Africa and defines the individual in terms of humanity or interdependency with others."[4]

In African philosophy, scholars often analyze or draw from proverbs and language use as a way to explore moral and political principles within an oral tradition. Because the characters of Wakanda are speaking a traditional African language, it is particularly important to consider proverbs and linguistic usage. Certain principles and approaches to life are contained within the language, the way of speaking. It is striking therefore that the character W'Kabi speaks isiXhosa but seems not to have heard of one of its key guiding values. Let me elaborate.

Philosophers in recent decades have explored the concept of *ubuntu* to unpack its moral and philosophical implications and to consider its modern-day application. A core idea of *ubuntu* is that one's humanity is intricately bound up with the humanity of the other. As Etieyibo observes, in order to be a person, one has to establish "human relations."[5] To be human, as ubuntuism holds, is to "affirm one's humanity by recognizing the humanity of others and, on that basis, establish relations with them."[6] Basic terms of such a relationship are expressed in the form of toleration, sharing, charity, respect, acceptance, hospitality, compassion, reconciliation, empathy, and reciprocity.[7] Or, as T'Challa says in the closing scene of the film, "We must find a way to look after one another as if we were one single tribe."

To be sure, traditional African societies were not homogeneous, nor were they entirely peaceful. Philosophers do not want to claim that all Africans lived in the perfect spirit of *ubuntu* before colonial interventions. Indeed, wars between different groups were common.[8] African philosophers also do not want to argue that pre-intervention society was inherently good and worthy of emulating. Such a "narrative of return," which essentializes what it means to be African and values principles *only* because they are traditional, would be misguided.[9] We can think here of how T'Challa comes to believe the traditional ways of his ancestors were wrong. Yet, we should nevertheless engage with what seems historically to have been a way of seeing the world and organizing society and consider the underlying values and their potential – especially when those philosophies and ways of life have typically been erased. In what follows, I present three examples of African philosophy on the question of our global duties, and highlight how they feature core values of relatedness, mutuality, and a sense of shared humanity.

"More Connects Us than Separates Us"

Etieyibo argues that if we unpack the concept of *ubuntu*, and the fact that we are persons through our recognition of others' humanity, then we should be drawn toward a cosmopolitan view: a view that holds the scope of our moral obligations is not affected by state (or other) boundaries.[10] While *ubuntu* was traditionally practiced in small communities, Etieyibo argues that the underlying philosophy does not have any grounds to justify it *having* to be only practiced within small communities. *Ubuntu* is based on our shared humanity, not on our shared kinship: it is I am because you are, not "I am because you are my cousin, or clansperson."

Some argue that today we are at the "end of *ubuntu*" for various reasons, including the strategic use and manipulation of the concept by politicians.[11] Part of the argument is that we no longer have the small communities required to make *ubuntu* work. Yet, we do not have the counterfactual example of how *ubuntu* would have adapted to the slow creation of larger communities and industrialization. So we cannot tell how much of the corrosion of the practice of *ubuntu* and its defining role in society is because of colonialist intervention and how much is down to the reality of living in large cities.

Of course, it seems reasonable to agree that *ubuntu* as practiced in a small-scale community would not function in the same way. But, is there a way the underlying values of *ubuntu* – the valuing of mutuality, compassion, respecting, and recognizing the humanity of the other – would have grown and adapted to being the guiding principles of a modern African state? Why did the creators of Wakanda not use this opportunity to imagine such a state? Given its centrality in considerations of the morality of the people of sub-Saharan Africa, particularly in Bantu-speaking communities, it is surprising that the proverb, word, or spirit seems largely lost in the Wakanda we find at the beginning of the film.

African Philosopher Michael O. Eze argues that *ubuntu* provides a foundation for a society that welcomes difference, that lays the groundwork for a "new paradigm of human citizenship that is both universal and provincial" where "we do not have the dilemma of choosing our own kind over the stranger for even the stranger is a potential relative."[12] This account speaks not to the tearing down of all borders or notions of community, but to viewing the rooted community as fundamentally open to others. Indeed, *ubuntu* can provide a new, stronger grounding for a cosmopolitan theory.

Traditionally in Western thought, the basis for a cosmopolitan view is that we are all fellow human beings and thus of equal moral worth. Human beings have been defined as those who share the quality of being able to reason. Eze argues that this Western cosmopolitanism, as is seen through colonialism, is "not so much about elimination of difference but an invention of a homogenous other."[13] Reason, Eze argues, is provincial: it can be dominated by culture, religion, and other features of our context.[14] It is not a reliable ground for a truly cosmopolitan theory. Eze argues instead that *ubuntu*, and its inherent relatedness, can do much better in justifying a cosmopolitan worldview, adding that *ubuntu* grounds a duty to "recognize others in their unique difference, histories and subjective equations" and that this sense of humanism "is not only a recognition of our kind."[15]

While cosmopolitanism based on reason requires recognizing in others the *same* ability to reason, a so-called Xerox of my being, the ethics of *ubuntu* in fact thrives on difference: "the other constitutes an inexhaustible source of our *reason* to be."[16] Human interaction is a mutual self-creating process, and there is nothing within the concept of *ubuntu* that prioritizes the recognition and interaction with those of "our own kind" over the other.[17] In fact, Eze argues that traditional communities would welcome the stranger and grant them epistemic preference (view them as the superior bringer of knowledge) because of their access to fresh ideas.[18] This interaction is motivated, Eze claims, by a "desire of harmonization of ethical virtues and common good."[19]

"I've Seen Too Many in Need Just to Turn a Blind Eye."

Ifeanyi Menkiti argues that proverbs and wisdom within African thought and tradition uphold mutuality and the sense of not holding one's self above others. He presents two proverbs from Igbo cultures (from Nigeria) that he argues can provide "ordering perspective with which we can approach justice."[20] The first, *ebele umu uwa* translates to "pity the children of the world."[21] The proverb is not a call to feel pity or mercy for those poor children out there, but rather an expression that includes one's self. It acknowledges that we are all in a situation of requiring pity. The point is not to put us down, but, as Menkiti explains: to "make possible the practice of reconciliation on an ongoing basis; [the proverb] makes possible also the acknowledgements that all of us need and can use, so as not to come down too heavily on ourselves and the moments of personal error, personal failure or professional defeat."[22]

For Menkiti, this position of pity and mercy enables one to "better position oneself to uphold the perspective of human dignity, even as failures and breakages occur all around one."[23] It thus encourages a worldview that holds "that human dignity is hard-won; it is precarious and constant effort is needed to uphold it."[24] The expression cannot be easily or simply translated, but the above discussion reveals that it is an inclusive statement, speaking to the reality we all find ourselves in, and a sense of mutually upholding human dignity within it (through pity, forgiveness, reconciliation). Indeed, Menkiti reinforces this sense of mutuality with another proverb: "aka nni kwo aka ekpe, aka ekpe kwo aka nni," which means "the right hand washes the left, the left hand washes the right."[25] He argues that we would do well to approach international relations through the lens of these "many innocuous rituals of daily life."[26]

These examples are not exhaustive of all that African philosophy can contribute to this debate, nor do they suggest there is complete consensus. They do suggest, however, that there is a strong strand of African philosophy that, drawing from traditional conceptions of justice and society, argues for accounts of what we owe each other that lean toward the cosmopolitan, toward the welcoming and inclusion of, dependence on, and respect for the other. Truly, it is striking that these themes are not given a more central place in the way of life of Wakanda, supposedly an example of an isiXhosa-speaking African community, unaffected by any external influences.

"What Would You Have Wakanda Do about It?"

African philosophy offers a stark contrast to typical Western contributions to the global justice debate. Western views tend to focus on how best to distribute resources because they're concerned with answering the question "what would you like us to do about it?" We do not spend enough time around typical Wakandans to get a good sense of their way of life. But the Wakandans featured in the film seem to embody this Western mindset. Beyond their borders exists only "the other," who is to be feared or on occasion assisted, but not valued. The foreigners we encounter in the movie are to be pitied (the Nigerian girls being kidnapped) or feared and mistrusted (Klaus, Killmonger, and even Agent Ross, to some extent). There is no sense in which foreigners should be valued for their shared humanity or what we can learn from "the stranger."

My argument is not that traditional African ideas should have been the dominant thinking of Wakandan society. Rather, my point is that it is strange that such ideas do not even feature on the lips of the elders or some characters, and given the long history of isolation, have not been the norm for a long time. The fact that N'Jabu and Killmonger are radicalized outside of Wakanda precisely reinforces this point – those who do go beyond the borders are the ones who begin to view others as "our people." The fact that Wakanda had not yet changed its position suggests that very few citizens ever meaningfully interacted with those beyond their borders, thus reinforcing their parochial perspective.

Ultimately, we see that T'Challa is convinced of the need to respond to the injustice of the world. Yet, despite what T'Challa says in his speech to the United Nations at the end of the film, his decision to "no longer watch from the shadows" appears to be motivated by the need to help, not by a sense of oneness with all of humanity, as understood through African philosophy.

Our People

I watched *Black Panther* in a theater in the Eastern Cape, South Africa, with a group of mostly isiXhosa-speaking students, who laughed and delighted in the passing comments in isiXhosa throughout the film. I led discussions and read essays on their responses to the film. It was a privileged experience, and a fantastic hook into a class on global justice and African philosophy.

Perhaps it is this context that amplified the dissonance between the film and African philosophy: on the one hand the voices of Wakanda spoke of "*our* way of life" and protecting *our* people: "I chose my people. I chose Wakanda."; "people who are not our own"; "I am not King of all people. I am King of Wakanda." On the other hand, the African philosophers we studied spoke frequently of "mutuality," "reciprocity," "relatedness" – of engaging with the other rather than fearing the other.

Wakanda is, of course, fictional. So, it does not need to be held accountable to empirical reality. Yet, Wakanda is clearly located in Africa and tries to represent a version of what Africa is, and could have been: a place that thrives in its own way. It is odd, then, that "the way" of the people of Wakanda appears to be largely shaped by a Western perspective rather than traditional African thought.

Much has happened with regard to the issue of global justice since *Black Panther*'s 2018 release – many around the world have joined in to support the American Black Lives Matter movement against systematic racism in US law enforcement and criminal justice systems, and the depth of global inequality and its dire consequences has been highlighted in a new and stark way through the COVID-19 pandemic. It will be interesting then to see how (or if) *Black Panther*'s sequel addresses these issues of injustice. Will the perspective remain Westernized? Or, will the filmmakers show a Wakanda that speaks more clearly to the histories of African philosophies and ways of life? And, what will be the effect of Wakanda's global outreach? Will Wakanda still view the world as others who need help, or will Wakandans embrace the concept of *ubuntu* and truly view the world as one?[27]

Notes

1. Miranda Fricker, *Epistemic Injustice: Power and the Ethics of Knowing* (Oxford: Oxford University Press, 2007).
2. Dennis Masaka, "'Global Justice' and the suppressed epistemologies of the indigenous people of Africa," *Philosophical Papers* 46 (2017), 70.
3. Michael Onyebuchi Eze, "I am because you are: Cosmopolitanism in the age of xenophobia," *Philosophical Papers* 46 (2017), 99.
4. Edwin Etieyibo, "Ubuntu, cosmopolitanism, and distribution of natural resources," *Philosophical Papers* 46 (2017), 141.
5. Etieyibo, 154.
6. Mogobe B. Ramose, *African Philosophy through Ubuntu* (Harare: Mond Books, 1999), 52.
7. Eze, 99.
8. Eze, 100.
9. Bernard Matolino and Wenceslaus Kwindingwi, "The end of Ubuntu," *South African Journal of Philosophy* 32 (2013), 197–205.
10. Etieyibo.
11. Matolino and Kwindingwi.
12. Eze, 98.
13. Eze, 101.
14. Eze, 100.
15. Eze, 100.
16. Eze, 101.
17. Eze, 101.
18. Eze, 100.
19. Eze, 100.
20. Ifeanyi A. Menkiti, "Africa and global justice," *Philosophical Papers* 46 (2017), 23.
21. Menkiti, 23.
22. Menkiti, 23.
23. Menkiti, 24.

24. Menkiti, 24.
25. Menkiti, 28.
26. Menkiti, 28.
27. This chapter would not have been possible without the interesting conversations with my Philosophy Honours classes at the University of Fort Hare, Alice, South Africa 2018 & 2019. Thanks are also owed to Stephen Cooke, Vuyani Ndzishe, and Ryan Roos, who commented on earlier drafts of this chapter.

5

T'Challa's Liberalism and Killmonger's Pan-Africanism

Stephen C. W. Graves

"Wakanda Forever" is the most memorable phrase from *Black Panther*, but what does it really mean? Given Wakanda's isolationist attitude and deep-seated sense of nationalism, it seems to mean "Wakanda for the Wakandans!" As portrayed in the film, this nationalism was constructed as a defense against the outside world. After all, as W'Kabi, who opposes accepting refugees from neighboring countries, says, "The problem with refugees is they bring their problems with them."

In brief, the history of Wakanda began thousands of years ago when five African tribes fought over a meteorite containing vibranium. United as Wakanda, they used the vibranium to develop advanced technology and isolate themselves from the world, posing as a third-world country. Ultimately, a visit from Thanos's army in *Avengers: Infinity War* led to the decision that Wakanda could no longer isolate from the rest of the world. As a result, nationalism gave way to liberalism.

Liberalism, as an international theory, encourages cooperation among nations for the sake of mutual benefits. The protection and promotion of human rights and freedom must come ahead of national interests and state autonomy. The hope is that war can be prevented or eliminated through institutional reform or collective action.[1] But does liberalism suffice? Perhaps a Pan-African alternative is preferable.

"Wakanda Has the Tools to Liberate'em All."

In 1992, N'Jobu planned an armed assault on the California National Guard in response to the beating of Rodney King and the Los Angeles uprising that ensued. He further planned to share Wakanda's technology with people of African descent around the world to help them throw off their oppressors. N'Jobu's plans were thwarted, but in 2016 N'Jobu's son, Killmonger, planned to share Wakandan weapons with operatives around the world.

Black Panther and Philosophy: What Can Wakanda Offer the World?, First Edition. Edited by Edwardo Pérez and Timothy E. Brown.
© 2022 John Wiley & Sons, Inc. Published 2022 by John Wiley & Sons, Inc.

After the death of his father at the hands of the former king T'Chaka, Killmonger grew up an orphan in poverty. His experiences of racial discrimination, the war on drugs waged in Black neighborhoods, over-policing, systemic poverty, and redlining, led him to the belief that Wakanda's advanced technology should serve the purpose of liberating oppressed African people around the globe.

Killmonger's philosophy of spreading Wakanda's wealth and technological advances to Black communities all over the world aligns with the Pan-African vision of such nationalists as Martin Delany, Marcus Garvey, and Malcolm X. The term "Pan-African" dates to the first Pan-African Conference, held in London in July 1900. The conference aimed to assemble "men and women of African blood, to deliberate solemnly upon the present situation and the outlook for the darker races of mankind" and to demonstrate that those of African descent could speak for themselves. Its "Address to the Nations of the World" condemned racial oppression in the United States, as well as throughout Africa, and demanded self-govern-ment for Britain's colonies.

W.E.B. Du Bois sought to continue the tradition of those of African descent speaking with one voice when he organized his own Pan-African Congress in Paris in 1919. Du Bois took the initiative to organize a second congress, held in 1921 in London, Paris, and Brussels, a third in London and Lisbon in 1923, and a fourth in New York in 1927. The congresses took a stand against racism and raised the demand for self-determination. They were, however, criticized as harboring moderate political views and for their exclusion of Marcus Garvey, perhaps the leading Pan-Africanist of the time.

Garvey had established his Universal Negro Improvement Association and African Communities League in Jamaica in 1914. Among its aims were "a universal confederacy amongst the race."[2] Time only strengthened Pan-African demands for an end to colonial rule. In Britain, George Padmore, Amy Ashwood Garvey, and the Pan-African Federation made preparations for a new gathering at the Manchester Pan-African Congress of 1945. The Manchester Pan-African congress of October 1945 marked a turning point in the history of the Pan-African movement. Since this meet-ing, the struggle for the emancipation of people of African descent focused on the continental homeland. When Kwame Nkrumah returned to Ghana in December 1947, Pan-Africanism moved into the realm of practical politics. With Ghana achieving independence in March 1957, and until the creation of the Organization of African Unity (OAU, May 1963), Ghana became the focal point of the struggle for African unity, with Kwame Nkrumah as the unofficial leader.

According to Nkrumah, political integration is a prerequisite for economic integration. As Nkrumah states, "unless Africa is politically united under an all-African union government, there can be no solution to our political and economic problems. We are Africans first and last, and as

Africans our best interests can only be served by uniting within an African community."[3] Muammar Qaddafi proposed a similar project at the 5th Summit of the OAU held in Qaddafi's hometown of Sirte, Libya, in September 1999. After the death of Nkrumah in 1972, Qaddafi assumed leadership of the Pan-African movement and became an outspoken advocate of African unity. "One Africa, One Hope" calls for the realization of the Pan-African ideal of African unity in order to achieve the elusive goals of peace, security, and development. Unfortunately, the relatively ineffective and powerless African union – modeled after the European union – that came into being in July 2001 was significantly different from the organization envisioned by Qaddafi.

In the world of *Black Panther*, Killmonger's plan to arm African descendants across the globe represents the beginning stages of the Pan-African ideal, where Blacks all over the world fight for liberation by any means necessary.

T'Challa's Liberalism

For centuries, Wakanda pursued a policy of isolation fueled by the desire to maintain its traditions and by the spirit of nationalism. Outside Wakanda were the scourges of colonialism, slavery, and wars of conquest. For Wakandans the question was whether to maintain their isolationist ways or to join the international community. Should they share their vibranium-based technology, or perhaps use it to support oppressed people across the globe? We get an answer at the end of *Black Panther*. T'Challa establishes an outreach center at the building where N'Jobu died, and he appears before the United Nations to reveal Wakanda's true nature to the world.

The United Nations is based on the notion that the member states have sovereign equality.[4] Each state, regardless of size or population, is legally recognized as equivalent with every other state. The inequalities between states, however, are codified through the veto power granted to the five permanent members of the security council: China, Russia, the United States, France, and the United Kingdom. Notably, only international problems are within the jurisdiction of the United Nations. The UN Charter does not "authorize the United Nations to intervene in matters which are essentially within the domestic jurisdiction of any state."[5] Increasingly, current wars have been civil wars, which do not legally fall under the provisions in the UN Charter. However, the prelude to and fallout from civil war can often demand UN attention: refugees seeking asylum often crossing international borders, and weapons of war being transported through transnational networks.

The UN is designed primarily to maintain international peace and security. Collective security is based on the proposition that potential aggressors will refrain from the use of force against another because they know ahead of time that their use of force will be met by all, or many, states joining together against the aggressor. The goal of achieving peace through collective security relies on several assumptions that will also help us understand why T'Challa believes that joining with the United Nations and building a community center is the best approach to solving the global oppression faced by people of African descent. The first assumption is that wars are preventable and will not occur if all parties exercise restraint. A second assumption is that aggressors, no matter who they are, should be stopped. This presumes that the aggressor can be easily identified by members of the international community. In many cases, though, it is difficult to tell who the aggressor is and who the victim is.[6] Lastly, collective security assumes moral clarity, meaning that the aggressor is morally wrong because all aggressors are morally wrong. As a result, those who are right must act together to meet the aggression. This also assumes that the aggressors know that the international community will act to punish the aggressor, or those committing the initial injustice.

In practice, collective security has been difficult to achieve since World War II. In most cases, states dare not interfere in actions taken by an ally or foe, even if that state was the aggressor, for fear of starting another world war.[7] The aggressor cannot always be easily identified and even if the aggressor can be identified, that party may not *always* be morally wrong. Trying to right a previous wrong is not necessarily wrong, nor is trying to make just a prior injustice always unjust. Ultimately, collective security in practice supports and maintains the status quo, leaving victims of oppression, both domestically and internationally, looking for answers.

Killmonger's Pan-Africanism

Pan-Africanism represents the expression of shared values and common interests of Africans across the diaspora. Intellectually, it tends to view Africans and descendants of Africa as belonging to a single race and sharing cultural unity. This group has a shared historical experience of domination and nationalist struggles for their cultural, economic, and political liberation. Pan-Africanism was thus conceived as a liberation movement designed to regroup and mobilize Africans in Africa and the diaspora against racial discrimination, foreign domination and oppression, and economic exploitation.[8]

Pan-Africanists led by Kwame Nkrumah of Ghana, and including Ahmed Ben Bella of Algeria, Patrice Lumumba of the Congo, Ahmed Sekou Touré of Guinea, and Modibo Keita of Mali, proposed, following the blueprint of "Africa Must Unite," immediate political and economic integration in the form of a "United States of Africa." This would consist of an African common market, African monetary union, African military high command, and a continent-wide Union government.[9]

Ignace Kissangou proposes the creation of a federation of African nation-states with a common defense and security policy, a continent-wide army, a common currency, and such Pan-African institutions as a security council for African development, an African parliament, and an African senate (or representative council of African institutions).[10] In 2018, in response to the visit of the British Prime Minister Theresa May, Julius Malema, the leader of one of South Africa's most significant opposition organizations, the Economic Freedom Fighters (EFF), evoked the spirit of Pan-Africanism. Malema called for a united Africa with a common language and an end to Africa's colonial borders. Ultimately, peoples of African descent, wherever they are, must take on the tradition of their forebear Pan-Africanists and unite their vision and talents to survive in the increasingly hostile global village.[11]

In a departure from liberalism toward a more realist theoretical approach, African Americans realized with frustration that the expectation that emancipation would end exploitation of Blacks and restore their dignity was mistaken.[12] We can view Killmonger as realistic in this way. He was educated and had traveled the world, witnessing violence and destruction and the oppression of dark skin people everywhere. Killmonger was not out to dominate the world and become a global dictator. His goal was liberation.

When Competing Philosophies Collide

T'Challa and Killmonger each see their respective philosophy as superior. Whereas Killmonger wants Wakanda to free oppressed Black communities all over the world, T'Challa wants to work through global institutions and the international community.

There are many positive elements of Pan-Africanism, and one cannot deny the collective conditions and oppression of Black people around the globe. Should African countries do for self, or should they rely and depend on other countries and other groups to defend and work in their best interests?

History has numerous examples of Africans uniting to oppose oppression. In eighteenth-century London, for example, African writers and campaigners such as Olaudah Equiano formed the Sons of Africa, perhaps the first Pan-African organization. Its members asserted their pride in a common African heritage and campaigned against Britain's role as the world's leading human trafficker at the time. The most important event to undermine both racism and the slave system during the eighteenth century occurred when revolution broke out in the French Caribbean colony of St. Domingue in August 1791. The result was the creation of Haiti, the first modern "Black" republic anywhere in the world. The revolution produced new heroes of African descent, such as Toussaint L'Ouverture and Sanité

Bélair. Moving into the nineteenth century, early Pan-Africanists included Martin Delany from the United States and Edward Blyden from the Caribbean. Delany, an abolitionist, writer, and medical practitioner, welcomed the "common cause" that was developing between "the blacks and colored races," clearly stating his policy: "Africa for the African race and black men to rule them."[13]

So what about Wakanda? Did Wakanda really just sit on its vibranium and wealth while African descendants were enslaved? Did they really just sit back and watch all of their neighbors experience colonialization? Did they do nothing about Apartheid? Did they ever reflect on these atrocities and think maybe they should do something, even if from the shadows?

Whatever some Wakandans may have thought, the nation as a whole did not act. It's no surprise, then, that Killmonger decided that disbursing arms to the African descendants was the best way to liberate them. While in the military, he had seen the benefits of war and the strength of arms. Can we really suppress our racial and historical ties of oppression in the name of international interdependence? Hadn't international security failed Black people? Would the United States ever grant the UN permission to intervene on racial violence and oppression within its own borders?

Pan-Africanism does not deny the idealistic hope and possibilities of collective action, and it does not denigrate the importance of international institutions. But it does recognize that that those outside of the diaspora have continually made little to no effort in assisting in the liberation of African descendants globally. Hasn't the status quo done a pretty good job of maintaining itself, even after the atrocities of World War II, and more recently the environmental disasters in Puerto Rico, New Orleans, and Japan? The system of international institutions and collective security may be a formidable opponent for superpowered aliens from outer space, but it is no match for the hegemonic superpower of states in the real world. It's easy to identify an alien threat coming from outer space, but a little more difficult to recognize human atrocities taking place across the sea by an important trading partner.

If anyone is going to save Africans, it is going to have to be Africans, on the home continent and across the globe. Africans must fight to save themselves and will be better off doing it together – and the African homeland is the most logical place for such a revival to take place. But why didn't Killmonger ask for financial assistance for Africans from Wakanda instead of weapons? Is violence the best way to liberate Black people? Or is it just the only thing that the oppressor respects?

What are the barriers to Killmonger's Pan-Africanism? First, and most importantly, selfishness and feelings of superiority by one nation, or group of people, over another. This is different from nationalism or protectionism where a nation establishes economic policy or creates institutions in the best interests of its own people. One can advocate for one's specific racial or ethnic group based on shared history, experiences, and culture without pronouncing one's group to be superior to another. But in the case of *Black Panther*, Wakanda clearly had it figured out. It was safe, secure, wealthy, and powerful. It also felt no real obligation to save anyone outside its borders or interfere with the oppression of Blacks throughout the world. In some ways, this is eerily similar to the way many Blacks in Africa and in the diaspora see African Americans. Like Wakandans in their defense bubble, African Americans may know very little of the conditions experienced by other Black peoples. With access to wealth and power, shouldn't African Americans do more for the liberation of oppressed Black peoples around the world? African Americans tend to feel more American than African, and they feel like they have a completely separate culture and set of beliefs than other members of the diaspora.

What if Killmonger had won and Black people around the world were able to liberate themselves? Then what? Despite a similar history and experiences, the lack of homogeneity amongst Black populations makes Killmonger's Pan-African vision difficult. Would they all migrate to one place? Would Wakanda accept Black people from across the globe into their separate world? If Blacks across the globe were willing to adopt Wakanda's norms and principles for the promise of security, would that be enough to establish unity? If united, Black peoples, both in the movie and in reality, would be an undeniable, dominant global force. Thus, it is in their best interest to unify.

T'Challa's action of throwing money into building a center in Oakland at the end of the movie is not the answer, however. We can understand Killmonger's frustration. Wakanda and T'Challa could do much more. They literally have the wealth and technology to completely rebuild and revitalize the entire community, but choose the route of building a community center instead.

Our current reality may be that Blacks are collectively better off with both Killmonger and T'Challa together. Killmonger represents realism, while T'Challa represents the liberal ideal. Blacks need Killmonger's global perspective and passion for justice and liberation, but they also need T'Challa's idealistic vision.

Notes

1. Karen Mingst, Heather Elko McKibben, and Ivan M. Arreguín-Toft, *Essentials of International Relations*, 8th ed. (New York: W.W. Norton & Co., 2019), 60.
2. Guy Martin, *African Political Thought* (New York: Palgrave Macmillan, 2012).
3. Martin, 58.
4. Mingst et al., 169.
5. Mingst et al., 171.

6. Mingst et al., 233.
7. Mingst et al., 234.
8. Mingst et al., 57.
9. Martin, 55.
10. Martin, 60.
11. Martin, 65.
12. Godfrey O. Ozumba and Elijah O. John eds., *African Political Philosophy* (London: lulu.com, 2017), 57.
13. Ozumba and John, 57.

PART II

Wakanda Forever!

6

Panther Virtue
The Many Roles of T'Challa

Mark D. White

T'Challa, the Black Panther, wears many hats, both at home and abroad. He is the chieftain of the Panther Tribe, which makes him the spiritual leader of his people as well as the king of Wakanda and its head of state. After he ended Wakanda's traditional isolationism, he acted as its ambassador to the outside world, meeting with global leaders and speaking at the United Nations – and even representing Earth in the Council of Worlds (at the request of Thor). Of course, T'Challa is also a world-famous superhero, protecting the innocent from the forces of evil on his own and as a core member of the Avengers, the Ultimates, and even the Fantastic Four for a while. And in his personal life – when he allows himself one – he is a son, a brother, and (occasionally) a husband, and in some future stories, a father as well.

T'Challa is also known throughout the world as a noble, honorable, and virtuous person – but what does this mean when he serves in so many roles, each with its own obligations, expectations, and moral problems? And what happens when two or more of his roles pull him in opposite directions? How does T'Challa remain noble and virtuous at these times of conflict – or *can* he – and what toll does it take on him?

The Virtues of the Black Panther

First, what does it mean to be virtuous? Virtue ethics is the oldest of the three basic Western systems of ethics, dating back to the ancient Greeks. Most versions of virtue ethics, including that of Aristotle (384–322 BCE), have as their ultimate goal a state of *eudaimonia*, a term that is best understood as "flourishing." Despite countless self-help books that use the term to support introspection and self-fulfillment, *eudaimonia* is achieved by "living well" and striving for "excellence" in one's actions in

Black Panther and Philosophy: What Can Wakanda Offer the World?, First Edition. Edited by Edwardo Pérez and Timothy E. Brown.
© 2022 John Wiley & Sons, Inc. Published 2022 by John Wiley & Sons, Inc.

the world. According to Aristotle, this can be done only by possessing and acting on character traits or *virtues* such as courage, honesty, and generosity. Cultivating and practicing these virtues not only makes one an ethical member of society, but is also the only way to achieve true happiness or *eudaimonia*.[1]

Many people throughout the Marvel Universe remark on T'Challa's virtues. In his first appearance in the pages of Fantastic Four, after T'Challa nearly defeated the entire team single-handedly and then promised to stand down so they could talk in peace, Reed Richards told the others, "a man such as the Black Panther does not give his word lightly – nor does he dishonor it, once given!"[2] The next hero to visit Wakanda was Captain America, widely regarded as a paragon of virtue himself, who saw in T'Challa "a leader born – in whose veins the blood of chieftains flows," after which the Black Panther returned the compliment, hailing Cap's valor upon his first meeting and telling him later, "there is no man I will be prouder – to die with."[3] Later, T'Challa told Cap of their bond of "sacred honor," and even after a tense period during which loyalties were tested, Cap called T'Challa "the most noble man I've ever met," and T'Challa affirmed that they were not just friends, but brothers.[4]

It isn't just his fellow heroes who acknowledge the virtues of the Black Panther. Everett Ross, the United States government agent assigned to accompany the king of Wakanda when visiting America – and who would later find himself entangled in many of his adventures – described T'Challa as "one of the greatest men of our time ... a man of great compassion and great nobility," not to mention heroism.[5] Namor the Sub-Mariner, king of Atlantis, who rarely has a kind word to say about anybody, told his fellow ruler he has "unshakeable moral fiber," and later told Shuri that her brother is a good man and "an honorable man."[6] Even Doctor Doom, a megalomaniac tyrant with a curious sense of honor himself, hailed T'Challa as "a true monarch and a man of integrity."[7]

But Virtue Needs Judgment

One key aspect that separates virtue ethics from its rival moral theories, consequentialism and deontology, is its focus on character. *Consequentialism* tells us to make choices that have the best results, usually put in terms of the "greatest good," and *deontology* tells us to follow rules, principles, or duties that represent what is right or just.[8] Both of these share a focus on action, whereas virtue ethics focuses on the person who is acting. Rather than follow a rule designed to maximize the good or do what is right, virtue ethics tells us to make choices based on character traits such as honesty and courage. Acting on these virtues will most likely lead to ethical results, whether in terms of the right or the good, but more important, they will imply good character on the part of the person performing them.

There seems to be a problem, though. "Be honest" doesn't seem to provide as much guidance in particular situations as "do what creates the most good" or "follow a certain rule." Does honesty mean revealing everything you think, or does it involve simply not lying? Is keeping your mouth shut honest? And does it matter to whom, or about what, you're being honest? Courage raises the same questions: Black Panther and Everett Ross may both be courageous, but we don't expect the same expressions of that virtue from both of them, even in similar situations.

This is where judgment comes into play. *Judgment*, or what Aristotle called "practical wisdom" (or *phronêsis*), is the ability to decide how best to act on one's virtues in a particular situation. In fact, the contents page of *Black Panther: Panther's Prey* #1 (May 1991) quotes Aristotle's *Nicomeachean Ethics* (Book IV), outlining what judgment involves: implementing a virtue "with the right person to the right extent and at the right time and with the right object and in the right way," which "is not easy, and it is not everyone who can do it." Sound judgment has to be developed, cultivated, and practiced, as with other virtues; in fact, it can be considered an *executive virtue* that helps us act on our more "basic" virtues.

Judgment is essential for putting our virtues to use in making decisions, even fairly common ones such as having to give bad news to a loved one or standing up to a bully in defense of ourselves or others.[9] In these situations, we use our judgment to make the choice that expresses our moral character and the virtues that comprise us, and maintains our moral integrity. Some situations are less common for us, but far more common for people in masks and capes. In choice situations that philosophers call *tragic dilemmas*, there is no option that seems good or right, and we cannot "escape with clean hands." This applies to the classic trope of the superhero having to choose between saving a number of innocent civilians or a close loved one; neither choice is acceptable, but a choice must nonetheless be made (unless the superhero thinks of a way out of it, which they usually do). For instance, after he destroyed all of Wakanda's vibranium to save it from falling into the hands of Doctor Doom, T'Challa told Daredevil that "a king must make terrible choices … I cannot regret them, I did what I had to do." Daredevil responded, "but they haunt you," a natural result of making a choice in tragic dilemmas.[10]

The Many Roles of the Black Panther … and the Conflicts that Result

Tragic dilemmas often arise because of a conflict of obligations, such as that between saving people in general and saving a person you're close to. Because of the number of roles and responsibilities he has, T'Challa often finds himself in such situations. Once, when T'Challa was thought dead, a traditionalist faction overthrew his government and put his wife, Storm of the X-Men, on trial, sentencing her to death. Rather than rush in and save her, T'Challa carefully plotted to win back his throne. When he defended this decision to the rest of the X-Men, he simply said, "I had to choose between my wife's life and the future of the entire country. I chose my country."[11]

Although the conflict between family and kingdom is perhaps the most personal of the conflicts T'Challa faces, by far the most frequent is that between his responsibilities as the king of Wakanda and as a superhero, especially as a member of the Avengers. As Everett Ross once said after T'Challa dissolved his government and nationalized all foreign businesses operating in Wakanda, "people keep mistaking him for a superhero – but the guy's a king. And, just when you least expect it – he starts acting like one."[12] The Avengers confronted this conflict head-on when it was revealed that T'Challa originally joined the team – on the invitation of Captain America no less – to spy on them and assess whether they posed a threat to Wakanda (a possibility that became all too real during the superhero Civil War years later).[13] Soon afterwards, the Avengers were forced to make a public statement when T'Challa initiated military action against the underseas kingdom of Deviant Lemuria, in which the Wasp referred to him as "King T'Challa" to stress the capacity in which he was operating (and that in which he was not).[14]

Judgment is necessary to decide how to act in any choice situation based on one's virtues, but it is usually needed even more when one has to balance several different roles, each with its own responsibilities and obligations. Although every superhero's moral code is different, most of them share basic elements, such as saving as many people as you can, avoiding killing anybody, and embodying basic virtues such as honesty and decency.[15] But a king, like all sovereigns, is responsible for the well-being, safety, and prosperity of his country and all of its citizens, and this often requires different moral decision-making. Thus, there are situations in which T'Challa must decide whether to act as a hero or a king, and his judgment may dictate different actions rooted in the same virtues.

When T'Challa believed that agents within the US government were helping to overthrow his own, he and the Dora Milaje drove a truck into a building and abducted a businessman involved in the operation. In a subsequent Avengers meeting, Iron Man confronted T'Challa about this, to which the king responded simply that "these are matters of national security," explaining that "factions of your government have committed an act of war against my throne," and rejecting their assistance, citing a conflict of interest in the Avengers' own charter.[16] As Everett Ross said later, "What kind of Avenger – or superhero – can this guy be? Answer: He's not a 'hero' at all – 'super' or otherwise! The guy is a king."[17] Even for the Black Panther, it can seem impossible to be both, and to remain virtuous according to one's own moral code at all times.[18]

Heavy Is the Head that Wears the Crown

T'Challa's duties as an Avenger come into conflict with his role as king of Wakanda, but other conflicts result from his role as a spiritual leader, which he regards as more important.[19] For example, during a war with the Skrulls, T'Challa bemoaned the fact that he was too busy directing the battle to help his people mourn: "My people are dying, and as their spiritual leader, I should be there for them. But I can't …"[20] This also brings up another role he has, that of military leader: Wakanda is often described as a nation of warriors, and even though it has never been conquered, it has been challenged on many occasions, often from within. T'Challa can be seen giving inspiring speeches to his fighting Wakandans in the aforementioned battle against the Skrulls. In an earlier battle in Niganda to save his sister Shuri from Killmonger, he instructed his people to focus on two things: rescuing the hostages and protecting "the innocent people of Niganda," among whom Killmonger is sheltering.[21]

Of course, simply being king carries immense responsibilities – and no one makes sure T'Challa knows this more than his mother, Ramonda. She told him he was neglecting his sovereign duties when he was spending too much time away from home, dealing with the superhero Civil War and serving as a member of the Fantastic Four with his wife, Storm.[22] Before T'Challa married, Ramonda would periodically make sure he remembered his responsibilities to choose a queen and produce an heir, the preoccupation of most kings around the world throughout history.[23] T'Challa would also confide in his mother about the burden of being king, claiming to be a captive of his role just as she was held captive in South Africa.[24] As he told her, "Every decision I make, I am imprisoned by the effect it will have on others. The prison bars are there, you just can't see them."[25]

All of these roles and burdens can be too much for a person, even as impressive a person as T'Challa.[26] When Wakanda stood on the brink of war with the underwater kingdom of Deviant Lemuria, Storm warned her future husband that he reminded her of Magneto in his benevolent ambition, and warned against the hubris that led to the mutant leader's downfall. In an emotional moment, T'Challa and Storm embraced and kissed, even though he was involved with another woman, and he immediately felt guilty. Storm assured him, "You are a human being … bones and flesh. A spiritual being trying to master a human experience. Holding yourself to impossible standards." T'Challa then revealed his guilt went much deeper, admitting to shame "of my confession, of my weakness, of my inability to rule as my father ruled, of my unworthiness of his legacy …"[27]

The more roles one plays, especially when so many people depend on their successful execution, the easier it is to fail at any one of them – but this is all too often the superhero's burden. Taking on too many roles is itself a failure of judgment: Aristotle writes that virtues are best implemented according to "the golden mean," neither too much nor too little, but in the right amount, the right way, and so on. Even the most virtuous superheroes usually take on too much responsibility, whether it's Captain America feeling he has to protect the American dream and all it stands for, or Doctor Strange taking on the charge of protecting the entire world from metaphysical threats.[28] Generosity, service to others, and beneficence are all virtues, but they must be practiced as such: to the right degree and balancing them with other virtues, including self-care.

To be fair, T'Challa does occasionally acknowledge this. Before he proposed to the other great love of his life, Monica Lynne, he told her, "If I don't keep alive the passions and ideals within me ... keep alive love because it can die so easily – then I will become a bad leader for my people."[29] Note he phrases this need for balance in terms of his overarching role as king, recognizing that successful integration of many duties – including duties to himself – is necessary to perform that role well. (If only he acknowledged this fact more often!)

King for Life ... Like It or Not

In the final issue of a recent run of his book that saw Wakanda adopting democracy and the title character leading an intergalactic rebellion against a symbiote-infected Killmonger, T'Challa confided in Storm that "I never wanted to be king."[30] He is not tribal chieftain, king, or the Black Panther by choice, even though he did fight for the honor. These were the roles expected of him by birthright. This fact makes his dedication to these responsibilities all the more impressive, while it makes the excesses he goes to in fulfilling them even more worrisome. It is one thing to devote yourself wholeheartedly to a task or goal you set for yourself, and another entirely to tie yourself to one set *for* you before you were born. As T'Challa told his mother, he is bound by these expectations and the responsibilities he bears, and while this may weigh heavily on him, for the sake of Wakanda, the world, and us – the comics readers and moviegoers – let's hope he never gives them up.[31]

Notes

1. For more on Aristotle's virtue ethics, see his *Nicomachean Ethics* (350 BCE), at http://classics.mit.edu/Aristotle/nicomachaen.html, as well as Richard Kraut, "Aristotle's Ethics," in Edward N. Zalta ed., *Stanford Encyclopedia of Philosophy* (Summer 2018 Edition), at https://plato.stanford.edu/archives/sum2018/entries/aristotle-ethics. On virtue ethics more generally, see Rosalind Hursthouse, *On Virtue Ethics* (Oxford: Oxford University Press, 1999) and Hursthouse and Glen Pettigrove, "Virtue Ethics," in Edward N. Zalta ed., *Stanford Encyclopedia of Philosophy* (Winter 2018 Edition), at https://plato.stanford.edu/archives/win2018/entries/ethics-virtue.

2. *Fantastic Four*, vol. 1, #52 (July 1966).

3. *Tales of Suspense*, vol. 1, #97 (January 1968), and *Captain America*, vol. 1, #100 (April 1968). This is not Cap's first visit to Wakanda, nor the first Black Panther he met: In *Black Panther*, vol. 3, #30 (May 2001), we learn that Cap met T'Challa's father T'Chaka during World War II, although in *Black Panther/Captain America: Flags of Our Father* #1 (April 2010), it was T'Chaka's father Azzuri whom Cap met on that visit.

4. *Black Panther*, vol. 1, #15 (May 1979), and *Black Panther*, vol. 3, #30. On Cap's own virtues, see my book *The Virtues of Captain America: Modern-Day Lessons on Character from a World War II Superhero* (Hoboken, NJ: John Wiley & Sons, 2014).

5. *Black Panther*, vol. 3, #30.

6. *Black Panther*, vol. 4, #21 (December 2006), and *Black Panther*, vol. 5, #11 (February 2010).

7. *Black Panther*, vol. 3, #27 (February 2001).

8. For more on these three moral systems, consult any introductory ethics textbook; for a very brief introduction, see my chapter "Superhuman Ethics Class with the Avengers Prime" in my edited volume *The Avengers and Philosophy: Earth's Mightiest Thinkers* (Hoboken, NJ: John Wiley & Sons, 2012), 5–17.

9. Actually, judgment is no less necessary to consequentialism or deontology: "Do the most good" and "do the right thing" are not exactly precise instructions either!.

10. *Black Panther: The Man without Fear!* #513 (February 2011).

11. *Doomwar* #1 (April 2010).

12. *Black Panther*, vol. 3, #19 (June 2000).

13. *Black Panther*, vol. 3, #8 (June 1999).

14. *Black Panther*, vol. 3, #27.

15. The eagle-eyed reader will recognize the first element as consequentialist, the second as deontological, and the third representing virtue ethics.

16. *Black Panther*, vol. 3, #9 (July 1999). Speaking of Iron Man, he and T'Challa share a talent for long-range planning, seeing many different angles to a problem and planning for every possible contingency; see, for instance, *Black Panther*, vol. 3, #44–45 (July–August 2002).

17. *Black Panther*, vol. 3, #30.

18. The field of *role ethics* studies whether different roles and responsibilities may justify different ethical standards; for a recent look at role ethics in terms of virtue ethics, see Christine Swanton, "A virtue ethical theory of role ethics," *Journal of Value Inquiry* 50 (2016), 687–702.

19. *Black Panther*, vol. 3, #19 (June 2000). (Sometimes, however, he needs to reminded of this, as Captain America does in *Black Panther*, vol. 1, #14, March 1979).

20. *Black Panther*, vol. 4, #40 (October 2008).

21. *Black Panther*, vol. 4, #36 (June 2008).

22. *Black Panther*, vol. 4, #35 (May 2008).

23. *Black Panther: Panther's Prey* #1; also *Black Panther*, vol. 4, #10 (January 2006).

24. *Marvel Comics Presents*, vol. 1, #37 (December 1989).

25. *Black Panther: Panther's Prey* #2 (June 1991).

26. He even has to Google himself regularly. When Storm catches him doing it, he

starts his defense with "part of my responsibilities include –" (*Black Panther*, vol. 4, #17, August 2006).

27. *Black Panther*, vol. 3, #27.
28. See Virtues of Captain America, 58–63, and "The Otherworldly Burden of Being the Sorcerer Supreme" in my edited volume Doctor Strange and Philosophy: The Other Book of Forbidden Knowledge (Hoboken, NJ: John Wiley & Sons, 2018), 177–190.
29. *Black Panther: Panther's Prey* #3 (August 1991).
30. *Black Panther*, vol. 7, #25 (July 2021).
31. I thank the editors of this volume and the series for advice on this chapter, and all the creators behind the *Black Panther* stories for inspiration, especially Christopher Priest, Reginald Hudlin, and Don McGregor.

7

Should Wakanda Take Over the World? The Ethics of International Power

Greg Littmann

What are you going to do when the rhinoceroses smash your door to pieces and charge into your living room? Will you try to make a stand as the Dora Milaje warrior-women pile in behind them, their vibranium spears spinning and slashing, leaving your curtains in ribbons in their wake? Outside, a thundering Wakandan hoverplane descends onto the road in a haze of exhaust. Resist if you like, but you don't stand a chance. The Wakandans have taken over the world.

And why not? They certainly have the power. Access to vibranium has given them a massive technological edge over the rest of us, complete with invisible planes, energy weapons, and Black Panther suits that store and release kinetic force. Ulysses Klaue, the international arms dealer who has a gun in his arm that can crush vehicles, assures CIA agent Everett K. Ross that the Wakandans have weapons that "make my arm cannon look like a leaf blower."

If the Wakandans did take over, couldn't they do a lot of good that way? As the opening history of Wakanda in *Black Panther* shows us, Wakanda has been flourishing peacefully over the past millennia, as the world outside was torn by war. If they took over, they could impose peace through superior force. Then they could get around to bringing justice to society, eliminating poverty and disease, and generally making life as good in other countries as it is in Wakanda.

Black Panther and Philosophy: What Can Wakanda Offer the World?, First Edition. Edited by Edwardo Pérez and Timothy E. Brown.

Wakanda Could Rule Them All

N'JOBU: I observed for as long as I could! Their leaders have been assassinated, communities flooded with drugs and weapons, they are overly policed and incarcerated. All over the planet our people suffer because they don't have the tools to fight back. With vibranium weapons they could overthrow every country and Wakanda could rule them all ... the right way.

T'CHAKA: You will return home at once, where you will face the council and inform them of your crimes.

Given what we know about Wakanda and about Oakland in 1991, N'Jobu's argument makes sense, doesn't it? In fact, given the contemporary context of Black Panther, released in 2018, N'Jobu's argument remains relevant. If Wakanda were in charge, the world might be a better place. And, it's not just N'Jobu's argument, it's also his son's. As Killmonger says to T'Challa and the tribal elders: "It's about two billion people all over the world that looks like us, but their lives are a lot harder. Wakanda has the tools to liberate'em all." Later, when Killmonger becomes king, he vows: "We're gonna send vibranium weapons out to our War Dogs. They'll arm oppressed people all over the world [...] The world's gonna start over and this time, we're on top."

Obviously, Killmonger is a power-hungry villain and the new world order he wants to set up would be no less oppressive than the one he'd replace. Killmonger foresees a "Wakandan Empire" in which people of African descent are "on top" and the formerly powerful are slaughtered, along with their children and "anyone else who takes their side." It should be clear enough that Wakanda should not follow *his* plan. But that doesn't mean that Wakanda shouldn't take over in order to bring justice to the world. What if they did it with a genuine intention to make things better for the people they rule?

The Greek philosopher Plato (428–348 BCE) argued in *The Republic* that political power in society should be concentrated in the hands of those most fit to rule. He rejected the democratic system of his native Athens, on the grounds that rule by the people is rule by the unqualified. Instead, a state should be run by the most reasonable and moral citizens. This arrangement would be in everyone's best interests. Plato writes: "to ensure that [an ordinary citizen] ... is ruled by something similar to what rules the best person, we say that he ought to be the slave of that best person ... It isn't to harm the slave that we say he must be ruled ... but because it's better for everyone to be ruled by divine reason."[1]

Plato recommended against foreign conquests, which he saw as pointless wars over needless luxuries. Still, all that would be needed to be added to Plato's model to justify taking over less enlightened nations for their own good is sufficient concern for their people's well-being. And doesn't

Plato have a point that the wisest should be running things? Given how much better the Wakandans have done than other countries in terms of avoiding war, hunger, disease, poverty, tyranny, and oppression, they definitely seem wiser than the people of other nations, don't they?

Asking whether Wakanda should take over the world isn't an idle hypothetical question. What we say about the duties of a fictional nation like Wakanda has implications for what we should say about international duties in the real world. How we would want Wakanda to treat us should guide how we treat the people of other nations and how they treat us.

The Right Way

Real world societies have often justified taking over other societies on the grounds that it's for the good of the society taken over. The Romans, for instance, justified their conquests, at least partly, by citing the benefits gained by the conquered, including peace, prosperity, and civilization. "Civilizing barbarians" meant introducing them to Roman technology, administrative and legal systems, and, as the Romans saw it, the superior Roman culture and way of life. The Romans were well aware that foreigners didn't want to be ruled by them and would fight not to be taken over. But that only went to show how foolish and ignorant they were. The Roman natural philosopher Pliny the Elder (23–79), in his *Natural Histories*, notes that if Rome were to conquer the barbaric Chauci tribe of the marshlands of Northern Europe, a people so unsophisticated and uncivilized that they subsist on fish and rainwater, the Chauci would complain that they had been reduced to slavery! They wouldn't realize what good fortune it would be for them to be conquered by Rome. Certainly, we would all enjoy good fortune if we had access to vibranium, right?

The mission to "civilize the uncivilized" was taken up by later European powers during the Age of Sail, as they began to set up empires across the world. Only this time, the imperialists could add the need to convert the world to Christianity to the reasons why they should be in charge. With the eternal future of all the heathen souls in the Americas, Africa, Asia, and elsewhere at stake, it seemed clearer than ever that the benefits of European civilization needed to be spread to less-enlightened peoples. For example, Pope Alexander VI (1431–1503) authorized Spain to occupy the Americas, in the interests of spreading Christianity. N'Jobu doesn't seem to be concerned about spreading Wakandan spiritual beliefs and, given how little regard Killmonger shows for Wakandan beliefs (especially when he burns the crop of Heart-Shaped Herbs), it's clear he's not concerned about sharing a belief in Bast with colonizers.

Imperialism had support among liberals as well as among conservatives. English liberal philosopher John Stuart Mill (1806–1873) argued that a period of European trusteeship was appropriate for non-European nations, so that they could be educated in enlightened European political doctrines, such as democracy, respect and toleration for different opinions, and equal rights for all humans, including equal rights between men and women.

English Poet Rudyard Kipling (1865–1936) popularized the expression "the white man's burden" through his 1899 poem of the same name. The "white man's burden" is the supposed duty of white people to rule others for their own good. Like Pliny, Kipling understood that rule by outsiders would be resented. He understood that non-whites didn't want to be ruled by whites. The poem warns that the "captives," who are "sullen peoples" or "half-devil and half-child," will not be grateful. The white man's "reward" will be "The blame of those ye better, The hate of those ye guard." The benefits of white rule mentioned in the poem include reductions in famine and sickness, the construction of ports and roads, and being guided "toward the "light" – toward reason, education, Christianity, and the adoption of European culture.

European imperialism still has defenders today. British Prime Minister Boris Johnson wrote of Africa in a 2002 column in *The Spectator* that "The continent may be a blot but it is not a blot on our conscience. The problem is not that we were once in charge but that we are not in charge anymore."[2] It's interesting to consider N'Jobu's and Killmonger's perspectives in light of these motivations behind colonization. Killmonger claims he knows "how colonizers think," yet, unlike N'Jobu and T'Challa, Killmonger doesn't seem interested in leading the world to the light.

"You Want to See Us Become Just Like the People You Hate so Much."

Kipling's poem, "The White Man's Burden," contains a warning to the "white man": "By all ye cry or whisper / By all ye leave or do / The silent, sullen peoples / Shall weigh your gods and you." Kipling acknowledged here that the character of Europe's civilizing mission depended not only on its theoretical justification, but on how Europeans actually behaved. Likewise, it's the actual history of empire, rather than its theoretical justification, that demonstrates what's wrong with one people presuming to take control over another for their own good.

Historically, where there is an empire there are, too often, terrible abuses of power. The Romans, for all their high ideals, exploited their subjects for economic gain and political glory. Their brutality, perhaps most famously immortalized by the atrocious practice of crucifixion, is notorious to this day. The Roman historian Tacitus (56–120), in the biography *Agricola*, criticizes imperial conquest through Galgacus, a British chief. Galgacus warns the assembled British warriors that Rome must not be allowed to conquer them, for the Romans are tyrannical and greedy, looking only to steal wealth and make slaves of the poor. He mocks the hypocrisy of Rome's pretense of benevolence, saying that "To robbery, murder and outrage, they give the lying name of government, and where they make a desert, they call it peace."[3]

The worldwide expansion of European empires that began in the sixteenth century and led to the colonization of Africa, India, and the New World was rife with atrocity. Around 12.5 million Africans were shipped to the New World as slaves. In North America, slavery lasted until 1865, and the descendants of these slaves continue to suffer injustices, including workplace discrimination, poor access to housing, and police brutality. In South Africa, Dutch colonists set up an apartheid state, which lasted until 1994, in which Blacks were second-class citizens by law. Other European colonies in Africa were established by Britain, Belgium, France, Germany, Italy, Portugal, and Spain. In the Belgian Congo, brutal conditions and punishments in the rubber industry killed an estimated 10 million Africans. In French Algeria, starvation, disease, and fighting killed about one-third of the native population.

In North America and Australia, the Natives were dispossessed of a continent by European colonists, and many were killed. In British India, between 12 and 29 million Indians starved to death, even as wheat was being exported from India to Britain. In 1943, up to 4 million Bengalis starved. Commenting on the Bengali famine, British Prime Minister Winston Churchill privately said: "I hate Indians. They are a beastly people with a beastly religion. The famine was their own fault for breeding like rabbits."[4] These are just a handful of examples, but volumes could be filled with the atrocities committed under empire. When the Wakandan scientist Shuri disdainfully refers to Ross, who is white, as "colonizer," this is the history that drives her contempt.

In the eighteenth and nineteenth centuries, European thinkers increasingly raised objections to the abuses and hypocrisies of European imperialism. For instance, English novelist Jonathan Swift (1667–1745), in his *Gulliver's Travels* (1726), has Gulliver explain European culture to an outsider. He tells them that, "If a prince sends forces into a nation, where the people are poor and ignorant, he may lawfully put half of them to death, and make slaves of the rest, in order to civilize and reduce them from their barbarous way of living."[5]

Even some racists objected to the abuses of European imperialism. German philosopher Immanuel Kant (1724–1804) believed that Europeans were naturally superior, but rejected the idea that Europeans should rule over others, and condemned the injustice in the way Europeans treated the foreigners they dominated. In his book *Perpetual Peace: A Philosophical Sketch* (1795), he claimed that the "European savages" who came to bring civilization were more barbarous than the people they supposedly came to benefit. Likewise, science-fiction writer H.G. Wells (1866–1946) in his novel *The War of the Worlds* (1897) presents a story of humanity's conquest and oppression by intellectually superior aliens from Mars. Wells's point was that the intellectual inferiority of non-Europeans was no justification for conquering and exploiting them, or treating them with brutality.

Some philosophers wrestled with the question of why empires went astray. French philosopher Denis Diderot (1713–1784), a passionate critic of European empire-building, theorized in *History of the Two Indias* (1770, with Guillaume Raynal) that the further a person is from their society of origin, the less they are liable to be constrained by the legal and moral principles of their society. Empires tend towards brutality and injustice as the human instinct for violence rises to the fore among imperial forces and agents. If Diderot is right, we would expect Wakandans to increasingly fail to live up to the high ideals of their culture the further they get from Wakanda itself. Ruling in New York, or Beijing, or Moscow, it would become all too easy for them to degenerate into brutality, being so far from the restraining influence of the moral and legal norms of home.

John Stuart Mill himself, while an advocate of imperialism, was horrified by the abuses and economic exploitation enacted through it. He warned that such abuses could render the imperial project illegitimate. In *Considerations on Representative Government* (1861), Mill offers four reasons why European rule of non-Europeans tends to go badly. First, outsiders to a society lack an understanding of local conditions and culture. Imagine a Wakandan who knows only the worship of the cat-goddess Bast and ape-god Hanuman, trying to mediate disputes between Christians, Muslims, and Jews, with no understanding of their traditions. Second, cultural differences between Europeans and the Natives they ruled made Europeans unsympathetic towards the Natives, with whom they didn't identify. To a Wakandan, you would be a strange, alien person with weird clothes and a bizarre culture. Would they be able to recognize your humanity under it all? Third, when Europeans came into conflict with Natives, European officials were more likely to sympathize with other Europeans, to whom they were culturally similar. Think of how Agent Ross is treated by the Jabari Tribe when he, Nakia, Shuri, and Ramonda turn to them for help. M'Baku listens to the three Wakandans, but when Ross tries to speak, they drown him out with barking.

Fourth, Europeans traveled to subject nations for the purpose of gaining as much wealth as they could as easily as possible. This naturally led to the exploitation of Natives. Think of how easy it is for Ulysses Klaue to justify stealing technology by classing the Wakandans as inferior. "You savages didn't deserve it" he snarls at the Black Panther, just before getting slammed into a car. Later, when Killmonger is stealing a Wakandan artifact from the Museum of Great Britain, he asks a curator, "How did your ancestors get these? Did they pay a fair price? Or did they just take it like they took everything else?"

Obviously, not every effect of contact with European civilization was negative. At least some of the time, Europeans really did spread scientific knowledge, useful technology like medicine and railways, educational and financial systems, and even important political ideas like democracy. They also, at least some of the time, built up local economies. But exposure to European ideas did not require domination by European powers. Neither did European investment nor access to European markets. So, whatever good things European civilization may have had to offer, it didn't justify invasion, forced rule, murder, or exploitation.

As N'Jobu and Killmonger would be the first to remind us, if we don't take over foreign nations, we can't force them to end unjust practices. For instance, as N'Jobu points out, Black people are overincarcerated in the modern United States. If Wakanda doesn't take over, then Wakanda can't fix this problem. Historically, nations have often faced such dilemmas, and imperial powers have often fought local practices that by their standards were unjust. For instance, the British rulers of India tried to undermine the hereditary caste system and banned the practice of suttee, in which widows were burned on their husband's funeral pyre. Further, though the British had benefited much from the slave trade, by the nineteenth century, they were committed to stamping it out. The question, as always, was whether the good that could be done was worth the cost.

So no, I don't think Wakanda should take over the world. History suggests that, for all the good intentions many of them might have, they would eventually abuse their power. T'Challa states that in Wakanda, "It is not our way to be judge, jury, and executioner for people who are not our own." That's a fine tradition! Similarly, we ourselves should be loath to have our nation run the affairs of another. It would be too simplistic to say that we should never take over and change things. For example, at the end of World War II, Germany and Japan had to be invaded, and for a time, run by the allies. I won't attempt to specify at what point international danger or looming atrocity is so awful that military intervention is the lesser of two evils. But we should be mindful of how badly international domination has gone in the past, even when inspired by good intentions. We must never grow complacent with power over others. Tellingly, much recent African philosophy has emphasized the notion of "neocolonialism." A term coined by French philosopher Jean-Paul Sartre (1905–1980) in 1956, neocolonialism is the practice of international domination through economic, cultural, and political means, rather than by direct force.[6]

"I've Seen Too Many in Need Just to Turn a Blind Eye."

So, how should Wakanda interact with the rest of the world? I'm with Wakanda's international spy Nakia, who wants to see Wakanda work to help the outside. Refusing to stay in Wakanda, she tells T'Challa, "I can't be happy here knowing that there's people out there who have nothing." T'Challa asks, "What would you have Wakanda do about it?" and Nakia replies, "Share what we have. We could provide aid … and access to technology and refuge to those who need it. Other countries do it, we could do it better."

Appropriately enough, the film *Black Panther* ends with the establishment of the first Wakandan International Outreach Centre in a poor neighborhood in Oakland, California. T'Challa tells Shuri, "Nakia will oversee the social outreach. And you will spearhead the science and information exchange." That's good news for humanity! Wakandan medicine alone, able to cure Ross's bullet wound in less than a day, might save or extend millions or billions of lives.

In his post-credits speech to the United Nations, T'Challa sees Wakanda as having a moral duty to share its knowledge and resources with the outside world. In fact, he thinks that the duty to outsiders goes so far that Wakandans should treat outsiders as if they were Wakandans too. He says, "We will work to be an example of how we, as brothers and sisters on this earth, should treat each other … We must find a way to look after one another as if we were one single tribe." This is an extraordinary moral step for a people whose catch cry is "Wakanda forever!"

Is T'Challa right that Wakandans owe outsiders so much? If he is, then presumably, other nations too must treat foreigners as brothers and sisters, and must look after them as though they are part of a single tribe (or nation). This would be an extraordinary moral step for our society more broadly too! We generally take it as a given that we should care more about the people of our native countries than about foreigners. Yet caring less about someone because they are of a different nationality seems no different, in principle, from caring less about someone because they are not of our ethnicity, or gender, or religion. If it's wrong for a white male Christian to care less about people if they are Black, or female, or Muslim, then shouldn't it be wrong for an American to care less about someone because they're African?

John Stuart Mill expressed his hope in *Utilitarianism* (1863) that his society would learn to condemn racism and sexism, just as it had learned to condemn historical injustices that were once accepted. He wrote:

> The entire history of social improvement has been a series of transitions, by which one custom or institution after another, from being a supposed primary necessity of social existence, has passed into the rank of a universally stigmatised injustice and tyranny. So it has been with the distinctions of slaves and freemen, nobles and serfs, patricians and plebeians; and so it will be, and in part already is, with the aristocracies of colour, race, and sex.[7]

Perhaps a future transition will lead us to recognize the aristocracy of nationality as well, and our duties to all humans.

Humanity forever!

Notes

1. Plato, *Republic*, 590c7–d3.
2. Boris Johnson, "The Boris archive: Africa is a mess, but we can't blame colonialism," *The Spectator*, July 13, 2016, at https://blogs.spectator. co.uk/2016/07/boris-archive-africa-mess-cant-blame-colonialism.
3. Tacitus, *Agricola and Germania*, trans. Harold Mattingly (Baltimore, MD: Penguin Classics, 2010), 30.
4. Richard Toye, *Churchill's Empire: The Word That Made Him and the World He Made* (New York: Henry Holt and Company, 2010), 237.
5. Jonathan Swift, *Gulliver's Travels* (Mineola, NY: Dover Publishing, 1996), 185.
6. Jean-Paul Sartre, "La Mystification néo-colonialiste (The Neo-colonialist mystification)," *Les Temps modernes* 123 (March–April 1956), 125.
7. John Stuart Mill, *Utilitarianism* (Mineola, NY: Dover Publishing, 2007), 100.

8

T'Challa, the Revolutionary King

Legitimation Crises in Wakanda

Kevin J. Porter

When T'Chaka dies in *Captain America: Civil War*, why does the throne fall to T'Challa and not to Shuri? *Black Panther* was lauded for its progressive depiction of women (because of strong characters like Shuri, Nakia, and Okoye), but the film falls short when it comes to the depiction of Wakanda's monarchy, which is founded upon *male primogeniture* (T'Challa is the firstborn son of T'Chaka), *warrior prowess* (a king may be replaced by another male of royal blood if he yields or dies in ritual combat), and, ultimately, *divine right* (the first Black Panther was a warrior-shaman who was called to serve by Bast, the Panther-Goddess). This is why T'Challa (not Shuri) assumes the throne, it's why M'Baku and Killmonger (not Nakia or Okoye) are able to challenge T'Challa, and it's why Killmonger is able to assume the throne when he wins his challenge.

What makes all of this salient is that T'Challa and Wakanda are not comfortably bracketed from viewer scrutiny by being placed, say, once upon a time in a galaxy far, far away. T'Challa is, for all intents and purposes, a king *right now* and *in our world*. He is not a king of antiquity (think Leonidas of Sparta), or of the remote past (think Henry VIII of England), or of a mythic past (think King Arthur), or of a pseudo-mythic past (think Aragorn of Gondor), or of some unearthly realm (think Peter of Narnia). T'Challa is also a *sovereign*, not a figurehead constitutional monarch who attends state dinners and serves as fodder for tabloids, and he's *dignified*: T'Challa may be teased, and he engages in self-deprecating humor, but he is never reduced to a caricature (think Burger King or King Kandy of Candyland).

It is significant that every character in *Black Panther* takes for granted that Wakanda has, should have, will continue to have, and should continue to have a divinely sanctioned and hereditary male monarch. Only once, and only briefly, is the notion of kingship seriously cast into doubt

Black Panther and Philosophy: What Can Wakanda Offer the World?, First Edition. Edited by Edwardo Pérez and Timothy E. Brown.

among the Wakandans themselves because Killmonger, seeming to have killed T'Challa in ritual combat, governs in ways too flagrantly contrary to Wakanda's traditions. In short, Killmonger's actions precipitate a *legitimation crisis* for Wakandan society.

"I'm the King Now."

The notion of a *legitimation crisis* derives from the work of the German philosopher Jürgen Habermas. In the social sciences, the term *crisis* refers to conditions in which "the structure of a social system allows fewer possibilities for problem solving than are necessary to the continued existence of the system."[1] The members of a society in crisis "feel [that] their social identity [is] threatened" as once-trusted social institutions disintegrate.[2] If the situation cannot be remedied, "the consensual foundations of normative structures are so much impaired that the society becomes anomic,"[3] lacking shared norms strong enough to bind its members together. Thus, a legitimation crisis occurs when the social mechanisms used to "maintain the requisite level of mass loyalty" necessary for a society to function start to collapse.[4] It follows that the most severe form of legitimation crisis would be one in which the very mechanisms meant to generate mass loyalty themselves undermine mass loyalty. For example, a king who acts unkingly, like Killmonger, may erode not only a society's trust in him as king, but also its acceptance of the very idea of kingship.

Killmonger takes actions and sets policies so arrogantly and divisively that they immediately test people's loyalty to him as king, forcing them to choose sides and, eventually, to take up arms against each other, worsening the legitimation crisis – in effect, returning to the state of war between tribes that the first Black Panther had ended when all the ancient Wakandans, except the members of the Jabari Tribe, "agreed to live under the king's rule." This founding act, taken as binding on Wakandans generation after generation until the end of time, would make perfect sense to James VI of Scotland (1566–1625), who argued as much in his tract "The True Law of Free Monarchies" (1598): "And it is here likewise to be noted, that the duty and allegiance, which the people swear to their prince, is not only bound to themselves, but likewise to their lawful heirs and posterity, the lineal succession of crowns being begun among the people of God, and happily continued in diverse Christian commonwealths."[5]

Wakanda isn't a Christian commonwealth, but the monarchy is certainly rooted in the spirituality associated with the Heart-Shaped Herb. Of course, Killmonger's disrespect for Wakandan spirituality and tradition is made immediately evident, most notably when he destroys the crop of Heart-Shaped Herbs, which also creates a legitimation crisis, given that no other king could rule after Killmonger (unless the tradition of the Heart-Shaped Herb is completely jettisoned). While this certainly fits his brash persona, it also serves as a criticism of Wakanda's monarchy, as Killmonger is startled at the possibility of another king succeeding him. As he says to the Shaman overseeing the herbs, "Another king? Yeah, go ahead and burn all that." Luckily, Nakia was able to steal an herb before the crop was destroyed, which, of course, eventually helps T'Challa restore his powers.

Unlike previous kings, who maintained a policy of isolationism in order to protect Wakanda's wealth, power, and technology from the world – and unlike T'Challa himself, who tells W'Kabi, leader of the Border Tribe, that "waging war on other countries has never been our way" – Killmonger is ready, seemingly within a few days of attaining power, to conquer the world in order to rule it "the right way." Despite his contempt for Western imperialism, Killmonger's response is to colonize the colonizers, enacting the most basic form of retribution and mocking what was once said of the British Empire: "I know how colonizers think. So we're gonna use their own strategy against 'em. The world's gonna start over, and this time, we're on top. The sun will never set on the Wakandan Empire."

The crisis swiftly comes to a head. T'Challa, seemingly risen from the dead after having suffered grievous wounds and a fall from a high cliff, openly challenges Killmonger's right to be called King of Wakanda. Killmonger cannot be king, at least not yet, claims T'Challa, because the ritual combat that determines kingship cannot end, so says tradition, until one of the combatants has either conceded or perished. "I never yielded!" says T'Challa. "And as you can see, I am not dead!" Killmonger, without the slightest hesitation, brashly waves away T'Challa and declares: "All that challenge shit is over with. I'm the king now." But is he? Wakandans rush to obey his orders to continue the preparations for waging war on the outside world, but should they?

Okoye had initially followed Killmonger because she respected the challenge ritual, especially since she thought Killmonger had won. As she told Nakia, "I am loyal to that throne, no matter who sits upon it." With T'Challa's return, Killmonger orders W'Kabi to "kill this clown," but Okoye decides to follow tradition, not Killmonger, saying to her husband W'Kabi that "the challenge is not complete." W'Kabi, whose sympathies lie more with Killmonger's vision of an expansionist Wakanda than with T'Challa's isolationism, briefly hesitates. But when one of the Border Tribe warriors nearby asks, "What will we do?" and action must then be taken, W'Kabi raises his curved blade, rouses his warriors, and charges at T'Challa. In response, Okoye renounces her duties to Killmonger and publicly defies him, declaring "You! Your heart is so full of hatred. You are not fit to be a king."

It's significant that Okoye is no longer questioning Killmonger's legitimacy on the grounds that the ritual combat has not been resolved in his favor; now it is his unfitness to be a king, regardless of the outcome of that combat, that is at issue. Even Shuri – hardly a traditionalist – recognizes Killmonger's illegitimacy, telling him: "You'll never be a true king." Thus, the undermining of Killmonger's legitimacy moves from a matter of procedure to a matter of principle – he isn't just illegitimate, he's unfit.

Notice that until T'Challa returned, Killmonger's legitimacy wasn't in crisis, at least for most Wakandans (who, like Okoye, assumed the ritual had been completed). Of course, everything is settled when T'Challa defeats Killmonger and, still more, when Killmonger chooses a warrior's death over ignoble imprisonment. In undoubtedly the greatest moment in the film, Killmonger refuses T'Challa's offer of Wakandan medical treatment for the fatal stab wound to his chest: "Why? So you can just lock me up? Nah. Just bury me in the ocean with my ancestors that jumped from the ships 'cause they knew death was better than bondage." With a final effort of will, Killmonger himself pulls the blade from his chest and slumps over, dead.

But, what would have happened if Killmonger *had* defeated T'Challa – and not through treachery or cheating, which would have undermined his claims of legitimacy, but *exactly as required by tradition*? Could Wakanda have survived in a form that would be recognizable to itself if T'Challa had not defeated Killmonger?

"I Want to Be a Great King."

With Killmonger defeated, all is set back to rights, for T'Challa doesn't just *happen* to be King of Wakanda but also *deserves* to be King of Wakanda. And, to carry that line of reasoning to its proper conclusion, he *deserves* to be king because he *is* the king of Wakanda. The ethical and the actual – the *ought* and the *is* – blur together. T'Challa has "the right to power" and to the allegiance of Wakandans, whereas Killmonger merely wielded power temporarily.[6]

The same principle is at work when, earlier in the film, T'Challa engages in ritual combat against M'Baku, leader of the Jabari Tribe. M'Baku gains the upper hand and declares that T'Challa is merely a "boy not fit to lead." As M'Baku starts grappling T'Challa into submission, the Queen Mother rouses T'Challa to victory by shouting: "Show him who you are!" And that is exactly what T'Challa does, regaining advantage, bashing M'Baku twice on the head, and overcoming a stab wound to the shoulder before shouting: "I am Prince T'Challa, son of King T'Chaka!" M'Baku is forced to his knees, and then, after displaying enough reluctance to avoid being called a coward, he yields for the sake of his people, if not for himself.

Whatever doubts T'Challa himself expresses about his readiness to be king, he never doubts that there ought to be a king or that he should aspire to be a great one. When T'Challa visits the Ancestral Plane for the first time, he meets the spirit of his father, T'Chaka. After hugging him, T'Challa takes his hand, kneels before him, and starts to apologize. But T'Chaka corrects him: "Stand up. You are a king." A few moments pass before T'Challa rises to his feet. "I am not ready," he tells his father, who replies,

"Have you not prepared to be king your whole life? Have you not trained and studied, been by my side?" But T'Chaka hasn't understood T'Challa's real concern. "That is not what I am talking about. I am not ready to be without you." For T'Chaka, this is a criticism: "A man who has not prepared his children for his own death has failed as a father. Have I ever failed you?" "Never," replies T'Challa.

So, when T'Challa is restored to the throne of Wakanda, viewers presumably feel some sense of satisfaction and relief that a terrible wrong has been righted. But why would viewers cheer for the restoration of a king when they themselves would not recognize the legitimacy of a theocratic dynastic monarchy or wish to be governed by one? As the political scientist and historian Benedict Anderson observes, "in fundamental ways 'serious' monarchy lies traverse to all modern conceptions of political life."[7] Certainly, for American audiences (and audiences in other countries with democratically elected governments), legitimacy of rule is rooted in the consent of the governed, as the philosopher John Locke (1632–1704) argues and as the United States Constitution enshrines. So, are we giving consent when T'Challa wins? Or, by viewing him as most deserving of the throne, are we saying we approve of his reign? Can consent be given to a king?

It is not easy to reconcile contemporary viewers to a form of government that would ordinarily be recognized as antithetical to progressive views of social justice and that, *at best*, could be treated as a harmless anachronism so long as the king were someone as enlightened as T'Challa. The fact that *Black Panther* pulls off this feat, making palatable what would otherwise be objectionable to most viewers, is attributable not only to the skillfulness with which it generally disguises or minimalizes the incompatibility, but also to the brazenness with which it justifies – even doubles down upon – that incompatibility.

Some viewers may not even notice the discordance between monarchy and progressivism because Wakanda is characterized throughout as a place that harmonizes opposites, such as nature/civilization, tradition/progress, and mysticism/science. Like *Avatar*'s Pandora, Wakanda is a place most of us wouldn't mind living in. Consider the Wakandan marketplace. A tram car moves slowly and silently down what appears to be a track laid in the dirt of the main thoroughfare while above, sounding no louder than a whisper, a high-speed train whizzes through a transparent tube. A man with traditional ear and lip plates wears what appears to be a leather jacket of contemporary manufacture and displays above the palm of his hand a holographic video showing people standing on a beach, perhaps dancing or tossing a ball. And so on. Through T'Challa, who considers nothing out of place as he smiles, completely at ease, while strolling through the crowd with Nakia, we are invited to accept Wakanda as "home." What is true in the marketplace is true throughout Wakanda, where we see advanced technology blended with traditional artifacts and practices – from Wakandans living in huts with animals enclosed in simple wood fencing to Shuri's lab, which appears to be part Batcave and part starship Enterprise. So, if Wakanda can reconcile tensions such as these, why not also those between monarchy and democracy?

"Just Because Something Works Doesn't Mean It Cannot Be Improved."

Another way to preserve the legitimacy of Wakanda's monarchy (other than ritual combat) is to conduct a mild critique of it, showing that criticism and improvement is permissible, perhaps even encouraged, within the monarchy itself. Like weakened germs in an inoculation, ideas that might otherwise threaten the monarchy are incorporated into it and neutralized in a way that adds vitality to the system and reduces "the risk of a generalized subversion."[8]

Shuri often serves to inoculate kingship in *Black Panther*. For example, despite holding the title of Princess, she repeatedly pokes fun at Wakandan traditions, but always as a smartass rather than a true rebel. Whereas knowledge and wisdom are often seen as the possession of the king and the tribal elders, Shuri, a precocious know-it-all, asserts that she has much to teach T'Challa and anyone else who clings to old ways of doing things that, while still functional, can always be improved. That she does this with humor (and a literal middle finger) makes her criticisms more palatable to contemplate, for T'Challa and for the audience.

Indeed, T'Challa, occupying the most privileged position, can smile bemusedly and shake his head at Shuri's outburst, and a child in the crowd can innocently (and comically) slap his hand to his forehead in disbelief; but the adults present are not amused at Shuri's transgressions. Annoyed, the Queen Mother seizes Shuri's wrist, and M'Baku, who has come to challenge T'Challa, adds a further justification for his actions: "We have watched and listened from the mountains! We have watched with disgust as your technological advancements have been overseen by a child … who scoffs at tradition!"[9]

Shuri herself undercuts her rebelliousness. Despite all her talk about how the extraordinary healing possible in Wakanda is performed "not by magic, [but] by technology," when she learns that T'Challa is too weak to be moved from the Jabari stronghold to her laboratory, Shuri joins in the Queen Mother's prayers to the ancestors and to Bast for T'Challa's recovery: "Praise the ancestors." And, as we have already seen, Shuri believes enough in kingship to know that Killmonger will never be the "true king" of Wakanda. So, does Shuri really believe things can be improved? Or, does she come to believe more in the traditions of Wakanda?

"You Get to Decide What Kind of King You Are Going to Be."

Shuri may be the most visible gadfly, but the harshest – and, ultimately, most effective – critics of Wakanda's kings are Killmonger, Nakia, and T'Challa himself. Together, they articulate a counterintuitive vision of kingship in Wakanda, more regressive than the one T'Challa inherited. This constitutes another strategy, which does not simply try to preserve the legitimacy of kingship but boldly expands it.

Killmonger, Nakia, and T'Challa agree in principle that *all* of the kings of Wakanda had promoted a disastrous policy of isolationism that ignored, and thereby abetted, the misery of countless others around the world, especially people of Black African heritage. Even someone horrified by the number of scars on Killmonger's body, each representing a person he has killed, may admire Killmonger's indignation when he stands as a prisoner before King T'Challa and the tribal elders and upbraids them for inaction in the face of injustice: "Y'all sittin' up here comfortable. Must feel good. It's about two billion people all over the world that looks like us, but their lives are a lot harder. Wakanda has the tools to liberate 'em all."

Nakia, too, feels she must act, even though this means living in self-imposed exile from home. When T'Challa asks her to remain with him in Wakanda, she refuses: "I can't stay. I found my calling out there. I've seen too many in need just to turn a blind eye. I can't be happy here knowing that there's people out there who have nothing."

T'Challa, meanwhile, takes the longest journey. Early on, he unreservedly loves and venerates his father, King T'Chaka. When T'Challa visits the Ancestral Plane for the first time, he asks the spirit of T'Chaka: "Tell me how best to protect Wakanda. I want to be a great king, Baba. Just like you." But, in small steps, T'Challa shifts from isolationism to interventionism – from saving Agent Ross to learning the truth about Killmonger's heritage and deciding that Wakanda's wrongs must be righted. As T'Challa angrily asks T'Chaka during his second visit to the Ancestral Plane: "Why didn't you bring the boy home? Why, Baba?" When T'Chaka explains that he did what he did for Wakanda, T'Challa, unable to contain his anger and dismay, bursts "You were wrong!"

But T'Challa goes further, extending the indictment to all of his predecessors. T'Chaka was just the latest – and now perhaps the last – King of Wakanda to believe that the rest of the world could not be trusted to know about or share in the great benefits of Wakanda's hidden resource, vibranium. T'Challa, gesturing vehemently at the spirits of the ancestral kings who have gathered near, cries out: "All of you were wrong! To turn your backs on the rest of the world!" T'Challa indicts himself, too – his old self: "We let the fear of our discovery stop us from doing what is right! No more!" Despite being beckoned to "come home and be reunited" with his father and the rest of his ancestors, T'Challa, like Nakia, cannot do so: "I cannot stay here with you. I cannot rest while [Killmonger] sits on the throne. He is a monster of our own making. I must right these wrongs."

Of course, T'Challa's desire to correct Wakanda's mistakes doesn't lead him to conclude that the tradition of kingship is a mistake, too – another wrong in need of righting. Where Killmonger coveted and adopted the title of King, even if his actions undermined the possibility of dynastic succession, T'Challa chooses to be King inasmuch as he wins the throne. He does so not because he desires authority for its own sake, but because he desires to change policy, not policy-making or policy-makers – he is, almost paradoxically, a *revolutionary king*.

T'Challa's revolution is radical in two senses. On the one hand, T'Challa *uproots* Wakanda's interactions with others (its foreign policy), which also requires a reorientation of how Wakandans understand themselves and treat each other (its domestic policy). On the other hand, he *returns to and deepens the roots* of kingship.

The King who had earlier conceded "I am not king of all people" finishes his journey in *Black Panther* by addressing the United Nations with words that eerily echo those of Jacques-Bénigne Bossuet (1627–1704), the French bishop whose *Politique tirée de l'Écriture sainte* (1679) lays out, through a series of articles and propositions, an extended apology for the divine right of kings, especially for the French monarchs of the seventeenth and eighteenth centuries:

T'Challa	Bossuet
"My name is King T'Challa, son of King T'Chaka. I am the sovereign ruler of the nation of Wakanda. And for the first time in our history we will be sharing our knowledge and resources with the outside world. Wakanda will no longer watch from the shadows. We cannot. We must not."	"*The love of God obliges men to love one another*" (Article 1, 2nd proposition),[10] and "*No man is a stranger to another man*" (Article 1, 4th proposition).[11]
"We will work to be an example of how we as brothers and sisters on this earth should treat each other."	"*All men are brothers*" (Article 1, 3rd proposition).[12]
"Now, more than ever, the illusions of division threaten our very existence."	"*The division of property among men, and the division of men into peoples and nations, ought not to alter the general society of mankind*" (Article 5, unique proposition).[13]
"We all know the truth. More connects us than separates us."	"*Common interest unites us*" (Article 1, 6th proposition).[14]

(Continued)

(Continued)

"But in times of crisis, the wise build bridges while the foolish build barriers. We must find a way to look after one another as if we were one single tribe."	*"The earth they inhabit together, serves as a bond amongst men, and forms the unity of nations"* (Article 2, 3rd proposition).[15]

Even the stirring battle cry "Wakanda forever!" has a parallel in Bossuet: "authority is immortal, and the State subsists for ever."[16]

"We Need a King."

T'Challa may be an enlightened monarch. He may even turn out to be the most enlightened monarch the world will ever know. But, unwittingly and with the best of intentions, he is a monarch who is nonetheless reaching toward absolutism; his vision of kingship, we may be astonished to realize, has more in common with Louis XIV than with the current heirs apparent of the unserious British monarchy, Prince Charles and Prince William. As *Black Panther* concludes, the lesson T'Challa has learned is one he has always known: Wakanda needs a king, it has always needed a king, and it will always need a king.

Wakanda, then, despite being the most advanced nation in the world in so many other respects, still has not faced, and may never face, the kind of *legitimation crisis* of kingship that started and was largely settled elsewhere in the world centuries ago. Furthermore, so long as the techniques by which the film *Black Panther* mildly tweaks and then forcefully reaffirms the very idea of kingship remain successful, most viewers may not even notice.

Notes

1. Jürgen Habermas, *Legitimation Crisis*, trans. Thomas McCarthy (Boston, MA: Beacon Press, 1975), 2.
2. Habermas, 3.
3. Habermas, 3.
4. Habermas, 46.
5. James VI, "The Trew Law of Free Monarchies," in Charles Howard McIlwain ed., *The Political Works of James I* (Cambridge, MA: Harvard University Press, 1918), 69. I have silently amended the text to improve readability.
6. See J.R.R. Tolkien, "On Fairy-Stories" (1947), in *The Tolkien Reader* (New York: Ballantine, 1966), 51. I am drawing on Tolkien's words about divinity, which has "the right to power (as distinct from its possession), the due worship." Just as God deserves to be omnipotent and to be worshipped, a king by divine right deserves power and allegiance.

7. Benedict Anderson, *Imagined Communities: Reflections on the Origins and Spread of Nationalism* (London: Verso, 1983), 19.

8. Roland Barthes, *Mythologies*, trans. Annette Lavers (New York: Hill and Wang, 1972), 150.

9. The Jabari Tribe chose isolation in the mountains rather than allegiance and submission to the first king and Black Panther, yet, for all that, M'Baku speaks as the voice of outraged tradition.

10. Jacques-Bénigne Bossuet, *The Political Science, Drawn from the Holy Scriptures* (1679) (London: George Keating, 1842), 2.

11. Bossuet, 5.

12. Bossuet, 3.

13. Bossuet, 20.

14. Bossuet, 5.

15. Bossuet, 9.

16. Bossuet, 15. This is part of Bossuet's support for the 6th proposition of Article 3: "*The Government perpetuates itself, and renders States immortal*".

9

T'Challa's Machiavellian Methods

Ian J. Drake and Matthew B. Lloyd

The *Black Panther* film depicts a conflicted, yet admirable and noble, king of a fictional and fantastical, utopian African nation known as Wakanda. Although a hereditary king, known by his given name T'Challa, he possesses the social empathy and political consciousness typically associated with the ideals of liberal, post-industrial democracies. By contrast, the original comic version of T'Challa is a traditional monarch, whose actions demonstrate his concern for maintaining power and securing his nation. In fact, with his strategic use of violence, his demonstrations of empathy and humanity, and his embrace of religious symbolism, T'Challa was classically "Machiavellian" in the comics.

The Machiavellian Model

Prior to the Renaissance, much of political thought and discourse in Western Europe was restricted to a discussion of what was proper in the eyes of God. Of course, politics as practiced was in no way "divine," but rulers always wanted – sometimes earnestly, sometimes cynically – their actions to be understood as providential. Rulers conceived of their legitimacy as emanating from God, and indeed, the "divine right of kings" was recognized throughout Christendom in the late Medieval Period.[1]

Niccolò Machiavelli's (1469–1527) *The Prince* reintroduced concerns about the utility of power, divorced from any concern with divine origins. Looking to historical examples as models for how power can be used for the ends of men instead of how power can be used in service of God, Machiavelli was cynical and believed that people are at root wicked and in need of social control. Thus, his advice for rulers offers guidance for how to keep populaces content so that rulers can maintain their hold on power.

Black Panther and Philosophy: What Can Wakanda Offer the World?, First Edition. Edited by Edwardo Pérez and Timothy E. Brown.

T'Challa, Prince of Wakanda

The Black Panther is a divinely ordained ruler, with his authority derived from his ancestry and the power his family has gained from its role in the religion of the Panther God. The Black Panther is both a superhero in the modern world and a traditional mythic figure in Wakandan culture.

T'Challa was first introduced in a two-part tale in *Fantastic Four* #52 (July 1966) and #53 (August 1966), where he was addressed as "Chieftain." Wakanda is steeped in religious tradition, though also highly scientifically sophisticated. T'Challa takes advantage of Wakanda's rich supply of vibranium – having the metal mined and sold abroad in order to bring great wealth to himself. Although T'Challa feels he has a great responsibility to care for his people, he does not share the wealth derived from the vibranium exports with the Wakandan people. Thus, T'Challa is able to afford a modern, technologically sophisticated palace, but the average Wakandan still lives in a primitive hut. Nevertheless, the comic leaves this wealth disparity unexplored, and T'Challa's story is, as he describes it in *Fantastic Four* #52, "… one of tragedy and deadly revenge." This description is apt, referring to the storyline in *Fantastic Four* #53 in which Klaue attacks Wakanda for its vibranium, not only destroying much of the land and people but killing his father, T'Chaka.

The comics series that introduces us to the problems faced by the Black Panther in Wakanda is entitled "Panther's Rage." Originally serialized in *Jungle Action* #6–18 (September 1973–November 1975), "Panther's Rage" is widely regarded as one of the earliest graphic novels, and is the first storyline to explore Wakanda's society and political structure. "Panther's Rage" chronicles T'Challa's return to Wakanda after an extended stay in the United States as a costumed superhero, most notably with the Avengers. Upon his return, T'Challa is shocked to discover that he must confront a usurper, the violent, merciless Erik Killmonger. The threat is immediately apparent when T'Challa witnesses an old man being assaulted and abducted by Killmonger's supporters on the outskirts of Wakanda. Though T'Challa prevents the abduction, he cannot prevent the old man's death. This event is emblematic of the threat his country faces on a societal scale. "Panther's Rage" is thus the story of how T'Challa maintains his control of the kingdom.

The Utility of Fear and Violence

In *The Prince*, Machiavelli gave frank advice to Lorenzo de Medici not merely on how to rule, but on how to rule with an eye toward keeping one's power. Machiavelli considered himself a realist about human nature. As he saw it, people might admire or love a ruler, but such admiration is short-lived and fickle. People respond best to fear. Thus, to govern the people and maintain power, fear could be generated in different forms: fear of death or arbitrary punishment at the hands of the ruler or the ruler's lieutenant, or fear of the loss of liberty and property through the enforcement of the law. Yet, Machiavelli also warned rulers to be mindful of being hated by the people. For example, he warned against arbitrarily taking people's property or women.[2] In short, Machiavelli advised princes to be prepared to deftly use fear to help preserve their power.

T'Challa, too, recognizes the economy of fear. In *Jungle Action* #7, Zatama, one of T'Challa's advisers, accuses him of always resorting to violence to achieve his goals: "Violence!! That's always your only answer, T'Challa." Later, in a loosely veiled reference to T'Challa, Zatama proclaims in *Jungle Action* #9: "We've got rulers who've acquired a taste for blood." In *Jungle Action* #10, another adviser, Taku, and T'Challa discuss their observations of Killmonger's attacks. Their exchange illustrates how one of T'Challa's closest advisers sees the Wakandan King. T'Challa complains of his rival: "Killmonger, the magnificent rebel ... but, he has no concern for the frailty of the victims he maims. He would govern this land if that's what you'd call it ... but he would only be concerned with his own designs." Taku responds: "The question you must ask yourself, my chieftain, is if you ... have been any different."

Machiavelli would approve of T'Challa's embrace of violence. As he saw it, people are naturally "wicked,"[3] and so a prince must be unkind in order to survive.[4] T'Challa wisely uses fear to maintain his power and thus maintain the stability and integrity of the Wakandan state.

T'Challa and the Five Qualities

Machiavelli was keenly aware of how a ruler should be perceived by his subjects, suggesting that a successful ruler will *appear* to possess five key qualities that meet with the approval of his subjects: mercy, faith, honesty, humanity, and religion.[5] T'Challa possessed – or appeared to possess – some of these qualities, and they proved useful to sustaining his position of authority and retaining the support of his people.

Appearances – rather than truth – matter for Machiavelli because appearances can be shaped to achieve the end of preserving the state. The truth can often be counter to one's aims, revealing unflattering realities. On Machiavelli's view, princes can obscure these realities by producing the image of strength, dedication, and faithfulness that rulers are expected to exemplify. Earlier versions of T'Challa, those seen in the Jungle comics of the 1970s, illustrate this Machiavellian kind of appearance-crafting. The recent film version is far less cynical, presenting a T'Challa who is humble, earnest, and far more idealistic.

Faith

In "Panther's Rage" T'Challa tries to prove to himself and his people that he has not broken faith with them by his prolonged absence in America. After his absence, T'Challa feels compelled to reassert control over his homeland where some of his subjects have lost their faith in him as a beneficent ruler. Upon his return, T'Challa learns what his absence has wrought. He hopes his return signals to his people that he has not abandoned them, nor forgotten his duty to his countrymen. In *Jungle Action* #6, the narrator states, "A moment before, he [T'Challa] was re-communicating with this land that is more than his name, re-establishing the link that has weakened since his absence from his kingdom." His time away from Wakanda has affected the relationship with his people. T'Challa fears his rule may be questioned, justifiably, since he has spent so many years away from the land he is charged with governing and protecting.

In the same issue, after having failed to save the life of an elderly countryman, T'Challa hears the words in the man's dying breaths that set the stage for the challenge the Black Panther will face: "Many of the people said you would never come back, that the Wakandans had lost their king. That you would desert us. But I knew they were wrong. You must believe … I never lost faith in you, T'Challa. I always … believed." T'Challa rightly fears that the rest of his subjects may not be so forgiving. After all, they blame him for the atrocities committed by Erik Killmonger in his absence. T'Challa's own adviser challenges him, "You were a wise and just leader in your early days … but now Wakanda separates – and one wonders – are you strong enough to pull it back together."

By the end of the series, T'Challa has dispensed with the would-be usurper, Erik Killmonger, and apparently demonstrated he is the rightful ruler of Wakanda and a worthy guardian of his people. Although T'Challa did in fact keep faith with his ideals, it was most important that he was seen as doing so. He gains (or regains or eliminates the doubts of) the faithful of Wakandan society, which is most important because his position has been secured, or at least strengthened.

Humanity

One of the men that Killmonger has enlisted to aid him in overthrowing T'Challa is Venomm, who has been taken captive by T'Challa and thereafter attempts an escape in *Jungle Action* #8. During the escape attempt, Venomm believes himself about to be killed by one of T'Challa's (the Black Panther's) lieutenants, W'Kabi. W'Kabi believed that they should have forced Killmonger's whereabouts from Venomm, thinking T'Challa was being too soft on the prisoner. T'Challa chastises W'Kabi, "And who would you have be his torturer, W'Kabi?" In this instance, T'Challa demonstrates his empathy for the followers, some unwilling or frightened, of Killmonger. T'Challa will not stoop to the methods of his adversary. Rather, he retains his dignity and seeks to have his followers do the same.

T'Challa is cognizant of the limits of cruelty in achieving his ends, and is aware of the need to maintain decency toward his enemies. He seems to heed Machiavelli's warning that cruelty "can enable one to acquire an empire, but not glory."[6] Glory is necessary to gain power, but also to retain it and help the homeland prosper.

The Uses of Religion

Wakandans have two major religions: worship of the White Apes and the Panther God. Fittingly, T'Challa embraces and utilizes their fear of the Panther God. As the Black Panther, T'Challa has special abilities of strength, agility, and heightened senses. In *Fantastic Four* #53, he explains to Ben Grimm, the "Thing," that the Panther Power is "a secret handed down from chieftain to chieftain. We eat certain herbs ... and undergo rituals ... of which I am forbidden to speak." In *Jungle Action* #13, T'Challa notes that his nation's "legends have been given the vulnerability of flesh," and his father, T'Chaka, was revered "like a god." Although T'Challa knows he is not a god, the Wakandan people regard him as such. As Machiavelli would advise, he uses this false belief to retain and extend his power. T'Challa's apparent divinity instills fear in the followers of the usurper Killmonger. For example, one supporter of Killmonger, Tayete, repeatedly refers to T'Challa as the "Panther Devil." As the narrator tells the reader in *Jungle Action* #12, "Tayete is convinced. T'Challa is not human. It is a deception that the Panther is in no hurry to discredit."

T'Challa never considers introducing democracy, even after his years in the United States as Black Panther. He may be a benevolent monarch, but he remains a monarch, seeming to share Machiavelli's opinion of human nature: people are fundamentally wicked and need to be controlled through their fear.[7] Although the religion that T'Challa embraced and encouraged in his people is, in some measure, real, the utility of that religion is the preservation of T'Challa's rule over his people. Near the end of *The Prince*, Machiavelli asks whether it is fortune (chance), God, or man that governs the world. He answers his own question with the claim that it is half fortune and half man. He conspicuously leaves God out of the equation. This was one of the reasons *The Prince* was not published during Machiavelli's lifetime. He died in 1527 and *The Prince* was first published in 1532. By 1559, it was put on the Catholic Church's list of proscribed books, the *Index librorum prohibitorum*, where it remained until Pope Paul VI abolished the list in 1966.

T'Challa's reverence for the religion of his people is at its most profound when he needs the religion to secure his rule. Significantly, T'Challa is never seen in public without the Black Panther garb. Even on a relaxing afternoon with his American girlfriend, Monica, as they go for a swim in *Jungle Action* #16, T'Challa continues to wear the "divine" attire, only raising his cowl so that he can kiss Monica. Not until safely inside his royal palace does T'Challa doff the garb of the Panther God. Clearly, he understands the power of the costume as a public religious symbol that sustains his power. Like his father, T'Chaka, he believes his people should view him as a god, even though his Panther Power is not truly divine.

Additionally, at those times when the Panther garb is bloodied and torn, T'Challa keeps the shredded garment on. He knows he is not a god, but he understands that most of the people see him as such. As the narrator in *Jungle Action* #13 tells the reader, "T'Challa wears the sacred attire of the Panther Religion. It is torn and crusted with blood and sweat, but it is no less sacred a garment." Although the omniscient narrator suggests divinity, T'Challa's own behavior indicates he finds more utility in the costume's performative value than in its inherent sacredness. T'Challa wears the Panther garb to publicly invoke the traditional beliefs of the Wakandans in the Panther God. Such intentions are clearly evident when Malice, one of Killmonger's lieutenants, tells T'Challa in the midst of an altercation in *Jungle Action* #8, "My mother thought you were a great wizard king who brought magic to our land, she remained an ignorant hill woman, but Killmonger has given me these powers and the chance for something more in my life. And your death will assure that chance."

In this exchange, Malice insists that she and the average Wakandan are encumbered by their traditional religious myths – and they could achieve freedom by killing the Panther God. Malice saw her mother, in particular, as a victim of these old tribal beliefs. T'Challa's death would free her (Malice) from what she sees as the oppression of living under T'Challa's reign and within the Wakandan religious state. As such, following Killmonger and aiding the usurpation effort is a path to power. However, T'Challa's death would also destroy the myths believed by the average Wakandan, and it is unclear how Wakandan society would be affected. T'Challa does not contradict the religion, but he does act as though the world is governed more by his choices and chance than by any divinely ordained process. In this sense, he is thoroughly Machiavellian and a modern, secular ruler.

A God on Earth

The T'Challa of the early *Jungle Action* comics is a Machiavellian ruler, who is willing to use traditional rhetoric, engage in the proper, socially accepted rites, and use the necessary tactics. As a result, his people believe he is a great ruler who deserves the deference and lifetime position of king. The people are quiescent and loyal, peace is attainable, and the monarchical institutions are preserved.

T'Challa never considers relinquishing power. He may wish to protect his people, but he has no faith in their ability to govern themselves. In fact, his people would apparently be bereft without him; they would certainly be the target of would-be tyrants, like Killmonger and his supporters. T'Challa's strength, his *virtue* or *excellence*, as Machiavelli would call it, is in providing physical (and thereby spiritual) protection for his nation and people. T'Challa is a prince – albeit an unusually benevolent one – and his concerns are always with preserving his power. He is fortunate to have vibranium and the wealth it provides, but the superstitions of the traditionalist populace inhibit their ability to fully profit from modern medicine and technology made possible by vibranium. Indeed, they often distrust the methods and motives of scientists and doctors.

A Machiavellian ruler is both enemy and savior, a veritable god on earth, whom his people should fear. T'Challa is never as cruel as some of Machiavelli's models, but he does preserve his divinely ordained kingdom by employing fear and religion to stay in power. In this fashion, the Black Panther is able to, as Machiavelli might have said, "speak well of evil."[8]

Notes

1. Alan Ryan, *On Politics: A History of Political Thought from Herodotus to the Present* (New York: Penguin, 2012), 334.
2. Niccolò Machiavelli, *The Prince*, trans. Harvey C. Mansfield (Chicago, IL: University of Chicago Press, 1998), 67, 72.
3. Machiavelli, 69.
4. Machiavelli, 61.
5. Machiavelli, 70.
6. Machiavelli, 35.
7. Machiavelli, 69.
8. Machiavelli, 37.

10

Understanding the Reigns of T'Challa and Killmonger through Hannah Arendt

Jolynna Sinanan

Black Panther (2018) was released in the middle of the Trump era, a time that saw an escalation of white supremacy movements and renewed concern about totalitarian governments. Fittingly, *The Origins of Totalitarianism* saw a spike in sales shortly after Trump's inauguration. This 1951 book by Hannah Arendt (1906–1975), a persecuted Jewish refugee, identifies conditions that can lead to totalitarian regimes. These conditions include: increasing xenophobia, racism, deep distrust of mainstream politics, an intensified alienation of the masses from government, and an accelerated increase in the number of refugees and stateless peoples coupled with the inadequacy and inability of nation-states to guarantee them rights.[1] Arendt's observations were relevant to the Trump era, but the issues she raises also resonate with *Black Panther*.

Indeed, one of the issues for T'Challa is how to respond to the refugees from broken African states while maintaining the isolationist interests of Wakanda. W'Kabi cautions T'Challa: "You let the refugees in, you let in all their problems." The isolationist code is challenged when Erik Stevens (Killmonger) swaggers through the doors of T'Challa's throne room (in handcuffs, he struts nonetheless) with his revolutionary vision for Wakanda and its technology to liberate the oppressed peoples of the world through violence.

So, is the King of Wakanda *just* the king of Wakanda? Or, does the King of Wakanda have a greater responsibility to the world? As we'll see, Hannah Arendt's concept of responsibility can help us understand the actions of two very different Wakandan kings.

Black Panther and Philosophy: What Can Wakanda Offer the World?, First Edition. Edited by Edwardo Pérez and Timothy E. Brown.
© 2022 John Wiley & Sons, Inc. Published 2022 by John Wiley & Sons, Inc.

Wakanda Forever or Wakanda First?

For Arendt, responsibility in individual action is always tied to being part of a wider collective. When Stan Lee and Jack Kirby created the character of T'Challa/ Black Panther in 1966, Kirby's rationale was straightforward in terms of the community of his readers: "I came up with the Black Panther because I realized I had no blacks in my strip. I'd never drawn a black ... I needed a black. I suddenly discovered that I had a lot of black readers. My first friend was a black! And here I was ignoring them because I was associating with everybody else."[2] In the initial years of *Black Panther* comics, T'Challa focused on protecting Wakanda, but as a member of the royal family he had very little shared experience with everyday Wakandans. In the comics, his affiliation with the Avengers taught him to become more of a team player and to contend with interests outside his own. In the 2018 film, T'Challa broadens his circle of concern after encountering Killmonger. At first, he declares to Killmonger "I am not king of the world." Later, though, he says to his father and ancestors, "you were wrong," and ultimately he announces to the United Nations that "we are one tribe."

For Arendt, one's responsibility is inextricable from the wider collectives and social groups (class, race, gender, etc.) one belongs to. Responsibility involves first, making oneself present to others through action, and second, making others present in one's mind by representing them.[3] T'Challa's kingly rule is rooted in Wakandan tradition and the collective. On the Ancestral Plane, When T'Challa confronts his father about Killmonger, T'Chaka responds: "He was the truth I chose to omit. I chose our people. I chose Wakanda."

By the end of the film, T'Challa embraces a more complex form of responsibility that is closer to what Arendt envisions. By creating a Wakandan International Outreach Centre and converting the housing estate in Oakland where Erik grew up, T'Challa moves past his earlier sense of what is morally right and just. In this action, T'Challa recognizes that the plight of the poor, marginalized, and oppressed is part of his responsibility as Wakandan king. Indeed, he attempts to right a family wrong that resulted in "the monster of our own making."

But what about Killmonger's responsibility? How does Killmonger fit into Arendt's framework?

Anarchist? Revolutionary? "Nah, I'm Your King!"

If T'Challa embraces too little change (at least at first), Killmonger calls for too much change. For Killmonger, liberation and revolution are violent, and violence is necessary for emancipation. As he says, "I want your secrets. I want your weapons. I'm gonna burn it all!" and "The world took everything away from me! Everything I ever loved! But Imma make sure we're even." After he is given the powers of the Black Panther from the Heart-Shaped Herb, Killmonger commands that the rest of the plants be burned. We see Erik watching the temple go up in flames, followed by un upside-down frame of Killmonger approaching the throne that rotates to the right side up – an inversion of the order of Wakanda. Shortly after Killmonger begins his reign with "We will arm the oppressed everywhere," Okoye describes him as full of hatred. We see his sadness and defeat as a child after his father has been killed, "Everybody dies. It's just life around here." But we witness no guilt or remorse as he wages his own war.

Arendt differentiates between matters of acting upon a sense of right and wrong driven by conscience (feelings of guilt) and matters of action motivated by being a part of a collective and community. Conscience doesn't necessarily indicate morality, just conformity and non-conformity. T'Challa's conscience is clear when he says, "I am not king of all people. I am king of Wakanda." Collective responsibility moves from the realm of personal judgment and individual conscience to political action, when a whole community takes it upon itself to be responsible for whatever one of its members has done, or whether a community is being held responsible for what has been done in its name.[4] Consider this exchange,

T'CHALLA: It is not our way to be judge, jury, and executioner for people who aren't our own.
KILLMONGER: Not your own? Didn't life start here on this continent? So ain't all people your people?

Killmonger's question reflects the conditions for collective responsibility, where "I must be held responsible for something I have not done, and the reason for my responsibility must be my membership in a group (a collective) which no voluntary act of mine can dissolve."[5] For Arendt, humans are political and social beings; individuals are always shaped by cultures, customs, and collectives that also shape consciousness of right and wrong. Responsible action results when "Through my initiative, I challenge my specific community and its traditions, because such challenges affect the whole of humanity."[6] Responsibility is the link between individual deeds and membership in collectives, and political life consists of the transformation (or the potential transformation) of identities (singular and collective) through individual acts.

"Do We Still Hide, Baba? Why?"

In the throne room Killmonger says, "It's about two billion people all over the world that looks like us, but their lives are a lot harder." Although his ambitions are rooted in an idealism fueled by his own wounded soul, his vision of global destruction is pretty much "Burn it all." In *Responsibility and Judgment*, Arendt explains "our decisions about right and wrong will depend upon our choice of company."[7] Violence and domination are explicitly part of Killmonger's plan for liberation. His less than kingly ideals and desire for warmongering come from being part of a collective outside Wakanda. He is an MIT-educated, US Navy SEAL, trained for Black Ops. Arendt says, "We can escape this political and strictly collective responsibility only by leaving the community, and since no man can live without belonging to some community, this would simply mean to exchange one community for another and hence one kind of responsibility for another."[8] Though Killmonger wants liberation, he becomes like the enemy he seeks to overthrow – an imperialist who seeks to be an authoritarian colonizer of sorts.

Despite his megalomaniacal plans, Killmonger is correct in pointing out the failure of Wakanda (which is what T'Challa comes to see). Wakanda used vibranium to become a technological utopia, "But as Wakanda thrived, the world around it descended further into chaos." By adopting a policy of hiding in plain sight, it abandoned its unmatched power to protect other Africans, so many of whom were lost to the slave trade and to the seas when they jumped from ships.

With Killmonger's death, T'Challa begins to direct Wakandan resources and technologies towards international social outreach to rectify the failures of generations of his ancestors. As he tells his predecessors on the Ancestral Plane, "You were wrong. All of you you were wrong." For Arendt, the center of moral consideration should be the world and not the self; the concern is whether an individual's conduct is good for the world they live in. When individuals engage in political considerations, they enact their capacity to shape the world they live in. "Non-participation in the political affairs of the world has always been open to the reproach of irresponsibility, of shirking one's duties toward the world we share with one another and the community we belong to."[9] Tellingly, one of Erik's deepest criticisms of T'Challa is that he denies his kingly responsibility to be a political actor in the wider world.

The women of Wakanda – Nakia, Okoye, Shuri, and Ramonda – are in constant conflict between collective and individual action. Ultimately they choose shared goals and the interests of their community, each for their own reasons. These admirable women share Arendt's disdain for indifference as one of the greatest dangers and threats to society. At the beginning of the film we see Nakia, a spy conducting her own operation to rescue captive women in Nigeria. She compels T'Challa to act in his capacity as king and be an influential political actor. Motivated by her love for him, she chooses to stay with T'Challa and continue to fight for Wakanda in its newfound global cause. Okoye, the fiercest warrior in the Dora Milaje, experiences conflicting loyalties to the throne; ultimately she upholds her principles by rebelling against a corrupt leader despite her duties to protect and serve him. Shuri embodies Wakanda's technological and scientific advancement and gives voice to the responsibility that such power implies, becoming an agent of change by leading the science and information exchange. And the Queen Mother Ramonda, who represents regal dignity and deep-rooted traditions, agrees to leave the capitol to appeal to M'Baku and the Jabari.

All of these women would agree with Arendt that responsibility involves political action. "I am responsible when my free doing stands for other others; when I accept my link to a particular community, to its traditions; when my acts are the continuation of the fate of members of that community. I am responsible only when, through my initiative, I challenge my specific community and its traditions, because such challenges affect the whole humanity. My responsibility fills the gap between my community and the world."[10]

Clearly, to build a better world we need to understand our communities. We need to know our shared goals and interests and how we can become individual agents of change in conversation with them.

"This Time, We're on Top."

The argument between T'Challa and Killmonger is unusual within the superhero genre; the villain wins and compels the hero to take a dramatic turn. Through T'Challa's actions in Oakland and through his speech at the United Nations, *Black Panther* affirms that Killmonger was right – the responsibility of a Wakandan king isn't just to Wakanda. Whether we use Killmonger's phrasing, "ain't all people your people," or T'Challa's, "we are all one tribe," the message is the same. And yet, Killmonger is also wrong, isn't he? Indeed, Killmonger's actions during his reign resonate with Arendt's warning against totalitarian regimes. Consider Killmonger's speech to the Wakandan council, which is one of his first acts as the new king:

> I know how colonizers think. So we're gonna use their own strategy against them. We're gonna send vibranium weapons to our War Dogs. They'll arm oppressed people all over the world, so they can finally rise up and kill those in power, and their children, and anyone else who takes their side. It's time they know the truth about us. We're warriors. The world's gonna start over and this time, we're on top. The sun will never set on the Wakandan empire.

Now consider the following excerpt from a speech Hitler gave in his 1924 hearing in Munich, where he and nine other Nazi party members were on trial for high treason after a coup was attempted in November 1923 against the Weimar Republic:

> The army which we have formed grows from day to day; it grows more rapidly from hour to hour. Even now I have the proud hope that one day the hour will come when these untrained [wild] bands will grow to battalions, the battalions to regiments and the regiments to divisions, when the old

cockade will be raised from the mire, when the old banners will once again wave before us: and the reconciliation will come in that eternal last Court of Judgment, the Court of God, before which we are ready to take our stand. Then from our bones, from our graves, will sound the voice of that tribunal which alone has the right to sit in judgment upon us.[11]

Hitler claims that only "the Court of God" can stand in judgment of his actions and those of the Nazi party. Likewise, when Killmonger orders the Heart-Shaped Herb to be burned, he essentially elevates himself to a level where no Wakandan can challenge him. This is the kind of thing Arendt warns about:

Totalitarianism is never content to rule by external means, namely, through the state and a machinery of violence; thanks to its peculiar ideology and the role assigned to it in this apparatus of coercion, totalitarianism has discovered a means of dominating and terrorizing human beings from within.[12]

Perhaps the comparison of evil villains (even those in the Marvel Cinematic Universe) to Nazis has become hyperbolic cliché – to the point that the meaning of the analogy gets lost or dismissed. Nevertheless, Killmonger seems to advocate killing millions of people, presumably white people, so that the world can start over with the Black people "on top." For Hitler it was a "Jewish question," for Killmonger it is a "Colonizer question." Their answers may be the same.

In Wakanda there is growing distrust, or at least disappointment, in T'Challa (certainly on W'Kabi's part) because of T'Challa's inability to bring Klaue to justice and his decision not just to save the "colonizer" Agent Ross, but to bring Ross to Wakanda. Killmonger is charismatic and taps into the xenophobia and hostile attitude against "colonizers."

At the challenge ritual, as T'Challa fails, Killmonger asks the audience, "Is this your king?" Of course, even if Wakandans want to answer yes (out of love for T'Challa) they can't, because their traditions (which Killmonger exploits) bind them to follow Killmonger. This is straight out of the totalitarian playbook. As Arendt cautions, the "true goal of totalitarian propaganda is not persuasion, but organization of the polity."[13] This is what Killmonger was doing from the moment he arrived in Wakanda with Klaue's corpse. Erik says he "knows how colonizers think," but we can infer that he also knows how Wakandans think. Thus, Killmonger is able to manipulate the situation to his advantage, playing W'Kabi and T'Challa, the Wakandan council, the Dora Milaje, and all the tribes of Wakanda (except for the Jabari). Ironically, it is Wakanda's very own laws that create the opportunity for Killmonger to seize the throne. In any case, Arendt's observations help us understand that Killmonger's reign was likely on a totalitarian trajectory. Had he succeeded, the result would've been similar to that of Thanos's snap in *Infinity War*, remaking the world in which the survivors would likely be traumatized by the magnitude of the loss.

Thankfully, for Wakanda and the world, T'Challa defeats Killmonger and stops his totalitarian reign before it really begins. In doing so, T'Challa doesn't just transform Wakanda's political ideology from isolationist to global, he transforms the world – not as a would-be totalitarian leader, but as a responsible steward of humanity.

Notes

1. Kathleen Jones, "Thinking with Hannah Arendt about responsibility," Learning for Justice, February 2, 2017, athttps://www.tolerance.org/magazine/thinking-with-hannah-arendt-about-responsibility.
2. Alex Abad-Santos, "Marvel's comic book superheroes were always political. Black Panther embraces that," *Vox*, February 22, 2018, at https://www.vox.com/2018/2/22/17028862/black-panther-movie-political.
3. Annabel Herzog, "Responsibility," in Patrick Hayden ed., *Hannah Arendt: Key Concepts* (London: Routledge, 2014), 186.
4. Hannah Arendt, "Collective Responsibility," in James W. Bernauer ed., *Amor Mundi: Explorations in the Faith and Thought of Hannah Arendt* (Dordrecht: Martinus Nijhoff Publishers, 1987), 45.
5. Arendt (1987), 45.
6. Annabel Herzog, "Hannah Arendt's concept of responsibility," *Studies in Social and Political Thought* 10 (2004), 52.
7. Hannah Arendt, *Responsibility and Judgment* (New York: Schocken, 2009), 145.
8. Arendt (1987), 45.
9. Arendt (1987), 48.
10. Arendt (1987), 48.
11. "Hitler Speech at Munich Trial 1924," at http://worldfuturefund.org/wffmaster/Reading/Hitler%20Speeches/Trial/hitletrial.htm.
12. Hannah Arendt, *The Origins of Totalitarianism* (New York: Harcourt Books, 1973), 325.
13. Arendt (1973), 361.

PART III
The Heart-Shaped Herb

11

Beastly Boys
The Racial-Sexual Politics of Meat

Sofia Huerter

From Ruth E. Carter's Oscar-winning costumes to the nearly all-Black cast to the use of Xhosa to the Kendrick Lamar songs featured on the soundtrack, *Black Panther* is self-avowedly Afrocentric, marking an undeniably important, albeit complicated, contribution to America's national conversation about race. What is perhaps less obvious is that *Black Panther*, in talking about race, also talks about gender, and the complex interrelationship between the two. One particularly interesting example can be found in the character M'Baku, a mountain warrior whose abstention from meat runs afoul of stereotypes about what a vegetarian looks like and, in so doing, challenges racist iconographies of Black masculinity. Another example is Killmonger, who confronts stereotyped notions of Black masculinity through his embodiment of Black patriarchy, portraying a version of a Black king that has more in common with a plantation owner than with the regal, African sovereign depicted by T'Challa. Indeed, the intersected layers of race, gender, and masculinity presented by M'Baku and Killmonger become even more significant when we consider the backdrop of Wakanda.

Unlike other African nations, Wakanda escaped the horrors of European colonialism, and consequently flourished into not only an Afrofuturistic wonderland but the most technologically sophisticated country on the planet. Wakanda therefore offers viewers an intriguing counter-mythology, a picture of what African nations might have become were it not for colonial rule. The reality, of course, is that the entirety of the African continent *was* eventually subject to colonization, and that the traumas inflicted by colonial violence continue to impact African peoples, including the African Diaspora, to this day. That last bit is important: as an African country that never suffered under colonialism, Wakanda lives squarely in the imaginations of people situated in its ongoing history. What we must be sure to keep in

Black Panther and Philosophy: What Can Wakanda Offer the World?, First Edition. Edited by Edwardo Pérez and Timothy E. Brown.
© 2022 John Wiley & Sons, Inc. Published 2022 by John Wiley & Sons, Inc.

mind, then, is that even in posing the counterfactual historical question (i.e. "What might have been?"), the Wakanda of *Black Panther* inevitably brings us back to where we already are.

Among other things, the cultural landscape out of which the *Black Panther* film was birthed is one where the first food behavior associated with masculinity is carnivorism. As Carol Adams argued in her landmark work, *The Sexual Politics of Meat*, in the United States, meat-eating is a highly visible reminder and reinforcer of patriarchal dominance.[1] According to Adams, there is a symbiotic, metaphorical relationship between the consumption of animals' flesh and gender politics. Whereas meat denotes stereotypically masculine traits like aggression and virility, vegetables have long been associated with feminine docility. "To vegetate is to lead a passive existence," says Adams, "just as to be feminine is to lead a passive existence."[2] The attributes of masculinity are thus ritually achieved, as Adams sees it, through the eating of masculine foods, with the inevitable consequence that, by violating this cardinal rule, vegetarianism becomes a marker of deviant masculinity among men, and is liable to be censured, correspondingly, with epithets like "pussy" or "faggot" (or my personal favorite, "soy boy") that mock them as effeminate. Perhaps this is why M'Baku initially doesn't want to yield when he challenges T'Challa; whereas T'Challa is somewhat feminized, being protected by a squad of women, M'Baku doesn't like to deviate from his masculinity. Let's see if we can understand why.

"Silence! I Make the Pronouncements, Girl!"

The notion of a deviant masculinity implies the existence of a hegemonic masculinity, and a hierarchical relationship between the two. Hegemonic masculinity is a way of being a man that facilitates patriarchal gender practices by concentrating those attributes associated with masculine power (strength, analyticality, independence, etc.) into an archetype of manliness.[3] Individual men become practitioners of hegemonic masculinity to the extent that they emulate this idealized way of being a man. Certainly, M'Baku and Killmonger (and even Klaue) ooze manliness. However, hegemonic masculinity is not equally realizable by all men; it requires certain resources, like wealth, social recognition, and access to (not to mention a desire for) women and heterosexual intercourse that are unevenly distributed along racial, sexual, religious, and economic lines. Thus, there is a gender politics at work even within masculinity, one that implies that patriarchy is "more implicated in the structure of social relations than has sometimes been admitted and at the same time not as monolithic as has been suggested."[4]

Much ink has been spilled over the patriarchal devaluation of all things feminine and womanly, but the disadvantages incurred by men who are not in line with hegemonic masculinity, let alone its food-based behaviors, has been less often discussed. This is especially true in the case of Black men, whose hypermasculinized representation in the media tends to make them appear as if they were the patriarchy's worst offenders. One of the most significant contributions of recent Black feminist scholarship has thus been to challenge this view, and to illuminate how the "demonization of black males as the epitome of brutal patriarchal masculinity deflects attention away from the patriarchal masculinity of White men."[5] This insight is expressed in bell hooks's writing on "plantation patriarchy," a term coined to describe the historical indoctrination of Black men into the gender politics of chattel slavery. For hooks, the subordinated status of Black men incentivized their conformity to the masculine norms exemplified by the White masters, who, through their commodification and control of slaves, assumed the role of patriarch on American plantations. One contemporary example of this dynamic can be found in *Black Panther* itself, specifically via the film's antagonist, the Oakland-grown Erik Killmonger.

"I Am the King Now!"

Killmonger comes to Wakanda as a conqueror, taking up his late father's mission to end the country's isolationist foreign policy and stage armed insurgencies the world over.[6] Although his express purpose is Black liberation, Killmonger's plan to achieve it is the familiar violence of colonial domination, and clearly has more to do with putting himself and his people at the top of the proverbial food chain. "The sun will never set on the Wakandan empire!" he declares, appropriating the adage of the bygone British empire, and in his blood-soaked zeal to seize the throne, Killmonger, not unlike the European colonizers before him, leaves behind a trail of Black bodies. No one is safe from Killmonger's warpath, not even his lover, Linda, once she stands in his way. Not for nothing, T'Challa denounces him as a hypocrite: "You want to see us become just like the people you hate so much," T'Challa says. "I learn from my enemies," Killmonger rejoinders.

The irony of Killmonger's plan, wielding the master's tools to dismantle the master's house, is palpable. As Adam Serwer notes, "It is somewhat bizarre to see people endorse a comic-book version of George W. Bush's foreign policy and sign up for the Project for the New Wakandan Century as long as the words 'black liberation' are used instead of 'democracy promotion.'"[7] Imperialism is both the ill for which Killmonger demands redress and the wellspring of his values, and in this latter fact, he is very evidently an adherent of plantation patriarchy, but he is also one of its tragic casualties.[8] Citing Killmonger's credentials in state-sanctioned murder, Agent Ross affirms the truth that Killmonger has assimilated to the American military–industrial complex. "He's not Wakandan," Ross laments. "He's one of ours." The method to Killmonger's madness thus serves as a cautionary tale: even in the struggle for liberation, not all skinfolk are kinfolk.

One problem noted by hooks is that, because gender is mediated by race, Black men have always lacked the means to embody the essential quality of the plantation's patriarchal icons: Whiteness. This idea is expounded in Hortense Spillers's pivotal essay, "Mama's Baby, Papa's Maybe," where she defends the "ungendering" of the Black subject as the primary dispossession resulting from chattel slavery.[9] Binary gender assignation has served less, in her view, to unify men and women across race under the shared mantles of manhood and womanhood than to cast into sharp relief how Black people are "out of step" with normative gender and kinship structures. For example, the sexual exploitation of enslaved women served not only to satisfy the carnal desires of White men and reproduce the slave labor force, but also to emasculate Black men who were married off as adoptive fathers to children sired by White masters, usurping the patriarchal convention according to which the sexual initiation of his wife, not to mention the rejection of any illegitimate children, is a husband's right. As lamented by the character Jake in Margaret Walker's *Jubilee*, "Marster had broke her in, and then 'give her to me.'"[10] What's more, *partus sequitur ventrem*, the legal doctrine providing that the bonded or freed status of the child followed that of the mother, situated Black men and their offspring outside the patriarchal system of filiation, and thereby condemned slaves to a kind of natal alienation, where the omnipresent possibility of separation made the traditional, nuclear family, with all its attendant rights and privileges, an impossibility – a dynamic that continues to play out in today's age of racialized mass incarceration.[11]

For Spillers, slavery both shaped and set in motion a specific symbolic order, what she calls "the American grammar," within which Black gender is always, inevitably, gender done wrongly – thinglike and sensuous.[12] It is in this context that Black men's internalization of hegemonic masculinity may result in a performativity that, even when it is identical in structure to the performativities of their White counterparts, can be systematically distorted as hypermasculine.[13] Masculine success, for example, is often conceived in terms of sexual access to women. However, as Amy C. Wilkins observes, "race intersects with gender and heterosexuality to unevenly allocate privilege and power, complicating the relationship between heterosexuality and masculinity for some men."[14]

In the years following Reconstruction, White Southerners were consumed by a fear of the Black rapist, whose imputed lust for White women deflected attention from White men and the cross-racial desire they had so brutally enacted prior to Abolition. Not supposing themselves to have such base urges, however, White men routinely blamed their sexual aggression on the inborn licentiousness of Black women, placing White women on a pedestal of chastity that made charges of rape committed by Black men all the more sensational.[15] The supermasculine image of Black men as over-sexed brutes is the contemporary outcome of this centuries-old identity-construction process. In many ways, M'Baku and Killmonger seem to conform to this image, especially in contrast to T'Challa and W'Kabi.

"I'm Kidding. We are Vegetarians."

It is my belief that meat-centered masculinity is part and parcel of planta-tion patriarchy. A clear reason for the establishment of the North American slave trade was the need for cheap labor in the newly established European colonies, and it was through this institution not only that the histories of Africa, Europe, and the Americas converged but also that the racialized association of meat-eating and masculinity began to crystalize on the plan-tation. Particularly during the global expansion of Britain, the consump-tion of meat became a marker of the culture's supposed evolutionary superiority, with the success of its colonial efforts being attributed, in no small measure, to its people's dietary habits.[16] According to Val Plumwood, author of *Feminism and the Mastery of Nature*, this line of thinking has as its basis a hierarchical dualism between reason and nature derived from the Platonic philosophical tradition. In this view, man constructs civiliza-tion by imposing order onto the otherwise unruly world of nature, and in so doing distinguishes himself from the "lower elements," namely the bes-tial and feminine.[17] Thus, the eating of meat, particularly the cooked meat of domesticated animals, came to have national significance in colonial England, because it demonstrated "an ability to triumph over and manage nature rather than be determined by it."[18]

  With the mastery of nature being figured as especially and normatively masculine, the consumption of animals, and its association with colonial prestige, took on a distinctly gendered dimension. Whereas the colonizer was masculinized, in a parody of heterosexual intercourse, through the penetrative power of conquest, those subjected to it were concomitantly feminized. To the minds of many colonized subjects, the only recourse against such effeminacy was virile masculinity of the carnivorous variety, as exemplified by the exhortation, during the British rule of India, that Hindus should forswear their prohibition on meat as a way of achieving parity with their oppressors.[19] Certainly, we can see Killmonger's actions existing on both sides of this axis – even M'Baku and the isolation of the Jabari reflect the dynamics of conquest and subjugation in relation to Wakanda. Empowerment was defined, in this instance, "not only by the normativity of the impulse toward masculine violence but more subtly by an injunction *not to fear* enacting such violence on others," including, but not limited to, the animals.[20]

With the putative transcendence of the human over nature being marked by the consumption of animal flesh, the near total subsistence of slaves on plant foods served similarly, on the American plantation, to spotlight their status as chattel. By the same token, White slavers were able to parlay their control over meat rations into a pseudo-benevolent form of patriarchal power. As recounted by Charles Ball in his autobiography, *Fifty Years in Chains*, "Whatever was given to us beyond the corn [...] was considered in the light of a bounty bestowed upon us, over and above what we were entitled to, or had a right to expect to receive."[21] The strategic distribution of meat had a domesticating effect on himself and his fellow slaves, Ball noted, that temporarily reconciled them to their fate. The rub is that slaves, too, could be rendered edible by their White masters, and not just in the metaphoric sense of being bought and sold, but also literally, when they were sicced upon by bloodhounds. Bénédicte Boisseronn, in her trenchantly penned *Afro-Dog*, explores dogs as an historical accessory to Black dehumanization, observing that "the dog bite, when orchestrated by the white against the black, is a racially driven kind of cannibalism that uses fangs as a means of transference ... demot[ing] the black race to the level of animal species, thus banning the so-called black race from human taxonomy."[22] By the same token, Black men were concomitantly configured outside of manhood.

In parallel fashion to the mythic Black rapist, the taboo of cannibalism, which was violated within the slave trade, has been symptomatically expressed in a fear of anthrophagy that has been part of the European psychosis since the colonial era, when the accusation was lobbed especially against Indigenous peoples who fought incursions into their lands. British historian Bryan Edwards, for instance, offered lurid, albeit unsubstantiated accounts of various African tribes as cannibals, describing the infamously resistant Igbo as "more truly savage than any other nation of the Gold Coast; inasmuch as many tribes among them ... have been, without a doubt, accustomed to the shocking practice of feeding on human flesh."[23] The reality – that it was slavery and European colonialism that cannibalized generations of Africans – stood "in contradistinction to the typical discourse about the practice that invariably indict[ed] the primitive other as cannibal."[24]

It is intriguing that *Black Panther* viewers meet M'Baku in the context of this historical milieu, where the invention of the New World (savage) man was realized. M'Baku is presented savagely when he challenges T'Challa, and again when Ramonda (and company) seek M'Baku's help after Killmonger assumes the throne. In this pinnacle scene, Agent Ross (the only White character other than Klaue and the museum lady) is shouted down whenever he attempts to speak: "You cannot talk," M'Baku literally barks, looking and sounding savage. "One more word and I'll feed you to my children." In the colonial imagination, African cannibals represented an unspeakable arrogation of power, in response to which the prime directive, in an analogue to phallic panic, was resisting ingestion. M'Baku's threat in the face of foreign intervention thus rehearses, as Janet Beizer quips, "the banally racist stuff of nineteenth-century exoticising," and, in one fell swoop, turns it upside down.[25] "I am kidding," M'Baku laughs uproariously. "We are vegetarians."

"So It Was Less a Murder than a Defeat."

Cinematic representation is saturated with the ideological residue of history's oft-repeated stories. Our perception of what is being played out on the screen trades on our relationship to the archive of collective cultural memory, which exhorts us to see things, not as they are, but "[as] they were handed down to us through mass-mediated representations."[26] The power of M'Baku's vegetarianism therefore lies in its manipulation of the very same tropological apparatus that primes us to fear his cannibalism, or to presume his insensitivity towards nonhuman animals. Rather than rehearse the trope to completion, M'Baku's vegetarianism turns the colonizer's othering gaze back upon itself, as if to ask, "Who told you that?" Whereas Everett Ross's pining for home doubtless includes the taste of a Big Mac, M'Baku, the colonist's bogeyman incarnate, disavows the consumption of flesh altogether, making him seem more enlightened and empathetic by comparison.

Empathy notwithstanding, M'Baku is, notably, a warrior. He is not a mewling patient of violence but has instead committed himself to its practice, even to its necessity, as has often been the case in overcoming the oppressive power of colonial rule. Killmonger's violence is similarly deliberate and, in its own way, is meant to honor the rage, yearnings, and aspirations of all those subjugated to, and displaced and discarded by, colonialism. From the moment he appears on screen to his final scene with T'Challa, Killmonger isn't just focused, he's willing to do whatever it takes to achieve his goal – whether it means killing his girlfriend, burning the fields of Heart-Shaped Herbs, or ordering W'Kabi and the Border Tribe to "kill this clown" and fight their own people. Even his death scene is defiantly masculine; not wanting to be saved, because he assumes that T'Challa will imprison him, he tells T'Challa to "Bury me in the ocean, with my ancestors that jumped from the ships, 'cause they knew death was better than bondage." Thus, Killmonger remains supermasculine as he pulls the blade from his chest and dies in the glow of the Wakandan sunset. "It's beautiful," he tells T'Challa.

In the case of M'Baku, his violence, even when it is insurrectional, refuses to mirror the violent absolutism of colonial terror. His diet thus becomes the stage of his politics, suggesting a moral asymmetry between his willingness to violence and the violence of colonial conquest manifested in its bloodsport kin: flesh-eating. As described by animal rights advocate Henry Salt: "The Englishman, both as soldier and colonist, is a typical sportsman; he seizes on his prey wherever he finds it with the hunter's privilege [...] He is lost in amazement when men speak of the rights of inferior races, just as the Englishman at home is lost in amazement when we speak of the rights of the lower orders."[27] By insisting upon his own right to violence while simultaneously refusing the carnophilic mandate of colonial masculinity, M'Baku honors the aspirations of all those dispossessed by its sequestering logic. Coupled with M'Baku's choice to save T'Challa and help him fight Killmonger, not to mention T'Challa's decision to (femininely) open up Wakanda (or W'Kabi surrendering to Okoye), *Black Panther* reveals the complexity inherent in the intersected layers of race and gender.

Notes

1. Carol J. Adams, *The Sexual Politics of Meat: A Feminist-Vegetarian Critical Theory* (New York: Bloomsbury Publishing, 2015).
2. Adams, 61.
3. Traditionally, patriarchy has been defined as a social structure in which men are the primary holders of power over and above women. For reasons which I hope to clarify shortly, I believe that this definition of patriarchy is antiquated and overly simplistic.
4. Marcia C. Inhorn, *The New Arab Man: Emergent Masculinities, Technologies, and Islam in the Middle East* (Princeton, NJ: Princeton University Press, 2012), 13.
5. bell hooks, *The Will to Change: Men, Masculinity, and Love* (New York: Washington Square Press, 2004), 130.
6. Killmonger's journey back to his ancestral homeland is conspicuously reminiscent of the Back-to-Africa movement and its influences on the separatist, Black Nationalist politics of the Black Panther Party.
7. Adam Serwer, "The tragedy of Erik Killmonger," *The Atlantic*, February 21, 2018, at https://www.theatlantic.com/entertainment/archive/2018/02/black-panther-erik-killmonger/553805.
8. Here, too, we see an echoing of the Black Panther Party, namely the arc from its noble beginnings to its eventual fracturing over the nature of violence and the legitimacy of its use. This is not to suggest that the Black Panther Party was particularly (or unwarrantedly) violent but rather that the issue of an armed insurrection against the US government, and the justification for it, proved divisive for the Party's leadership.
9. Hortense J. Spillers, "Mama's Baby, Papa's maybe: An American grammar book," *Diacritics* 17 (1987), 64–81.
10. Margaret Walker, *Jubilee* (New York: Bantam Books, 1966), 14.
11. The term "natal alienation" is described by its progenitor, Orlando Patterson, as "alienation of the slave from all formal, legally enforceable ties of 'blood'." Orlando Patterson, *Slavery and Social Death: A Comparative Study* (Cambridge, MA: Harvard University Press, 1982), 7. What is entailed by natal

alienation, then, is not the absence of familial relationships but the fact that such relationships confer no legal standing for their constituent members.

12. Spillers's "American grammar" harkens Lacan, whose "symbolic order" denotes a network of social and linguistic categories, like "man" and "woman," which are at once produced and reiterated by individual subjects through practices of identification; in an effort to render themselves intelligible, subjects act these as though they were following a script. Where a bad performance is met with admonition, a good performance might be met, contrariwise, with approbation.

13. This is not, of course, to suggest that Black men never do perform hypermasculinity but rather that, were they to mirror their masculine performances to those of White men, theirs would often come out for their worse.

14. Amy C. Wilkins, "Stigma and status: Interracial intimacy and intersectional identities among Black college men," *Gender & Society* 26 (2012), 165–189. doi:10.1177/0891243211434613.

15. For more, see Madelin Joan Olds, "The Rape Complex in the Postbellum South," in Kim Marie Vaz ed., *Black Women in America* (Thousand Oaks, CA: Sage, 1995), 179–205.

16. For instance, William Smellie, in his *Philosophy of Natural History*, described the people of India as a "meager, sick and feeble race," and blamed vegetarianism for their military ineptitude. William Smellie, *The Philosophy of Natural History*, 3rd ed. (London: Hillard, Gray, Little, and Wilkins, 1829), 144.

17. Val Plumwood, *Feminism and the Mastery of Nature* (London: Routledge, 1993).

18. Claire Rasmussen, "Domesticating Bodies: Race, Species, Sex, and Citizenship," in Judith Grant and Vincent Jungkunz eds., *Political Theory and the Animal/Human Relationship* (Albany, NY: State University of New York Press, 2016), 88.

19. In his autobiography, Mahatma Gandhi links meat-eating, masculinity, and colonialism as he recalls being influenced by the trope, often touted by Indian nationalists, that meat-eating was a sign of modernity, and feeling a consequent compulsion to couple Indian resistance with a meat-centered diet. "'We are a weak people because we do not eat meat,'" he recalls one friend saying. "'The English are able to rule over us, because they are meat-eaters'." M.K. Gandhi, *An Autobiography or The Story of My Experiments with Truth*, ed. Tridip Suhrud and trans. Mahadev H. Desai (New Haven, CT: Yale University Press, 2018), 77.

20. Judith Kegan Gardiner, *Masculinity Studies and Feminist Theory* (New York: Columbia University Press, 2002), 315.

21. Charles Ball, *Fifty Years in Chains, or, The Life of an American Slave* (Indianapolis, IN: Asher & Co., 1859), 127.

22. Benedicte Boisseronn, *Afro-Dog: Blackness and the Animal Question* (New York: Columbia University Press, 2018), 70–71.

23. Bryan Edwards, *The History, Civil and Commercial, of the British West Indies*, vol. 2 (London: T. Miller, 1819), 90.

24. Alan Rice, "'Who's eating whom': The discourse of cannibalism in the literature of the Black Atlantic from Equiano's 'Travels' to Toni Morrison's 'Beloved,'" *Research in African Literatures* 29 (1998), 115.

25. Janet Beizer, "Eating others: Cannibalizing and power in France," *Dublin Gastronomy Symposium*, May 29, 2018, at https://arrow.tudublin.ie/cgi/viewcontent.cgi?article=1138&context=dgs.

26. Lutz Koepnick, "Honor Your German Masters," in Randall Halle and Margaret McCarthy eds., *Light Movies: German Popular Film in Perspective* (Detroit, MI: Wayne State University Press, 2003), 351.

27. Henry Stephens Salt ed., *Killing for Sport: Essays by Various Writers* (London: George Bell and Sons, 1919), 150.

12

Panther Mystique
Wakandan Feminism Demystified

J. Lenore Wright and Edwardo Pérez

The women of Wakanda are no ordinary women. They are Wakandan women. They hold positions of power and enjoy professional parity with men. Shuri oversees Wakanda's vibranium and technology, with her exceptional mind elevating her above her male counterparts. Okoye, Wakanda's greatest warrior, commands the Dora Milaje and serves as T'Challa's chief bodyguard (she also belongs to Black Widow's ragtag Avengers team in *Avengers: Endgame* after the Thanos snap). It is no surprise that the Dora Milaje are trained warriors who take on Thanos's forces in *Avengers: Infinity War* and *Avengers: Endgame*. Nakia, a war dog, possesses physical and philosophical alertness equal to T'Challa's along with some wicked military skills. Ramonda displays true wisdom and courage (and because she's played by Angela Bassett, you know she can break kneecaps whenever necessary).

Wakandan women can play stereotypically male roles because of the political construction of Wakandan identity. Wakandan kinship emerges from a distinctive social location that transcends sex differences, a world of political conflict, spiritual diversity, and technological advancement. Because of Wakanda's tie to a warring past and investment in a technological future, both men and women must operate within multiple systems of meaning, systems that surpass the ordinary world of meaning making. Wakandan semiotics incorporate physical strength, spiritual awareness, political acumen, and keen intellects into identity politics. Strong, wise, intellectual women are therefore normal rather than deviant. Although sex differences are largely irrelevant to the achievement of Wakandan goals, one wonders how the lives of Wakandan women compare to liberated women around the world.

Black Panther and Philosophy: What Can Wakanda Offer the World?, First Edition. Edited by Edwardo Pérez and Timothy E. Brown.
© 2022 John Wiley & Sons, Inc. Published 2022 by John Wiley & Sons, Inc.

Wakandan women emerge, for starters, in a radically different cultural context than women of color in other countries and cultures. They function as a majority racial group in an advanced society organized around (at least some) egalitarian principles. Their embodiment of dominant cultural norms and physical traits authorizes their high social standing, a standing undergirded by a cultural hegemony that non-Wakandan women of color lack. Their majority status opposes the minority position of African American women and the subjugation of African, Asian, and other women of color. It also appears that women's historic, cultural, political, and economic poverty – a phenomenon that circumscribes all women's lives – is largely absent among these female characters. (Perhaps they can teach us how to advance diversity, equality, and inclusion). Their exercise of equality, by contrast, begs critical, feminist questions: can feminism demystify the exemplary world of Wakanda? Is the world of Wakanda as rosy and riveting as it appears?

Despite their tacit representation of feminist ideals, Wakandan women resist the full-throated feminism we associate with the modern era: the no-husband, no-children feminism championed by the French philosopher Simone de Beauvoir. Rather, the interdependency of Wakandan women reflects a multiplicity of feminist views, a multiplicity aptly explained by the feminist theorists Angela Davis and Audre Lorde. Davis was among the first philosophers to argue that feminism is plural rather than singular.[1] Feminisms include, as she sees it, Black Feminism, a form of feminist theory that seeks to understand Black women's experiences of oppression. And, Lorde adds, feminisms include feminism of color, a feminism that challenges the exclusion of women "who have been forged in the crucibles of difference."[2] Taken together, Davis and Lorde advance a fleshed-out feminism – a feminism that acknowledges embodied and lived female differences and the truth "that survival is not an academic skill."[3] Their work sheds important light on Wakandan women's struggle for recognition in the face of a particular panther mystique.

"This Corset Is Really Uncomfortable."

In her published speech, "The Master's Tools Will Never Dismantle the Master's House," Lorde asserts that "women of today are still being called upon to stretch across the gap of male ignorance and to educate men as to our existence and our needs. This is an old and primary tool of all oppressors to keep the oppressed occupied with the master's concerns."[4] Her argument encapsulates the male–female dynamic in most parts of the world, including the world of Wakanda. When Zuri asks the tribes if anyone of royal blood wishes to challenge T'Challa for the throne, we know Nakia and Shuri can issue legitimate challenges if they wish to do so.

They do not. But had they done so, they might have prevailed as victors given their fighting skills and T'Challa's compassion (would T'Challa have yielded?). Of course, it's M'Baku who challenges T'Challa. M'Baku chastises the observing crowd for their submission to Shuri prior to the battle: "We have watched with disgust as your technological advancements have been overseen by a child ... who scoffs at tradition!" Given the cultural context, Shuri's sex alone is not the source of M'Baku's deep offense. Rather, her flouting of traditions sends him over the edge: traditions that derive from embedded, patriarchal patterns of male dominance and leadership. She must be a child, after all, if she stubbornly refuses to hand over management of Wakandan technology to a male leader (we're guessing he discounts her driving ability and dismisses the panther suit housed inside a necklace too).[5] And she must be a child if she flouts the challenge ritual with its tribal costumes and roles, costumes and roles designed to reinforce power historically vested in men. Even if being a woman is not inherently threatening, being a woman in a world like Wakanda where there is limited access to, and intense competition over, power raises the threat level significantly. Women can rule so long as they rule like men (there's no room for throwing like a girl in Wakanda). Female equality comes with conditions, à la Lorde. Teaching Wakandan men that women have their own ideas, methods, and visions for leadership is one of these conditions. Some men, however, are not very teachable.

In 1966 Black Panther, the Marvel comic superhero, made his debut during the height of second-wave feminism. The ethos of Wakanda, Black Panther's home, embraces the movement's mood: women are more than mothers, housewives, and caregivers (even if some men miss the memo). In the West, explicitly feminist sentiments emerged in the seventeenth century, though the term *feminism* is a later creation. Canonical texts and organized activism unfolded in a series of intellectual waves beginning in the eighteenth century (feminism has entered its fourth wave). Mary Wollstonecraft in England and Olympe de Gouges in France, for example, appropriated French Enlightenment ideals of equality, liberty, and fraternity to argue for women's political rights and social inclusion.

Building upon first-wave feminism, two defining texts – Simone de Beauvoir's *The Second Sex* (1949) and Betty Friedan's *The Feminine Mystique* (1963) – initiated a second wave of thought with individual freedom as its goal (Beauvoir is the proverbial mother of second-wave feminism). Beauvoir's and Friedan's works codify key foundational principles of feminism that subsequent waves develop and deploy.[6] Their recognition that cultural views of women radically shaped female freedom opened the door to feminisms of difference. By posing the metaphysical question *What is a woman?* as an existential question, Beauvoir invited an anthropological reply – "One is not born, but rather becomes, woman."[7] She argued that the roles a woman plays are not inherent to the female sex. Rather, they are constructed by society and inscribed onto women through processes of normalization (a sex/gender division is inherent to twentieth-century feminism). When we identify an baby's biological sex as female, we say, "it's a girl," and subsequently (and to some degree unconsciously) assign to the infant a set of culturally bound, sex-based expectations. Over time, these expectations grow into bodily inscriptions: normative standards of how a woman should look, act, and think, as well as what economic positions she should occupy (or not occupy). These expectations may vary in degree from group to group, but collectively they express a universal view that woman is the second sex, an opposing alterity to the human archetype embodied and idealized in man.

M'Baku expresses the stereotypical male reaction to women who want more from life than their normative, secondary, caregiving status. His critique of Shuri's flouting of tradition emerges from her apparent violation of social norms. Although we never see Jabari women and do not know how they are viewed or treated, the Jabari Tribe shuns technology and vibranium. Is M'Baku reacting to Shuri's displacement of male authority, thereby reinforcing her femininity by speaking of her diminutively as a child? Or is he issuing a cultural critique of Shuri, suggesting she herself is guilty of betraying Wakanda by violating Jabari norms as she embraces and advances technology? Would M'Baku critique a male leader of the Wakandan Design Group in the same vein?

Friedan expanded upon Beauvoir by highlighting the oppressiveness of female domesticity. After surveying Smith College alumnae (she mailed out a questionnaire in 1957) and learning how desperately they desired an identity beyond the home, she called their feeling "the problem that has no name," a feeling of utter unfulfillment common to college-educated women homemakers. The problem baffled physicians and confused husbands and men in general: *how could keeping house and rearing children leave women unfulfilled?* But the interviewees consistently reported that although they loved their children and husbands, they despaired at the thought that homemaking is the sum total of their identities. "Is this all?" they wondered. Friedan coined the phrase *the feminine mystique* to capture the situation.[8] As Friedan explains, "The feminine mystique says that the highest value and the only commitment for women is the fulfillment of their own femininity," and that "femininity is so mysterious and intuitive and close to the creation and origin of life that man-made science may never be able to understand it."[9]

Back in Wakanda, M'Baku's renouncement of Shuri's non-domestic activities makes an implicit appeal to the feminine mystique. Shuri should stop playing in her silly little lab and focus on real female gifts, like natural, maternal love. He seems to endorse the feminine mystique: "the root of women's troubles in the past is that women envied men, women tried to be like men, instead of accepting their own nature, which can find fulfillment only in sexual passivity, male domination, and nurturing maternal love."[10] Is Shuri wrong to "behave like a man," lured by technology into forsaking her feminine ways? (We can imagine M'Baku's answer.) Would society function better if women would accept their naturally passive state and submit to male authority? (Maybe Shuri can go back and fight M'Baku on behalf of women everywhere.)

Friedan's account of "the problem" with homemakers resonates with women across centuries and cultures. She identified an archetype of femininity that holds today: an idealization of housewife-mothers – *women who never had opportunities to pursue activities outside the home* – as the model *par excellence* of womanhood.[11] Recent critiques of Beauvoir and Friedan have, however, highlighted just how white their analyses are. Beauvoir speaks for women situated like her: smart, educated, well-heeled, well-positioned, and yes, very white indeed. Friedan represents an elite bunch of society gals whose worlds reflect a minority slice of modern American life. Their white-woman analyses raise the question of difference, a question Lorde was brave enough to ask: "How do you deal with the fact that the women who clean your houses and tend your children while you attend conferences on feminist theory are, for the most part, poor women and women of Color?"[12]

Lorde and Davis add valuable perspective to second-wave feminism's emphasis on transcendence. While white women have sought transcendence in the form of overcoming domesticity (and, with it, femininity, as Beauvoir powerfully asserts), Black women have sought to transcend racial prejudice and poverty by gaining access to education, opportunities for economic advancement, and social acceptance. Put differently, the social barriers that white and Black women seek to transcend are radically different. Just as women of color have had to educate men about their circumstances, Lorde rightly claims (and rightfully objects to the fact) that women of color must also "educate white women – in the face of tremendous resistance – as to our existence, our differences, our relative roles in our joint survival. This is a diversion of energies and a tragic repetition of racist patriarchal thought."[13] Freedom rests on women's ability to join in a collective fight to challenge their predefined social situations. By drawing strength and inspiration from the women of Wakanda, real women can subvert their respective (assumed) places and personhoods.

Ruby Hamad extends the critique of second-wave conceptions of transcendence, arguing that white feminism (what she also calls White Womanhood) has been used as a weapon against women of color – from the treatment of Native and Aboriginal women and female slaves, to harmful depictions of fictional characters in *The Hunger Games*, and finally to demeaning portrayals of politicians such as Alexandria Ocasio-Cortez.[14] "Because women of color are always perceived as lesser women," Hamad writes, "then whatever the intersection – be it gender identity, sexuality, disability, or something else – every experience of marginalization is made more acute when race is thrown into the mix."[15] Wakandan women show us that transcendence is not an abstract, philosophical idea. Transcendence is a social endeavor, an embodied struggle for freedom from a particular face of oppression, to borrow the language of Iris Marion Young.[16]

Feminists should, as Lorde suggests, specify the meaning of transcendence. And feminism itself would be enriched by an analysis of the particularity and variability of transcendence. Yet it does not follow that some women are free while others are oppressed (it's just that some women are subject to fewer faces of oppression). From Beauvoir's perspective, defining woman as womb, woman as Other, and woman as the second sex is produced by a structural positioning of man as the human archetype. By position and definition, women are inferior to men. If we can free humans from this structural arrangement (here is the opening to post-structuralism and third-wave feminism), then we can free women to become who they are. For Friedan, confining woman to the role of "housewife-mother" with its embedded, yoked concepts of domesticity and femininity sets women up for the problem that has no name. And, if we steal a page from Marvel, when we see the truth of women's oppression, we should resist grounding this truth in sameness so that we can move toward meaningful analyses and exercises of transcendence for all women. White women, for example, regardless of class, education, and sexual preference, are higher on the hierarchy of oppression than women of color.[17] Being a Black wife or mother is, to use Lorde's word, different. As Trudier Harris puts it, the list is more pointed for Black women: "Called Matriarch, Emasculator and Hot Momma. Sometimes Sister, Pretty Baby, Auntie, Mammy and Girl. Called Unwed Mother, Welfare Recipient and Inner-City Consumer, the Black American Woman has had to admit that while nobody knew the troubles she saw, everybody, his brother and his dog, felt qualified to explain it to her."[18] For Alice Walker:

> Black women are called, in the folklore that so aptly identifies one's status in society, "the mule of the world," because we have been handed the burdens that everyone else – everyone else – refused to carry. We have also been called "Matriarchs," "Superwomen," and "Mean and Evil Bitches." Not to mention "Castraters" and "Sapphire's Mama."[19]

Hamad articulates other demoralizing labels for women of color, such as "Jezebel," "Pocahontas," and "China Doll," among others.[20]

Killmonger calls Ramonda "Auntie" in *Black Panther*, suggesting a shared cultural meaning rooted in race. But do colloquial terms for Black women apply to Wakandan women?[21] Are Wakandan women burdened with identities that signal oppression? Analyzed through the work of Patricia Hill Collins, Wakandan women borrow a strategy from Black female intellectuals that enables them to throw off cultural labels and define themselves anew. Collins argues that "Black women intellectuals from all walks of life must aggressively push the theme of self-definition because speaking for oneself and crafting one's own agenda is essential to empowerment."[22] In the process of self-definition, "Black women journey toward an understanding of how our personal lives have been fundamentally shaped by intersecting oppressions of race, gender, sexuality, and class."[23] Looking through this lens, we see that Shuri, Okoye, and Nakia have deployed a process of self-definition that empowers them to occupy roles and identities of their choosing.[24] Their version of transcendence is continuous with and speaks powerfully to the Black female experience in the United States.

M'Baku's dismissive mansplaining undermines everyone outside of the Jabari – Shuri as well as Ramonda and Nakia when they seek his help after Killmonger takes the throne. His dismissiveness codes as anti-culture rather than anti-sex, however, in light of his isolationist tendencies. Given women's high status in Wakanda – *and given the principle of second-wave feminism that views of woman shape female freedom (and the Black feminist addition that transcendence from oppression must be defined)* – it becomes clear that Wakandan women are not "Otherised" and oppressed in the same way as women of color in the United States, at least not to the extent that Lorde, Davis, Hamad, and Collins observe wherein stereotypical images "are designed to make racism, sexism, poverty, and other forms of social injustice appear to be natural, normal, and inevitable parts of everyday life."[25] The Dora Milaje are natural and normal (just as vibranium-armored rhinoceroses and flying ships are natural and normal). Wakanda teaches us that societies that overcome tradition – by transcending, for instance, sex-based roles and identities – foster connection and community.

Wakandan women appear to be born into their state of equality. Historically, oppressed groups have come into and then moved out of (some forms or faces of) oppression. Africans and Jews, for example, enjoyed freedom prior and subsequent to their respective enslavement and imprisonment. They, therefore, have a historic record of oppression: a before-during-after oppression narrative to reference and share.[26] But for women, Beauvoir contends, there is no such pre-oppressive state, no history of non-oppression, no record of oppression's causes or commencement. Women not only become who they are (wombs, Others, secondary sexes), they become who they are because their lives are constitutive of ontological oppression. In short, all women, regardless of race, class, culture, ethnicity, sexual orientation, gender identity, ability, and so forth, are oppressed. Wakanda, however, as represented in *Black Panther*, has no such pre- and post-record of female oppression because sexism, if it exists, has no real force in Wakandan culture. There is no tradition of women's structural inferiority, though hierarchy (monarchy) and patriarchal habits persist. Individuals are defined by their political wits, not biological sex. Wakanda invites women to experience a reality not yet realized anywhere else in the world: *the freedom to define what and who one is, and the power of interdependence to lift others out of oppression.*

The power of Wakanda is embedded in Lorde's, Davis's, Hamad's, and Collins's collective call for solidarity across difference. Second-wave feminisms, including Black feminism and feminism of color, are right to reject the use of sexist and dehumanizing labels to mark women as property, as lesser humans, as Other, regardless of race, color, or culture. They are also right to affirm, as does Lorde, a collective female voice that speaks across differences and valorizes the beauty of diversity within women's experiences:

> Interdependency between women is the way to a freedom which allows the I to be, not in order to be used, but in order to be creative. This is a difference between the passive be and the active being. Advocating the mere tolerance of difference between women is the grossest reformism. It is a total denial of the creative function of difference in our lives. Difference must be not merely tolerated, but seen as a fund of necessary polarities between which our creativity can spark like a dialectic. Only then does the necessity for interdependency become unthreatening. Only within that interdependency of difference strengths, acknowledged and equal, can the power to seek new ways of being in the world generate, as well as the courage and sustenance to act where there are no charters. Within the interdependence of mutual (nondominant) differences lies that security which enables us to descend into the chaos of knowledge and return with true visions of our future, along with the concomitant power to effect those changes which can bring that future into being. Difference is that raw and powerful connection from which our personal power is forged. As women, we have been taught either to ignore our differences, or to view them as causes for separation and suspicion rather than as forces for change. Without community there is no liberation, only the most vulnerable and temporary armistice between an individual and her oppression. But community must not mean a shedding of our differences, nor the pathetic pretense that these differences do not exist.[27]

By problematizing the meaning of transcendence – by identifying variation in women's situations and locating additional barriers to female freedom – Black feminism and feminism of color open the door to female difference and mutual transcendence. Differences in bodies, locations, and power call for feminists to rethink what it means to be a woman. The future is female. The future is feminist. The future is Wakanda.

"The Real Question Is, What Are Those?"

Shuri teases T'Challa about freezing when he sees Nakia. She also complains about her corset. Her mother scolds her for vocalizing what amounts to too much information, which raises the question of Shuri's intent. She seems (dare we invoke M'Baku) rather childlike in her playful banter, as if she hasn't fully come of age and matured into a romantic subject herself. One advantage to presenting herself as a spirited playmate rather than potential partner is that Shuri escapes the male–female dyad entirely: a coupling dynamic that reconstitutes male dominance by capitulating to (Jabari-like) patriarchal structures. Shuri ensures, in other words, that she is not defined by a man – by the need to have one or want one, romantically or sexually. She reclaims the power to define herself (think Hamad and Collins) and sublimates internal desire by creating protective gear for T'Challa (think Beauvoir and Lorde). Every gadget she designs is meant to keep him safe. By transferring any familial feelings for T'Challa to Wakanda as a whole, she values community above domesticity and femininity.

Shuri's elevation of community exemplifies embodied Black feminism: she repudiates white womanhood with its embedded concepts of domesticity and femininity. In Beauvoir's and Friedan's analyses, female performances of domesticity and femininity make women into singular, passive, submissive (aesthetic and sexual) objects.[28] Female recognition is conditioned on woman's abilities to nurture the man with whom she is coupled (heteronormativity and monogamy are implied). White women are left alone, Beauvoir and Friedan maintain, to negotiate any power they accrue, which is why they align themselves with men rather than other women. Shuri wants no part of this oppressive scheme. While her jettisoning of romance calls into question her femininity (and sexuality, perhaps) – Shuri does not flirt with Bucky – it highlights her commitment to Black feminist work.[29] Shuri's barrier to self-definition is not, like Beauvoir's and Friedan's, the nuclear family organized around one man. Shuri's barrier is economic control (the Wakandan world revolves around power). Taken together, Shuri's rejection of romance and embrace of community puts her squarely in the category of "womanish."

The term *womanist* as Walker defines it consists of four elements, of which the first is:

> Womanist. 1. From womanish. (Opp. of "girlish," i.e., frivolous, irresponsible, not serious) A black feminist or feminist of color. From the black folk expression of mothers to female children, "you acting womanish," i.e., like a woman. Usually referring to outrageous, audacious, courageous or willful behavior. Wanting to know more and in greater depth than is considered "good" for one. Interested in grown up doings. Acting grown up. Being grown up. Interchangeable with another black folk expression: "You trying to be grown." Responsible. In charge. Serious.[30]

To look at Wakandan women from this new angle, we must ask whether it is possible that M'Baku's references to Shuri as a child are his way of outing her as womanish by effectively saying, "you acting womanish" or "you trying to be grown" in Walker's positive sense of the term. Certainly, Shuri is responsible and serious. Moreover, her willful subversion of tradition empowers her to take charge of Wakanda by protecting T'Challa from external threats.[31] It's also an example of how Black feminism differs from other feminisms: *communal freedom is prioritized above individual freedom*. Because of the value shift embedded in Black feminism and feminism of color, these bodies of thought warrant their own label: *womanist philosophies*. Womanist philosophies offer new challenges and opportunities for demystifying Wakandan feminism. We wonder, for example, whether it is right to label Wakandan women "womanists"? And we ask, do Black women with power and equity who were born into an isolated, non-oppressive nation share any cultural resonance (or cultural similarity) with "black folk" and their self-defining characterizations? Let's turn to Okoye and Nakia for analytical guidance.

"I Would Make a Great Queen because I Am Stubborn."

Bald and fierce, Okoye epitomizes a warrior (who hates wigs and who would choose a spear over a gun any day). Yet, Okoye also exhibits an affinity for femininity (and domesticity) when she refers to W'Kabi as "My Love," when she cries as Killmonger beats T'Challa, and when she tells Nakia that "my heart is with you" when Nakia leaves to find M'Baku. Okoye also nurtures feminine bonding with Natasha Romanoff in *Avengers: Infinity War* and *Avengers: Endgame*. And she is romantically linked to W'Kabi, a heterosexual coupling common to *Black Panther*. On the one hand, Nakia's behaviors suggest an alignment with white womanhood, that is, with white women who share her economic status, social power, and romantic arrangement. On the other hand, her behavior subverts normative white womanhood by repudiating passiveness and submissiveness, aligning her with womanist norms and behaviors. W'Kabi is, after all, submissive to Okoye, not just by surrendering to her at the end of *Black Panther* but insofar as Okoye, Wakanda's best warrior, accompanies T'Challa to Korea, not W'Kabi.

Nakia also plays with the differences between feminist and womanist norms. She displays femininity in her relationship with T'Challa by flirting with him, kissing him, and professing her love for him, behaviors that reflect white feminist analyses of womanhood. Yet, like Okoye, Nakia performs womanhood in a masculinized mode, which is central to womanist commitments to preserving community and controlling power plays. Is Nakia aiming to ameliorate the boundary between feminist and womanist views? Emphasize their shared commitment to transcending oppression? Is Okoye, by contrast, seeking to reassert a clear distinction between the two?

Both Okoye and Nakia are presented throughout *Black Panther* as physically strong, intellectually capable warriors – as women who perform womanhood in masculine and feminine modes. Nakia, however, seems to balance her masculine and feminine traits more easily than Okoye. For example, in Korea, Nakia is more at ease with the mission, sweet talking the Korean woman to gain entrance into the club and exhibiting general comfort with playing the part of T'Challa's female companion. Okoye, on the other hand, looks uncomfortable, not just because she's wearing a wig, but because she has to perform womanhood in overtly feminine ways.

As we've seen, the historic "Otherizing" of woman is produced through a structural, binary positioning of man as the human archetype. If we could free humans from this structural arrangement, then we could free women to define what and who they are independently of other women and men. We should also add that freeing humanity from this structural arrangement would also release them from compulsory heterosexuality (man and woman would no longer serve as logically opposed human types and, therefore, naturally coupled human types). The integration of difference into feminist philosophy – through womanist philosophies, certainly, but also through post-structural analyses – invites a critique of these dualistic presuppositions (man:woman/white:Black/human:other) and makes room for post-structural and third-wave feminism. Judith Butler, for example, draws on post-structural methods to challenge the "sex-gender" distinction assumed by second-wave feminism. Both white and Black second-wave theorists accept the view that biological sex is a naturally occurring human state (female) and gender is a constructed, normative set of behaviors imposed on this natural state (woman). Butler deconstructs this distinction by arguing that sex, like gender, is taken up in performances of womanhood. In other words, there is no natural, meaningful state of "sex" separate from the performance of sex we call "gender." And gender, as Butler explains, is best understood as "performativity [...] a reiteration of a norm or set of norms, and to the extent that it acquires an act-like status in the present, it conceals or dissimulates the conventions of which it is a repetition."[32] Just as different cultures adopt different norms of masculinity and femininity (all artificial and arbitrary, according to Butler), feminist and womanist philosophies assume different conceptions of what it means to perform womanhood. Their differences emerge out of their respective values (individual vs. community, domesticity vs. self-empowerment) and shape their gender performativity in unique ways.

In Korea, Okoye must perform womanhood in feminine modes with which she is uncomfortable. Her discomfort suggests that she operates much more out of a womanist philosophy than Nakia, who performs femininity rather easily. Reading Nakia as "feminist" also explains why she has a much easier time navigating the world beyond Wakanda. By the same token, reading Okoye as "womanist" explains her ease in Wakanda, a comfort level Nakia lacks.

Recognizing feminist and womanist elements within Wakanda helps explain the masculine and feminine performances of Wakandan women (and men). Most Wakandan characters exhibit both masculine and feminine norms regardless of their gender identities, a fluidity enabled by their culture's joint feminist and womanist goals. T'Challa and W'Kabi are feminized as much as Nakia, Okoye, and Shuri are masculinized because they embody both American and Wakandan cultural norms. Integrating womanist views into Wakandan norms frees women and men from the heteronormativity of second-wave feminism. We do not see Ramonda arranging a marriage for Shuri, nor do we see T'Challa being forced to pursue Nakia because he needs an heir. Rather, T'Challa respects Nakia's right to perform womanhood in diverse ways, including in how she relates to men. She is nurturing (feminine) but also independent (masculine), telling T'Challa "I would make a great queen because I am stubborn, if that is what I wanted."

Gender performativity in Wakanda reflects feminist and womanist elements. Shuri can be irreverent. Nakia can be stubborn and nurturing. Okoye can loathe wigs. T'Challa and W'Kabi can be sensitive and submissive to women. And they can all be fierce warriors with deep layers of emotionality. Because oppression in the United States is shaped by race, class, and gender, transcending oppression requires diverse feminist and womanist strategies: freeing oneself from gender conformity and economic poverty and assuming responsibility for self-definition and community empowerment (transcendence modeled by Wakandans). Wakandans also deploy love as a strategy for transcending particular experiences of oppression, empowering them to transcend ordinary codes of masculinity and femininity. We see this freedom exhibited in their love for Wakanda ("Wakanda Forever!") and in each character's devotion to their individual causes. By deploying love as a mechanism for transcendence, the women of Wakanda perform womanhood in feminist and womanist ways: actively rather than passively (Beauvoir and Friedan) and interdependently (Lorde and Walker) with females supporting one another even when they disagree.

"What Has Happened to Our Wakanda?"

Ramonda, Shuri, and Nakia seek M'Baku's help collectively, bringing Agent Ross along because he's a friend of T'Challa and because he took a bullet in the back to save Nakia's life. They exemplify what both Beauvoir and Lorde observe as women's real power – interdependency – "which is so feared by a patriarchal world."[33] In Lorde's words, "for women, the need and desire to nurture each other is not pathological but redemptive."[34] Engaging interdependency and embracing differences among women is a necessary step toward collective female liberation. We reiterate Lorde's famous call for communal action: "As women, we have been taught either to ignore our differences, or to view them as causes for separation and suspicion rather than as forces for change. Without community there is no liberation, only the most vulnerable and temporary armistice between an individual and her oppression. But community must not mean a shedding of our differences, nor the pathetic pretense that these differences do not exist."[35]

We have argued through our analysis of Wakandan women that Lorde's introduction of difference into the scheme of second-wave feminism helps give rise to womanist thought, a distinctive Black voice refined by Black feminists and feminists of color. Walker's womanist characterization aptly describes Wakandan women and enriches our reading of their trek to the Jabari. There is no clearer example of womanist philosophy than the joint decision of the Queen Mother, the Princess, and a War Dog spy (and to be fair, a CIA agent who represents colonizers) to offer the last Heart-Shaped Herb in Wakanda to M'Baku, who is almost as much an enemy as Killmonger. They act in unison, per Walker, and play to one another's strengths and to the strengths of M'Baku, per Lorde. They amplify rather than elide difference.

Wakandan women are equal and different *but never separate*. Okoye professes absolute loyalty to Wakanda's monarchy, telling Nakia, "I'm not a spy who can come and go as they so choose! I am loyal to that throne, no matter who sits upon it." Shuri and Nakia, on the other hand, criticize (even flout) Wakandan traditions and rituals (Nakia asks if it even matters that Killmonger won the fight with T'Challa). Their freedom to disagree, to define themselves differently, is authorized by their womanist commitment to community. They may define themselves differently in relation to community, but they nevertheless support one another and work collectively to protect Wakanda from outside power grabs. This powerful example of interdependency enriches feminist philosophy and elevates womanist thought.

Indeed, without the women of Wakanda working together, it is likely that Killmonger would have fulfilled his plan and T'Challa would have died rather than been resurrected. We also see powerful examples of female community in *Avengers: Infinity War* and *Avengers: Endgame*, where we get glimpses of women superheroes working together, despite their differences, to help defeat Thanos and save the world. Iron Man may get all the glory, but Natasha Romanoff, Okoye, and Captain Marvel keep Earth spinning during the blip (with the help of Rocket and Rhodey), while Steve Rogers holds therapy sessions, Tony Stark builds a lake house, and Thor gets drunk playing Fortnite (not to mention other great female characters, such as Wanda and even Shuri). It is unlikely that the men would be able to defeat Thanos on their own without a gauntlet of Infinity Stones.

"What Can Wakanda Offer the World?"

Why do Beauvoir's and Friedan's second-wave analyses of womanhood, bound up with femininity and domesticity, still resonate with women around the world? Their analyses unveil the mystique of womanhood: the mysterious elements of gender performativity that constrain and oppress women (and men). Freedom from oppression requires, as they aptly argue, transcendence from femininity and domesticity – and, as Lorde, Walker, and others add, transcendence from female isolation and male hegemony. Taken together, feminist and womanist analyses carve out a new path toward female liberation, a path materialized in the mysterious world of Wakanda.

Demystifying Wakanda requires us to recognize and reckon with *The Panther Mystique*: uncoerced appropriations of masculine and feminine norms for the sake of collective, communal freedom. Wakanda's progressive concept of freedom may be best captured in T'Challa's smile, with Nakia and Okoye by his side, when he's asked at the United Nations what Wakanda can offer the world. Wakanda issues a (feminist and womanist) collective call for solidarity across difference. We desperately hope that the future is Wakanda.

Notes

1. Angela Davis, *Women, Race, & Class* (New York: Vintage, 1983).
2. Audre Lorde, "The Master's Tools Will Never Dismantle the Master's House," in *Sister Outsider: Essays and Speeches* (Berkeley, CA: Crossing Press, 2007), 110–114.
3. Lorde, 110–114.
4. Lorde, 110–114.
5. Because, given the Marvel Cinematic Universe timeline, Shuri's nanotech panther suit in *Black Panther* precedes Tony Stark's nanotech Iron Man suit in *Avengers: Infinity War*. So, yeah, she may be young, but she's genius young.
6. Beauvoir's *The Second Sex*, published in 1949, was technically published at the end of feminism's first wave. However, her observations are generally thought to lay the groundwork for the second wave, making her a precursor to work like Friedan's.
7. Simone de Beauvoir, *The Second Sex* (New York: First Vintage Books Edition, 2011), 283.
8. Betty Friedan, *The Feminine Mystique* (New York: W.W. Norton & Company, 1963).
9. Friedan, 91–92.
10. Friedan, 91–92.
11. Friedan, 92.
12. Lorde, 3.
13. Lorde, 3.
14. Indeed, nearly every chapter title in her book reinforces her thesis. For example, chapter 1 "Lewd Jezebels, Exotic Orientals, Princess Pocahontas: How Colonialism Rigged the Game Against Women of Color," chapter 3 "Only White Damsels Can Be in Distress," chapter 4 "When Tears Become Weapons: White Womanhood's Silent War on Women of Color," chapter 5 "There Is No Sisterhood: White Women and Racism," chapter 6 "Pets or Threats: White Feminism and the Reassertion of Whiteness," chapter 7 "The Rise of Righteous Racism: From Classwashing to Lovejoy Trap," and

chapter 8 "The Privilege and Peril of Passing: Colorism, Anti-Blackness, and the Yearning to Be White." Ruby Hamad, *White Tears/Brown Scars: How White Feminism Betrays Women of Color* (New York: Catapult, 2020).

15. Hamad, 13.
16. Iris Marion Young, "The Five Faces of Oppression," in *Justice and the Politics of Difference* (Princeton, NJ: Princeton University Press, 1990), 39–65.
17. Ashley Tauchert, "Are women oppressed?" *Critical Quarterly* 50 (2008), 145–164.
18. Quoted in Patricia Hill Collins, *Black Feminist Thought: Knowledge, Consciousness, and the Politics of Empowerment* (New York: Routledge, 2000), 69.
19. Alice Walker, "In Search of Our Mother's Gardens," in Angelyn Mitchell ed., *Within the Circle: An Anthology of African American Literary Criticism from the Harlem Renaissance to the Present* (Durham, NC: Duke University Press, 1994), 405.
20. Hamad.
21. Sonia Sanchez, in her poem "Introduction (Queens of the Universe)," explains the list this way: "We Black/woooomen have been called many things: foxes, matriarchs, whores, bougies, sweet mommas, gals, sapphires, sisters and recently Queens. i would say that Black/woooomen have been a combination of all these words because if we examine our past/history, at one time or another we've had to be like those words be saying." John H. Bracy, Jr., Sonia Sanchez, and James Smethurst eds., *SOS-Calling All Black People: A Black Arts Movement Reader* (Boston, MA: University of Massachusetts Press, 2014), 114.
22. Collins, 36.
23. Collins, 114.
24. Unlike T'Challa, who doesn't seem to have a choice about whether he wants to be king and/or Black Panther, which may explain why he feels uncertain about how to do both.
25. Collins, 69.
26. Beauvoir makes this case in the Introduction to *The Second Sex*. Consider, for example, the year 1619, when enslaved Africans first arrived in Jamestown, implies a pre-slavery existence as much as the year 1865 implies a post-slavery existence in America and the beginning of a Jim Crow existence.
27. Lorde, 2–3.
28. Alena Plháková and Katerina Pavelková, "Implicit theories of masculinity and femininity," *Ceskoslovenska Psychologie* 51 (2007), 89–98.
29. Plháková and Pavelková, 90.
30. Alice Walker, *In Search of Our Mother's Gardens: Womanist Prose* (New York: Harcourt, 1983), xi.
31. For example, the other three definitions state: "2. Also: A woman who loves other women, sexually and/or nonsexually. Appreciates and prefers women's culture, women's emotional flexibility (values tears as natural counterbalance to laughter) and women's strength. Sometimes loves individual men, sexually and/or nonsexually. Committed to survival and wholeness of entire people, male and female. Not a separatist, except periodically, for health. Traditionally universalist [...] Traditionally capable [...] 3. Loves music. Loves dance.

Loves the moon. *Loves* the spirit. Loves love and food and roundness. Loves struggle. Loves the Folk. Loves herself. *Regardless.* 4. Womanist is to feminist as purple is to lavender." (Walker, xi–xii).

32. Judith Butler, *Bodies that Matter: On the Discursive Limits of "Sex"* (New York: Routledge, 1993), 12.
33. Lorde, 111.
34. Lorde, 111.
35. Lorde, 112.

13

The Ancestral Plane
Metaphysical Mystery or Meaningful Metaphor?

Dean A. Kowalski

Imagine you have the chance to visit with a deceased family member – a grandparent, parent, or child – someone you dearly loved. How would you react to such an opportunity? What might you say?

In *Black Panther*, T'Challa and Erik "Killmonger" Stevens experience audiences with their (respective) departed fathers. The Heart-Shaped Herb of Wakanda makes this possible. After ingesting the herb and undergoing a ceremony that includes being buried, they are transported to the Ancestral Plane. Three scenes in the film depict the Ancestral Plane (T'Challa visits twice), and each is important to the *Black Panther* storyline. But these plot points raise intriguing philosophical questions: Where do they go, exactly, and how, once transported, are they able to communicate with the dead? Of course, these questions would also pertain to your (hypothetical) case: What would have to be true if you were to visit a deceased loved one?

As we'll see, *Black Panther* suggests a metaphysical theory known as substance dualism in its depictions of the Ancestral Plane. The truth of this theory would allow for out-of-body personal encounters. This theory is well known, but also controversial. As we'll also see, fortunately, the film may not require the truth of substance dualism. Careful analysis of the second and especially the third Ancestral Plane visits downplays the metaphysical, leading toward a metaphor for better understanding one's place in the world.

"He Was There! He Was There, My Father."

King T'Chaka has been tragically killed by a bomb during his United Nations address. His son, T'Challa – who had already assumed the duties of Black Panther from his aging father – is set to succeed him as the king. Wakandan custom dictates that before assuming the throne, the prince

Black Panther and Philosophy: What Can Wakanda Offer the World?, First Edition. Edited by Edwardo Pérez and Timothy E. Brown.

must accept all challenges by ritual combat. To prove his true worth, T'Challa drinks a red liquid that strips him of his Black Panther powers and awaits any and all challengers. All of the great tribes decline – except the isolationist Jabari Tribe, whose imposing leader, M'Baku, explains: "We have watched with disgust as your technological advancements have been overseen by a child … who scoffs at tradition! [pointing at T'Challa's sister Princess Shuri.] And now you want to hand the nation over to this prince who could not even keep his own father safe. Mmm? We will not have it." T'Challa accepts M'Baku's challenge. M'Baku fights gallantly, but T'Challa prevails, and bolsters his worthiness for the throne by sparing M'Baku's life. The shaman Zuri announces, "I now present to you King T'Challa, the Black Panther!"

The coronation ceremony continues with much less fanfare in the Hall of Kings. As T'Challa, bare-chested, lies on his back in the ceremonial red sandpit, Zuri prepares the Heart-Shaped Herb potion. As Zuri pours it into T'Challa's mouth, he solemnly states, "Allow the Heart-Shaped Herb to restore the powers of the Black Panther and take you to the Ancestral Plane," and as T'Challa closes his eyes, Zuri continues, "T'Chaka, we call on you. Come here to your son." As T'Challa relives a series of flashbacks, including holding his father as he dies, Zuri's attendants cover T'Challa with the red sand. With T'Challa completely covered, the screen goes black.

T'Challa rises from the ground, not in the entombed Hall of Kings, but in what appears to be an African savanna where the sky is rippled in majestic blues and purples, giving off a twilight ambiance. T'Challa is no longer bare-chested, but wears a regal white gown. He sees three black panthers sitting in an acacia tree. Getting to his feet, T'Challa walks to the tree and stops before it. One panther leaps to the ground, and after some localized flickering of purple and blue hues, King T'Chaka appears in the panther's place. They embrace, wrapping their arms around one another, and smile. T'Chaka pats his son's back affectionately. T'Challa whispers, "Baba." T'Challa pulls away, but grasps his father's hand and, overcome with grief, kneels before him, saying, "I'm sorry." T'Chaka admonishes him: "Stand up. You are a king."

T'Challa, now more astonished than grieved, rises slowly and takes full advantage of his opportunity to converse with his father again. "I am not ready to be without you," admits T'Challa, to which T'Chaka answers, "A man who has not prepared his children for his own death has failed as a father. Have I ever failed you?" "Never," replies T'Challa. The new king inquires, "Tell me how to best protect Wakanda. I want to be a great King, Baba, Just like you." T'Chaka advises, "You're going to struggle. So, you need to surround yourself with people you trust. You're a good man with a good heart. And it's hard for a good man to be King." At that moment, Zuri abruptly yanks T'Challa out of the ceremonial red sandpit, instruct-ing the new king to breathe. As T'Challa regains his breath, he smiles and informs Zuri, "He was there! He was there, my father."

It's an emotionally compelling scene (even the music is dramatically solemn), revealing a vulnerable side to T'Challa that balances his otherwise regal confidence. But, again, aside from the fictional wonders of Wakanda, how is it possible?

"The Heart-Shaped Herb Did That?"

Breathtaking and bathed in lavish light, the Ancestral Plane provides the viewer a sense of majesty. It's just the sort of place one would expect to find an ancestor – and the depiction of T'Challa's ancestors as panther spirits who can shapeshift into their former selves adds to the magnificence of the plane. Given the nature of the scene, our wonder also leads us to ask how T'Challa was transported anywhere, when his body was lying in a ceremonial red sandpit. And, how was he able to physically embrace his father, when his father no longer exists, but is now a decaying corpse, buried somewhere in Wakanda?

Philosophically speaking, these sorts of questions are often asked when considering the prospects of personal existence after one's bodily death. Is it possible for a human person to live on after one's body ceases to function? If there is nothing about persons in addition to their bodies, then the answer seems to be no. But if persons are something in addition to their bodies, then it seems possible for this something – whatever it is – to live on after the body dies. This something is typically called a soul.

Substance dualism affirms that persons are a duality of two distinct things, a union of body and soul. Some facts about you cannot be quantified, such as your feelings and emotions – how much you miss your loved one and the regret you feel for all the things left unsaid. Or, like T'Challa confessing that he's not ready to be without his father. We can understand it, but we can't quantify it. So, if such mental states cannot be quantified, then they are not physical, because anything physical – your height, weight, blood type – can be quantified.

Your mental states – pangs of jealousy or joyful bliss – are qualitative in nature, more amenable to description than measurement. They have subjective meaning that can only be experienced by the person having them and cannot be observed directly from the outside by anyone else. Because these feelings are difficult to connect securely with any physical fact about your body, substance dualists argue that there must be non-physical facts about us, and such facts "reside" with the non-physical spirit or soul. Substance dualists further hold that your non-physical facts, including the soul itself, account for who you "truly" are – your beliefs, choices, desires, and memories – while your body, the non-thinking, fleshy component of you, is the physical aspect of your self. Combined, they comprise the fundamental nature of any human person.

The words "soul" and "spirit" are never used in the *Black Panther* movie. However, the film does suggest an intriguing analogy to understand substance dualism. Recall the car chase scene in Korea. Shuri is piloting one of the cars remotely from her lab in Wakanda. A careful examination of that vehicle will reveal only wires, metal, rubber, and plastic. Although the driver's seat is empty, the car could not do what it does without a driver. When that car is destroyed, Shuri is jettisoned from its interface; she lands with a thud on her laboratory floor.

Substance dualism says similar things about the human body. A careful examination will reveal only muscle, bone, skin, and fluids. But the human body could not do what it does without the soul. Persons make choices, express feelings, and share memories. The human body, according to substance dualism, is incapable of doing any of these all by itself. The soul is akin to the driver of a car. Although it is not physically present in the body, it is fitted to the body just as Shuri is (remotely) connected to T'Challa's Lexus. Furthermore, when the body dies, its relationship to the soul is dissolved. Whether it is jettisoned is unknown, but it is possible that it continues to exist and function apart from the body.

René Descartes (1596–1650) is a well-known substance dualist, and, in fact, substance dualists are often called *Cartesian dualists*. Descartes explains his theory this way:

> Because we have no conception of the body as thinking in any way, we have reason to believe that every kind of thought which exists in us belongs to the soul … We must [also] know that the soul is really joined to the whole body, and that we cannot, properly speaking, say that it exists in any one of its parts to the exclusion of the others.[1]

Many substance dualists like Descartes believe in the possibility of life after bodily death. The soul, metaphysically distinct from the body, can function apart from the body, allowing you to retain your various mental functions, including your memories.

So, to answer some of the questions raised by the Ancestral Plane, we might say that T'Chaka's soul lives on in the Ancestral Plane. Although his body died in Vienna, his essence lives on, possessing all of his thoughts, feelings, and memories. Assuming substance dualism where the body and soul, although connected in life, can be dissolved in death, *Black Panther* suggests that the Heart-Shaped Herb is able to dislodge the soul of a living Black Panther, which is what happens to T'Challa and Killmonger. With the soul dislodged from the body, the Heart-Shaped Herb apparently is also able to direct the soul where it needs to go to visit its ancestors. For T'Challa, this is the Ancestral Plane. For Killmonger, it's the Oakland apartment where he grew up with his father, N'Jobu – because that's also where N'Jobu was killed. Furthermore, it is interesting that T'Challa is buried in preparation for his Ancestral Plane visit. Indeed, this seems to be a regular feature of any Ancestral Plane visit. Why? It might be that burying the visitor brings about a near-death experience – recall that one's breathing seems suspended when buried – and if the body is close to death, the soul is more prone to become separate from the body. Just as T'Chaka's soul became separate from the body upon his death, a near-death experience may aid T'Challa's attempt to visit with his father again.

"Do Not Tell Me What Is Possible, Tell Me the Truth!"

While the belief that human persons are the union of body and soul is common, the peculiar relationship between the physical and non-physical worlds is one of the great puzzles facing metaphysics in general and substance dualism in particular. Put another way, the issue is not merely how the soul might dislodge from the body when T'Challa visits the Ancestral Plane. We must also ask how the body and soul are properly related to each other in *this* life.

Descartes realized the significance of these interrelationships and their implications for his worldview:

> By means of these sensations of pain, hunger, thirst and so on, nature also teaches me that I am present in my body not merely as a sailor is present in a ship, but that I am most tightly joined and, so to speak, commingled with it, so much so that I and the body constitute one single thing. For if this were not the case, then I, who am only a thinking thing, would not sense pain when the body is injured; rather, I would perceive the wound by means of the pure intellect, just as a sailor perceives by sight whether anything in his ship is broken.[2]

Here Descartes anticipates the objection that the body and soul cannot be radically distinct because our experiences tell us that our physical and mental lives are closely intertwined. His response is that the so-called commingling of the body and the soul allows for the two to interact. Indeed, most substance dualists follow Descartes and ascribe to *interactionism*, which is the idea that the soul and body cause changes in each other. Interactionism is the "explanatory glue" holding Cartesian dualism together, and without it, the Cartesian dualist can't account for our experience of a unified wholeness of our physical and mental lives. When you suffer a wound – as T'Challa does during his combat with M'Baku – you don't merely recognize the damage intellectually –you *feel* it – and interactionism is supposed to explain why.

Descartes further argues that, although the soul is "commingled" with the whole body, the interaction takes place in the brain's pineal gland.[3] Descartes believes that the pineal gland is infused with what he called (according to standard translations) "animal spirits," which transfer information from the body to the mind and vice versa. However, as many soon realized, Descartes's "solution" only succeeds in inviting further questions: How do these spirits accomplish information transfer between mind and body? If the spirits are physical, then how do they impact the non-physical mind? If the spirits are non-physical, then how do they come into contact with the physical pineal gland?

Yet, these sorts of philosophical concerns are not limited to the pineal gland. The issue is not *where* body and soul interact, but *how* they are able to interact at all. The deeper problem is the nature of interactionism itself. How can one's soul be both radically distinct, and thus separate (and separable) from one's body, and also causally conjoined to it, and thus able to account for all that human persons accomplish?

These sorts of questions were posed to Descartes from the beginning. For example, Princess Elisabeth of Bohemia, who was something of a student of Descartes, elegantly asked her teacher:

> Tell me how the human soul can determine the movement of the animal spirits in the body so as to perform voluntary acts ... For the determination of movement seems always to come about from the moving body's being propelled – to depend on the kind of impulse it gets from what sets it in motion, or again, on the nature and shape of this latter thing's surface.[4]

It seems that the body and the soul are not the sorts of things that could interact. Physical objects are propelled by contact, but non-physical objects can't come into contact with anything.

As it pertains to *Black Panther*, note that if T'Chaka and T'Challa were mere souls in the Ancestral Plane, they could not embrace. T'Chaka could not pat his son's back and T'Challa could not grasp his father's hand. These activities require physical attributes, but the soul is non-physical. Furthermore, non-physical souls cannot be seen, because sight requires light reflection; if souls are non-physical, they are not the sorts of things that could reflect light. And though drinking the Heart-Shaped Herb potion may heighten one's physical abilities by chemically altering one's body, it is a complete mystery how any chemical could affect a non-physical soul. Finally, the analogy of Shuri's remotely controlling T'Challa's car breaks down. Although she is not physically present in the car, she utilizes energy and technology – that which falls under the laws of physics – to drive it. As she might remind us, she works "not through magic, but technology." Shuri accomplishes this from Wakanda, but the soul is literally nowhere and cannot work within the laws of physics. For the soul to do what it does indeed borders on magic.

Some people might object that all this is too literal or over-thought. Despite Shuri's dismissiveness about magic, why does everything need to follow the laws of physics? There are many mysteries that scientists have yet to understand, perhaps the soul is among them. To be fair, those who disagree with substance dualism usually admit that interactionism is not *logically* impossible. It's not like the idea of a married bachelor or a round square, for example. However, philosophers try to arrive at reasonable, likely, and justified beliefs about the way things are, not just ways they *could* be. Magic is possible, but we have no reason to believe that it actually occurs. In fact, given other beliefs that we are justified in having, it seems most likely that it does not occur. For example, the kids on the basketball court in Oakland marvel at the Wakandan ship materializing in the sky, but it's not magic, as Shuri begins to explain to them. Adopting interactionism requires us to revise or reject much of what we know about biology, chemistry, and physics, which doesn't seem reasonable. Thus, until we have better reason to question basically everything we know about the world and how it works, perhaps we should remain dubious of interactionism.

"You Can't Let Your Father's Mistakes Define Who You Are."

Given these metaphysical difficulties, let's reexamine the Heart-Shaped Herb's role in bringing one to the Ancestral Plane. Ingesting it increases one's strength, speed, agility, and stamina. It is akin to Captain America's super soldier serum, which reminds us of that awesome footrace between T'Challa and Steve in *Avengers*: *Infinity War*. It might be that the Heart-Shaped Herb alters brain chemistry to heighten one's mental acuity and sharpen one's memory (assuming that the brain, and not the soul, is responsible for our mental states). The Heart Shaped Herb potion, then, helps T'Challa and Killmonger achieve greater focus on each man's past and allows a better perspective on who each one is now. Of course, one's past is greatly influenced by one's parents. So, it is no wonder that each man visits his father. On this emerging account, visiting the Ancestral Plane does not involve the soul being dislodged from the body or being transported anywhere. Rather, it is a metaphor for better understanding how one's past can shape who one becomes.

When Killmonger drinks the potion and is buried in the ceremonial pit, he experiences his childhood apartment. It appears unchanged since the day his father died, but with the characteristic purple and blue majestic night's sky seen through the vertical blinds. He quickly finds his father's journal. In it, he discovers his grandfather's royal ring on a gold chain and places it around his neck (even though he is already in possession of it). But the scene also shifts between a young Erik who discovers his father's dead body and an adult Killmonger who is revisiting his past and having an audience with his deceased father. Prince N'Jobu suddenly appears and asks, "What did I tell you about going through my things?" Now smiling, he also asks, "What did you find?" Erik responds: "Your home." N'Jobu sighs and inquires, "No tears for me?" Young Erik is not phased. He answers, "Everybody dies. That's just life around here." N'Jobu is filled with regret. He wishes that he had taken his son to Wakanda. Now, he will be an outsider – one who is lost and abandoned. Killmonger opines, "Well maybe your home is the one that's lost. That's why they can't find us." Killmonger is subsequently pulled from the ceremonial red sandpit, ending his reunion with his father.

This scene seems to reinforce Killmonger's belief that Wakanda could have done more to help those in need. Recall his challenge to T'Challa and the council elders, "Y'all sittin' up here comfortable. Must feel good. It's about two billion people all over the world that looks like us, but their lives are a lot harder. Wakanda has the tools to liberate 'em all." After all, Prince N'Jobu entreated his brother T'Chaka to also take action. Recall N'Jobu's stirring words from the opening scene: "I observed for as long as I could! Their leaders have been assassinated, communities flooded with drugs and weapons, they are overly policed and incarcerated. All over the planet our people suffer because they don't have the tools to fight back. With vibranium weapons they could overthrow every country and Wakanda could rule them all … the right way." T'Chaka did not heed his brother's advice. Rather, he killed him and left young Erik behind. Now that Killmonger is King of Wakanda, he will not fail as his father did before him. He will take action to benefit the oppressed of the world. Perhaps one might question the way in which he will provide it, but it seems that his choice was heavily influenced by his past and the person he has become.

During T'Challa's second Ancestral Plane visit with his father, T'Chaka believes it is time for his son to join him and the other ancestors. But this scene is all about T'Challa and his new revelations about Killmonger. T'Challa admonishes his father, "Why didn't you bring the boy home? … You were wrong to abandon him … All of you were wrong! To turn your backs on the rest of the world! We let the fear of our discovery stop us from doing what is right! No more!" Interestingly, during this third Ancestral Plane visit, it is not a night's sky we see, but a bright new day filled with yellow and orange hues. This is symbolic of T'Challa's choice to break with tradition and move Wakanda away from its long-standing isolationist policies. T'Chaka was a great king and a good father, but he was not perfect. T'Challa has learned from his father's strengths and shortcomings to become his own man and king. Thus, he does not stay with his father in the Ancestral Plane; he goes back to take the mantle from Killmonger. Subsequently, he buys the apartment building in Oakland where Erik grew up and will transform it into the first Wakandan International Outreach Centre. He then makes his plans official by announcing them before the United Nations Assembly: "Wakanda will no longer watch from the shadows. We cannot, we must not. We will work to be an example of how we as brothers and sisters on this Earth should treat each other."

The importance of the Ancestral Plane as a metaphor for acknowledging your past but not being bound by it when striving to become your own person holds regardless of whether substance dualism is true. Perhaps T'Chaka and N'Jobu exist as disembodied souls and perhaps the Heart-Shaped Herb has the ability to bring about the mystical event of communing with the dead. But the decisions T'Challa and Killmonger made – for good or for ill – remain important by connecting them to who their fathers were, what they stood for, and how they tried to accomplish their goals. By taking stock of one's past, one is in a better position to shape one's future.

"Come. Much More for You to Learn."

We may never know for sure whether substance dualism is true, how bodies and souls interact, if they do, or whether there is personal existence after bodily death. (If there is, I hope to meet Chadwick Boseman and shake his hand, or whatever the afterlife equivalent of that would be.) But apart from those complex metaphysical questions, there is much to learn about your past. Taking stock of how your parents influenced your past is crucial, and it is perhaps why we wonder about meeting them again one last time after they are gone. Of course, your past shapes your present, and you must consider carefully what is involved in changing your future. You don't need to be King of Wakanda or drink the Heart Shaped Herb potion to engage that process. Like T'Challa, you merely need to live the examined life, and philosophy can help.

Notes

1. René Descartes, *Passions of the Soul* (1649), trans. E.S. Haldane and G.R.T. Ross, quoted in *René Descartes: Philosophical Essays and Correspondence*, ed. Roger Ariew (Indianapolis, IN: Hackett Publishing, 2000), 298, 307.
2. René Descartes, *Meditations on First Philosophy, Meditation VI* (1641), trans. Donald Cress, quoted in *Rene Descartes: Philosophical Essays and Correspondence*, ed. Roger Ariew (Indianapolis, IN: Hackett Publishing, 2000), 136.
3. See Descartes, *Passions of the Soul*, Part I, articles 31–34.
4. Quoted in *Philosophic Classics, Vol. III*, ed. Forrest E. Baird and Walter Kaufmann (Upper Saddle River, NJ: Pearson-Prentice Hall, 2008), 53.

14

The Afterlife of Erik Killmonger in African Philosophy

Paul A. Dottin

There is a long history in Western thought of attributing the origins of civilizations in sub-Saharan Africa principally either to societies not in Africa or to societies in Africa's north. For centuries, philosophers, archaeologists, anthropologists, historians, linguists, theologians and writers of fiction have argued – and some still do – that ancient and premodern African civilizations owe their genesis and greatness to non-Africans or, at least, Africans whose complexions were closer to the color of copper than to the color of coal. Historian Edith Sanders labeled this intellectual tendency to judge as patently absurd the proposition that civilizations had developed indigenously in any part of Black Africa as the "Hamitic Hypothesis."[1]

Regrettably, Black Panther lore often follows a version of this hypothesis when recounting Wakanda's origins. In the comics, for example, though sub-Saharan Africans appear to have lived in Wakanda for at least 10,000 years – 5000 years before historical ancient Egypt was unified under its first pharaoh – Marvel's Egypt is still positioned as the original transmitter of civilization to Wakanda, not the other way around.[2] Millennia later, a group of Marvel supervillains discover that a "cache of tomes" saved from the burning of their Egypt's Great Library of Alexandria was secreted "south" and "led to the foundation of the country of Wakanda."[3] The Hamitic Hypothesis operates even in the final resting place for dead Black Panthers called "the Necropolis." King T'Challa and his best friend, the white superhero Mr. Fantastic, travel there on a "journey of knowledge" to repel malevolent supernatural incursions into the ruler's African state.[4] They descend deep beneath Wakanda to its hidden "Wall of Knowledge."[5] T'Challa says it is "part of an older, ancient Wakanda."[6] Mr. Fantastic is surprised to see intriguing "perfectly preserved … designs" etched across its surfaces.[7] "The Northman," as the resident North African deity they discover nearby would later call the hero, identifies these etchings tentatively as "pre-Demotic, but clearly Egyptian iconography."[8] T'Challa confirms his friend's educated guess by revealing that Wakanda's

Black Panther and Philosophy: What Can Wakanda Offer the World?, First Edition. Edited by Edwardo Pérez and Timothy E. Brown.
© 2022 John Wiley & Sons, Inc. Published 2022 by John Wiley & Sons, Inc.

patron "Panther God" is actually Bast, the Egyptian cat-goddess, and that it was she who had "brought us knowledge."[9]

The Hamitic Hypothesis lurks in T'Challa's corroboration. Note that Demotic script is a writing system developed during historical Nubia's reign over Egypt during its latter Twenty-fifth Dynasty (747–656 BCE).[10] Applied to Wakanda, one could infer that Bast may have edified Wakanda at a time when ancient Black "Sudanese" Nubians had conquered Egypt and became its pharaohs. However, the "*pre*-Demotic" script Mr. Fantastic saw was likely the "Hieratic" priest-script used during this Twenty-fifth Dynasty but also predating this dynasty by thousands of years.[11] The ideological implication is this: though the *racist* premise propelling the Hamitic argument would be weakened by the proposition of pharaonic Nubian contact with Wakanda, the questionable *cultural* trajectory of the hypothesis would yet remain undeflected. Marvel's Egypt would still operate as *the* civilizing force upon Wakanda even when its Egypt was likely led as well by Blacks.[12]

But what of the "special knowledge" T'Challa and Mr. Fantastic sought? As the story goes, the founding of Wakanda begins in Egypt with the defeat of Amun-Ra by the death-god Anubis.[13] However, Anubis's sought-after prize, Amun-Ra's heart, is stolen away by Bast who delivers it south to the early so-called primitive Wakandans. This special delivery of wisdom from North Africa seems to ignite Wakanda's culture in East Africa[14] where it is adopted as Wakanda's metaphysical uber-principle, *the Great Circle*.[15] According to T'Challa, "with [this] knowledge, Wakanda became the greatest nation of all."[16] Time and again, the message in *Black Panther* lore is that Wakanda's enlightenment was a gift, one given to it by faraway foreign gods or coming from faraway foreign peoples.

Author-essayist Ta-Nehisi Coates and director-screenwriter Ryan Coogler, the most recent crafters of the world of Wakanda in comics and film, respectively, have deviated significantly from this decades-long Hamitic tendency by incorporating numerous sub-Saharan African ideas and images into their works. Coates has expanded the pantheon of Wakandan gods well beyond Egyptians. There is now Mujaji, the South African Lovedu people's "god of sustenance"; Nyami, the Akan sky-god; and Kokou, the Yoruba god of war.[17] Coates has even introduced two Saharan "Elder Gods" who predate the pantheon. Those "Lost-Found Gods" named Nommo ("by which everything lives") and Ammah ("by which everything dies") were inspired by Mali's Dogon religion.[18] Coogler's choice of Hindu deity Hanuman as the divine patron of M'Baku's Jabari Mountain Tribe is strange, but in comic books, this Hanuman is the "White Gorilla God" modeled after the "god of judgment" Ghekre, a simian deity of the Ivory Coast's Akan Baoule people.[19] Moreover, regardless of a deity's original ethno-cultural origin, each god holds the title *orisha*, the Yoruba word for a deity subordinate to the Supreme Being. Furthermore, the entire pantheon of Wakandan gods is now known collectively as *the Orisha*.

Clearly then, Coates and Coogler are engaged in a struggle over African representation in popular culture. In philosophical terms, what Coates and Coogler are advancing is a *conceptual decolonization* of the Wakandan afterlife away from a pernicious Western philosophy of culture towards an enabling African philosophy of mind.[20]

"In My Culture, Death Is Not the End."

Conceptual decolonization is an intercultural philosophy developed by the Akan philosopher Kwazi Wiredu which is critical of the "undue influence" of Western concepts and categories originally imposed on African religions and philosophies during colonialism that often distort comprehension and application of African thought-systems well after the continent's political independence.[21] The contention here with *Black Panther* lore is not whether Egyptian history, culture, and religion should populate tales of Wakanda. They should. Ancient Egypt was an African civilization (though not an entirely racially Black one or white one). To disqualify and erase Egypt's presence from Wakanda for reasons of cultural or color purification would be "madness."[22] The issue is, rather, that fictionalized Egyptian notions have overshadowed other African ideas about the afterlife in *Black Panther* lore or have overcrowded conceptual space that promising fictionalized non-Egyptian African content could have shared.

The Coates–Coogler expansion of the Wakandan afterlife in name, membership, and deed toward West African and transatlantic African diasporic ideas, concerns, and sentiments puts Erik Killmonger's last words in *Black Panther* into a different light. Recall his "just bury my body in the ocean with the ancestors that jumped off the ships because they knew death was better than bondage." This final request remains poetic, principled, and political – but now it seems it was also pragmatic. Remember that before his death, Killmonger had already spoken in person to a dead man, his father N'Jobu. Recall that before his death, Killmonger had this face-to-face someplace like (but so unlike) his childhood Oakland apartment. It is entirely reasonable, therefore, to think that Killmonger knew – not hoped for or prayed for but *knew* – that something of his consciousness, his self-awareness, his will, in short, his *subjectivity*, could survive past the death of his physical body. So, Killmonger may not have been speaking figuratively just before he pulled the head of a spear from out of his chest. Given what he knew of life after death as a state of being and the afterlife as a setting for being, it is likely Killmonger was being quite literal when he requested an oceanic afterlife. Not literally to be buried at sea, though. Rather, he desired a metaphysical state of being and setting for being wherein he could continue on, and perhaps even rule over and rule from. If so, a West African-ized afterlife would probably be preferable to Killmonger, given his affinity for the region's cultures, as he demonstrated to the museum curator's everlasting regret. But which West African cultures' metaphysics suit Killmonger's concerns?

At least one strong candidate is mentioned in the *Black Panther* film: Ghana's Ashanti.[23] Ashanti are arguably the most famous members of the larger Akan ethnic group from which Akan traditional religion and modern philosophy have developed. In the *Black Panther* comics, we find another robust contender: Nigeria's Yoruba. From this ethnic group's religious divination tradition, modern Yoruba philosophy was formed. If we interpret Killmonger's last words not only as a dying man's final request or as a poignant declaration of his politics but also as a call for a new philosophy of mind in Wakanda, then arguably Akan and Yoruba West African philosophies are best equipped to theorize Killmonger's afterlife prospects. How so?

"Allow the Heart-Shaped Herb to ... Take You to the Ancestral Plane."

There are three metaphysical problems confronting Killmonger's postmortem existence in the Wakandan afterlife. They are the problems of substance, subjectivity, and setting. The problem of substance may be addressed through Wiredu's Akan theory of *quasi-physicalism*. The problem of subjectivity primarily through Leke Adoefe's Yoruba theory of *quasi-historical self-actualization*. Finally, the problem of setting can be triangulated through a combination of African cosmological theories.

No matter how many times the spiritual plane and the earthly plane were crossed mystically, those crossings probably would not have made sense to Killmonger intellectually. An "Ancestral Plane"? Really? His time spent at the United States Naval Academy at Annapolis, as well as at MIT, and in inner-city Oakland would have taught him not to believe in fairy tales. Killmonger would never put his fate in the hands of faith, not even after he found out he could talk to his dead dad. He would demand rational explanations about supernatural phenomena since the survival of his subjectivity after death would depend on substantial answers.

Even if Killmonger's knowledge of African traditional religions were thin, he still would have thought that the dichotomy Wakanda's mystics draw between an earthly plane and a spiritual plane makes little sense. As Wiredu quite plainly puts it, "the African world of the dead ... is in no sense another world, but rather part of this world, albeit a conceptually problematic part."[24] It seems then that Wakanda is suffering from a second type of conceptual colonization, one that had seeped into *Black Panther* lore through some of its writers who had unwittingly infused its comics and related films with a confounding Western ontological theory. That theory, known in Western philosophy as *substance dualism*, drastically reduces the plausibility of Killmonger's survival by introducing a fundamental tension into the makeup of reality that is almost impossible to surmount.

Many substance dualists today are still sympathetic to the reasoning of the seventeenth-century philosopher René Descartes, who believed that a human being is composed of physical and non-physical substances: a body and a mind.[25] The body (including the brain) is material and therefore subject to the laws of physics. The mind's qualities are exactly opposite. It is immaterial and immune to the laws of physics. As strange as it sounds, Descartes did not believe the brain does the thinking for a person; the mind does. For dualists, the mind is one's sentience, one's consciousness. It is a person's truest identity, and, being immaterial, the mind is what endures spiritually even after the body dies. Substance dualists would say that this is what happened to Killmonger after he died; his mind lives on. But how is this possible? If he is now completely separated from his former physical body, how can his mind maintain any coherence? And how could Killmonger's immaterial mind interact with his material body in the first place even when he was completely alive? These types of questions have been debated for centuries among dualists and raised endlessly by their critics.

We can see in *Black Panther* lore the challenges that substance dualism poses to Wakandan physics and metaphysics. In a late 1980s comic book mini-series, Bast was so disgusted with Wakanda's isolationism in the face of Apartheid in Azania (the comic's version of South Africa) that the goddess abandoned T'Challa. Bast possessed a Black prisoner tortured in Azania and mutated him into a superpowered man-cat in order to fight back.[26] T'Challa eventually defeated his more radical replacement by having the Azanian chase him through "a shrub of paralyzing electrodes, a river of de-vitalizing fluid, and a series of muscle retardant inductors in the ground" all located in the "electronic jungle" that Black Panther used years earlier to defeat the Fantastic Four.[27] Triumphant, King T'Challa proclaims to the cat-goddess the essential reason for his victory: "Although your spirit could not be touched, you now possess a body with completely neutralized muscles and nerves."[28] T'Challa's strategy against Bast is clearly based on substance dualist reasoning. Not being able to engage his former divine patron's mind/soul directly, T'Challa attacked the physical body Bast inhabited. T'Challa fought and defeated Bast as a dualist would.

So, could possession of another person be Killmonger's second chance at life after death? Probably not, for how could, after all, T'Challa have possibly beat Bast on a dualist philosophical basis? If Bast truly were the "Panther-*Spirit*" she was called throughout the series, how could it as a spiritual entity be capable of interacting at all with the physical body of a man, much less healing a badly tortured one and transforming him into a man-sized wildcat? Neither T'Challa nor Bast give a cogent explanation as to how the orisha overcame the fundamental incompatibility between the physical and the spiritual. From an African religio-philosophical perspective, Wiredu contends that "all the orders of being [physical and spiritual] are conceived to interact in a law-like manner." But there is no sign in the comic book series of a principle or mechanism anchoring the purportedly different orders of Wakandan reality under a single "law." But then again, in the *Black Panther* film, there is: *the Heart-Shaped Herb*.

From his first fight with T'Challa, Killmonger knew that consuming the Herb would affect a person's physical abilities. He did not know of its spiritual properties until he drank it and communed with his dead father. "Allow the Heart-Shaped Herb to give you the powers of the Black Panther and take you to the Ancestral Plane," a grove-keeper advised Killmonger as she poured it as a brew into his mouth. After his spiritual communion concludes, the first words out of his mouth are "The Heart-Shaped Herb did that?" His incredulity would have made any defender of dualism within earshot nervous. Descartes's solution to such a physical/spiritual interaction problem was to locate the connection between body and mind/soul at the pineal gland of the brain. Killmonger would think that ridiculous. So, the Heart-Shaped Herb is the pineal gland of Wakanda's split reality? Wiredu's research shows that in Akan and most other traditional African cosmologies "the natural / supernatural dichotomy ... [has] no place."[29] Why in Wakanda, then? The linking of bodies and souls through herbs and glands should be quite unnecessary.

Maybe it takes the Devil himself to overcome the dichotomy that Descartes could not. In the late 1990s, Black Panther battled Mephisto, the Devil of the Marvel Universe. T'Challa knocked him out with one punch![30] Since Killmonger may have guessed he might well end up in the archdemon's clutches due to all the "necessary evils" the mercenary committed throughout his career, Killmonger would want to know how his flesh-and-blood royal cousin was able to put the powerhouse evil spirit flat on its back. Simple. To overcome the substance dualism hurdle that should have made Mephisto untouchable, T'Challa just needed to alter the "molecular constant of the universe"![31] Okay, not quite. T'Challa got his scientists to whip up a "remodulating force field" around Mephisto as he battled him in Brooklyn.[32] Trapped on the physical plane, the malevolent spirit was thus vulnerable to T'Challa's very solid right cross and very sharp vibranium claws. To add insult to injury, T'Challa then told the Devil himself, "You are dying. So long as a part of you remains bound to the earth, your power remains diminished."[33] That is how incompatible spiritual and physical substances can be in *Black Panther* lore. No one – not Descartes, not divinities, not demons – can reconcile the irreconcilable without solutions to substance dualism that are fantastic even in the fictional world of the Black Panther.

From these examples, we can see that Wakanda has had a substance abuse problem for a long time. Subscribing to substance dualism would render any possibility of Killmonger living past death over before it started because a postmortem existence in dualist terms is patently illogical and virtually impossible to achieve practically. In short, substance dualism would make Killmonger's existence after death unbelievable. Coming to this logical and practical conclusion would be utterly fatal to Killmonger's subjectivity, which theoretically would have survived after death as had his father's. Killmonger would need survival scenarios that were intellectually convincing. Consequently, Killmonger would have sought out theoretical alternatives less destabilizing to the prospect of continuing his existence postmortem. Wiredu's theory, *quasi-physicalism*, would have alleviated some of Killmonger's substance abuse problems.[34]

Quasi-physicalism is an Akan/African framework for reconceptualizing supposedly antithetical physical and spiritual substances in a manner that at least logically does not make ordinary and surreal phenomena incompatible. For several reasons, Killmonger would find quasi-physicalism superior to substance dualism as grounds for his survival post-death. First, quasi-physicalism rejects the idea that reality is split into fundamentally different physical and spiritual components. Instead, it seeks to enlarge the range of what physical reality could be considered to be. This enlarged categorization of reality is open to the possibility that so-called spiritual entities and environs do exist. Second, according to Akan philosopher Safro Kwame, quasi-physicalist philosophers align with African traditional sages in thinking that although such spiritual phenomena (if real) are obviously not the same physically as everyday persons and places, the actual difference between them is not a substantial one.[35] Rather, it is to say that the Ancestors, the Orisha, Satan, the Supreme Being, and where each resides in the afterlife differ substantially from humans and their habitats mainly by having a different degree of physicality, not because they are composed of different substances altogether. Third, but unlike African traditional sages, a modern quasi-physicalist's expanded sense of reality is more "epistemologically humble."[36] Philosophical quasi-physicalists would not support the claim that souls, demons, and gods *must* exist. They contend instead that *if* souls, demons, and gods exist, they are probably comprised of physical matter of some sort and not immaterial spirit stuff. Rather than relying on faith to support their intuitions, philosophical quasi-physicalists look forward to a scientific basis being found eventually for their substance theory of mind, perhaps through cutting-edge quantum physics. What keeps a quasi-physicalist's mind open but grounded prior to those hypothetical scientific discoveries being made is their knowledge that "all forms of materialism are relative to the physics of the day, however unmaterialist their theories may sound to their predecessors."[37]

Having witnessed (and weaponized) first-hand what is physically possible by employing Wakanda's amazing technologies, Killmonger would have been intrigued by quasi-physicalism's broader conception of what is possibly physical and hence physically possible after death. The African theory could free Wakanda's religion from substance dualism, a form of "conceptual inertia" in its metaphysics emanating from the West, Wiredu would surmise.[38] Quasi-physicalism would offer an African alternative to wrongheaded thinking that would get in the way of Killmonger living a more substantial life in the afterlife.

"I Know How the Colonizer Thinks."

Traditional African sages believe quasi-physical beings exist. Modern quasi-physicalist philosophers say they might. However, it would take more than having substance for Killmonger to survive in the afterlife. Every animated being Killmonger or T'Challa saw in the Ancestral Plane possessed something else: *subjectivity*. Subjectivity can be defined as a volitional self-awareness, a consciousness capable of intentionality. Wiredu has argued that in order to be an agent in this world or the next, an ancestor or deity would require the functional equivalent not only of a body (substance) but also of something akin to a mind (subjectivity).[39]

For substance dualists, this subjectivity would be understood as *mind*. However, mind in their way of thinking is thought objectified. It is more than just a substance *with* subjectivity. Mind is a substance that *is* subjectivity. In contrast, mind in traditional Akan/African perspectives remains minimally the activity of thinking or maximally the underlying capacity for thought. While mind is treated as an object in everyday casual Akan speech, it is typically not taken to be a metaphysical thing deserving of philosophical reflection or religious contemplation. Hence, like Wiredu, Killmonger would probably think the whole mind-is-a-substance spiel to be more dualist "gibberish."[40]

But Killmonger would also have been critical here of some of Wiredu's thinking. Wiredu is better at saying what the functional equivalent to mind in quasi-physical entities *is not* than he is at saying what that functional equivalent to mind *is*. Killmonger would not gamble what might remain after death of his intentional self-awareness on this potentially lethal omission. He would have again quested through sub-Saharan thought to better his post-death prospects for survival. Yoruba religion's and philosophy's ideas on subjectivity would have attracted him with their potentially useful configurations of determinism and willpower. Zuri, Wakanda's shaman supreme, could have explained to Killmonger how adopting the Yoruba notions of *ori-inu* and *ipin* would force the American to rethink his own personal ontology in lifesaving ways[41] – if Killmonger had not killed him!

Ipin is a person's destiny.[42] It can be understood as the broad strokes of fortune and misfortune in one's life dictated before birth by Oludumare, the Yoruba Supreme Being. Killmonger in Coates's comics would recognize *ori-inu* in part from when he defeated Bast, an orisha, at *Orisha Gate*, home of Wakanda's pantheon. This Killmonger would know that "ori" in Yoruba means "physical head" while "*ori-inu*" refers to a person's metaphysical "inner head," the more philosophically interesting idea. Killmonger would loathe the idea of determinism, divine or otherwise. However, Yoruba philosopher Leke Adeofe's theorization of the ontological relationship between *ipin* and *ori-inu* could have allayed some of the mercenary's reservations. *Ipin* is actually "quasi-historical," according to Adeofe.[43] This means destiny's prenatal determination is actually somewhat susceptible to manipulation. That is what makes *ipin* a "-historical" formation.

However, forces attempting to affect destiny are often incapable of altering that predestination significantly or at all. This is what makes *ipin* a "quasi-(established fate)" phenomenon.

Ori-inu is "self-actualization" in Adeofe theory.[44] This means that no matter how prescribed a destiny is for a particular person, that destiny becomes a crucial part of that person's identity only when it is claimed as a possession through one's personal initiative. This is what makes *ipin* potentially a "self" in the sense of *that* destiny became *my* destiny as a result of *my* acting intentionally upon it. Yoruba philosopher Segun Gbadegesin symbolizes this possessive investment and thus personal attachment argument by using the images of *owo* (hand) and *ese* (leg) to connote the ever-busy hands and endless leg-work required to actualize [45]*ipin*.[45] *Ipin* is the raw potentials of life, which vary from person to person, of which an individual usually does not know the precise details or any at all of what they are fully capable of achieving with the right effort. One gets the impression overall that destiny is like wet-but-hardening concrete that yet may be molded somewhat – especially during life's make-or-break moments – into desired shapes (outcomes) possibly but not assuredly through effort and skill.

Cast in Yoruba philosophical terms, the subjectivity that Killmonger wants to persist after death takes on new unconventional meaning. Subjectivity is not something one can simply test for like a brainwave or a personality type. Subjectivity is a kind of personal *identification* toward the effort(s) exerted *itself* to realize the potentials one's destiny has allotted. In Yoruba religion, the closest approximation to Adeofe's theory of subjectivity is found in the story of Afuwape, an orisha who performs the contradictory acts of kneeling or humbling himself before a destiny while simultaneously choosing or being agential towards that destiny.

But what is Killmonger's destiny? As far as can be made out, it is an *ipin* comprised of two interwoven investments. The earlier investment is personal – revenge upon his Wakandan kin for his father's execution and for his abandonment as a boy. The latter investment is political – liberation of the "two billion people all over the world that looks like us." It is an unfulfilled destiny, however, because the 30-something's life was cut a good 40 years short of the normal human life span foreseeably required to achieve such improbable longshots even with vibranium weapons of mass destruction. Death, or a life after death in a world where sons can talk to their dead fathers, would hold out a much better chance for what Wiredu might characterize euphemistically regarding Killmonger's case as the anti-hero's "continuation of pre-mortem concerns."[46]

Those concerns, that destiny, may never have come to pass for Killmonger. Destiny is not definite. Nevertheless, this is Killmonger's destiny – "The Avenger will avenge, he cannot but avenge," as it is written in Yoruba divination literature.[47] By claiming this destiny by consciously identifying with it through his intentional pursuit of it through admirable works (such as overcoming poverty, graduating from Annapolis and MIT) and even through despicable deeds (such as wet-work assassinations, murdering Zuri and others, and burning the Herb grove), that destiny is now Killmonger's subjectivity. It *is* Killmonger. This subjectivity is one that respects determinism but rejects fatalism. Subjectivity in this Afuwape mode would come closest to reconciling the realist and revolutionary strains in Killmonger's being and replicating them in the afterlife.

"Everybody Dies, It's Just Life around Here."

So, in African theories, Killmonger could live after death. But just where exactly after death could he live? Ironically, it is in the afterlife, and not during any mortal combat, that Killmonger's life is most at risk. Once his quasi-physical substance/quasi-historical self-actualization subjectivity left his body, the key metaphysical questions became whether he would continue existing, and if so, under what circumstances. Before Coates's involvement in *Black Panther*, the Wakandan afterlife was a largely undifferentiated "Spirit-World." Coates's and Coogler's imaginings of that afterlife along with notions from earlier writers can help us postulate existential scenarios of different degrees of viability for Killmonger's substance-subjectivity.

Killmonger in Limbo?

"Burial is the commonest method of dealing with the corpse in African cultures," according to Kenyan theologian John Mbiti.[48] Religious studies scholar A. David Lewis writes that "[f]or a body to be left unburied sounds nearly worse than death and … is seen as such in some cultures."[49] Lewis highlights three times lack of burial signals a spiritual crisis in the *Black Panther* movie. First, when T'Chaka kills his brother N'Jobu in Oakland. Second, when Killmonger tosses T'Challa over the waterfall. Third, when Killmonger dies on the mountain.[50] Among African traditionalists, special funerary rituals must be conducted for a person's soul to actually depart and commune with other quasi-physical beings.[51] None of the three men are buried properly (ritualistically) soon after apparent bodily death, and thus face consequences in the afterlife. Recall T'Challa's falling out with his father's spirit occurred there *after* his belated burial under snow and ice. Along with ingesting the Heart-Shaped Herb, it seems that being buried by some particulate matter also may be necessary to go beyond the mortal coil satisfactorily.

Mbiti describes a sense in African religions of a state of "lingering" for the soul between this life and the next.[52] Arguably, this is the "stepping-off point" T'Challa tells Black Widow about in *Captain America: Civil War*.

Perhaps the closest comic book version of this state/setting is found when Shuri was defeated by the "Mad Titan" Thanos's minion, Proxima Midnight, and trapped in a "living death" state.[53] T'Challa puts Shuri in a stasis-pod to stabilize what is left of his sister. But even though he is now Wakanda's King of the Dead and has the power to stalk souls, T'Challa laments that "[t]he woman frozen before me was not Shuri ... there was no scent, no trail about her ['soul'] ... She was not even a woman. She was a door."[54]

This limbo is probably where Killmonger's substance-subjectivity is now, since his body died in the film. Bereft of ritual burial, he has probably not moved onward from that death into a more permanent afterlife.

Killmonger in the Ancestral Plane?

Killmonger chose "death over bondage." He apparently wants to join the ancestors. Yet, as South African anthropologist Meyer Fortes discovered, in many African cultures "death is a necessary but not sufficient condition for the attainment of ancestorhood."[55]

The "Ancestral Plane" is the term used in the *Black Panther* film for where the dead-yet-alive reside. This is where we first see T'Chaka after his assassination, on a surreal grassland, first as a panther, then looking like the old man he was when he died. Apparently, the Ancestral Plane is also where Killmonger's father, N'Jobu, now resides in an uncanny version of the Oakland apartment he died in. In the comics, the Ancestral Plane has two iterations. The older is the *Panther Pavilion* (i.e. the Necropolis) where all former Black Panther warriors are buried but whose substance-subjectivities yet remain active and engaged (when summoned) in mortal affairs. "The dead counsel us, inspire us, sometimes even save us," Shuri in the comics reminds T'Challa.[56] The more recently conceived iteration is called *D'Jalia*, the "Wakandan Plane of Memory."[57] This is where the culture heroes of the nation reside after body-death. It is described variously as "a place long forgotten" and "the ancient place, the future place."[58]

Killmonger said he wanted to join the ancestors, but this may not have been his actual metaphysical intention. Becoming an ancestor to keep his subjectivity and substance safe would have come with several drawbacks for Killmonger's postmortem identity. First, according to Wiredu, the main reason ancestors exist, unlike unspecified spirits, is to "help the living to realize human purposes."[59] Second, the ancestors must help make compulsory established social mores. They cannot create new values or conventions. Third, ancestors cannot act out of self-interest. They "can only enforce rules whose basis or validity is independent of their own wishes or decisions."[60] As an ancestor, Killmonger would find these restrictions insufferable. Therefore, contrary to his stated wishes, it is unlikely becoming an ancestor is Killmonger's endgame.

Killmonger in Oblivion?

There are at least two renderings of oblivion in *Black Panther* lore. The better-known by far occurs when Killmonger visits an afterlife setting strangely like his childhood apartment in Oakland. He does not go there actually to communicate with his father, N'Jobu. Killmonger is actually surprised to see him there "alive." When he does speak to his father, there is little sign of tenderness or reverence from the son. "No tears for me?" N'Jobu wryly notes. "Everybody dies, it's just life around here," his son states stoically. In a traditional African metaphysical frame, this lack of devotion by the physically living toward the physically dead is existentially dangerous to the deceased's continued existence, its continued "personal immortality."[61] Dead relatives in one's family lineage especially, such as fathers and sons, should be remembered ritually on special occasions and informally in daily life. Otherwise, as Mbiti warns, a physically dead person can become "nobody and simply vanishes out of human existence like a flame when it is extinguished."[62] N'Jobu tells his son as much: "They will say you are lost … Instead, we are both abandoned here."

So, within a more distinctly Yoruba-Wakandan metaphysics, we can interpret the final fate of N'Jobu as a kind of oblivion rather than a lingering in limbo. He is being gradually forgotten by Killmonger, and therefore degrading existentially. Whereas N'Jobu was once probably a vivacious ancestor to Killmonger (through his son's adoration before stoicism set in), N'Jobu's subjectivity – his personal immortality – has since withered.[63] N'Jobu is now fading, evaporating, going from being an ancestor, a quasi-physical entity with a strong identity and clear destiny, to becoming a spirit, a quasi-physical entity with a dissipating identity and unfulfilled destiny. This version of oblivion would, in theory, be the more sentimental one, the version wherein identity loss is accompanied by a debilitating loss of intimacy.

The second kind of oblivion is also emotional but more ideological. In his recently retconned origin story in comics, Killmonger communes with Bast and K'Liluna (Bast's sister-goddess Sekhmet, in disguise) in *D'Yshalah*.[64] D'Yshalah is "[t]he great shoreline of the universe," as Killmonger calls it, an afterlife "where the wronged dead wait for justice in the world of the living."[65] But Killmonger's description of D'Yshalah as a place resonates more strongly historically and religiously with the Middle Passage, the transatlantic slave trade in West and Central Africa peoples, than with Egyptian passages up and down the Nile. Killmonger's final request in the film, to be buried at sea in the spirit of those who chose suicide over slavery, now makes more cosmological sense in light of this afterlife. Typically, in traditional African thought, "the high point of the post-mortem journey is the crossing of a river."[66] Forced further out to sea metaphysically by the brutality of the slave trade, the consequent oceanic afterlife for African victims would mean existing – unjustly – in a state of "collective immortality," an amalgamation of subjectivities whose distinct identities have been lost over time.[67]

Killmonger's substance and subjectivity would be absorbed into the tragically undifferentiated mass of enslaved African spirits, if he chose to join
them in their aquatic afterlife. To be in D'Yshalah would mean becoming
an "empty name," under most circumstances.[68] For Killmonger, it would
almost certainly mean that he would eventually lose whatever remained of
his personal identity when he first entered that afterlife. Why then, would
Killmonger make joining this transatlantic afterlife his request for a final
fate? The reason can be surmised through another afterlife possibility
found both in *Black Panther* lore and in traditional African metaphysics:
D'Yshalah offered the best chance for Killmonger to become an *orisha*.

Killmonger in Orisha Realm?

In films involving the *Black Panther* mythos, there is no mention of orishas by that name. In *Black Panther* comic book lore we know there is an
entire pantheon called such.

But there is the rub. Orisha Gate, the afterlife/other-life realm where
Wakanda's orisha reside, is populated by deities – gods – only. Killmonger
was completely human before body-death. How then could he ever come
to reside with such rarified company? Moreover, generally in African traditional ontologies of beings, a soul "becomes less ... not more a person"[69]
as it becomes over time an amorphous spirit. If Killmonger dwelt in
D'Yshalah, would not that signal he is even less capable of becoming an
orisha than if his subjectivity resided in some other setting?[70] How then
could he become an orisha?

In both *Black Panther* comic book lore and in African/Yoruba religion,
it is metaphysically possible for Killmonger to alter his ontological state
and cosmological setting. First, according to Mbiti, within African metaphysics although a spirit is a degraded human soul, it is still higher up the
ontological ladder of beings and therefore closer to the Supreme Being.
Second, though the vast majority of collective immortality-status spirits
lack distinct identities, some maintain them. The more remarkable or fortunate may be accorded by their devotees a robust "mythological personality built around fact and fiction."[71] Third, and more particular to Yoruba
ontology, some exceptional ancestors can assume the powers of true gods
through the "sheer force of their character."[72] Fourth, the profound adulation or faith people direct toward a person can supercharge that person up
the ontological ladder to orisha-level.[73] Storm, the X-Man, confirms this
when T'Challa asks the mutant if she is actually a goddess. Storm replies,
"the more the people believed, the stronger I grew ... And that is what I
know of gods. Their native powers may be formidable but it is the faith of
others that elevate them beyond the mortal coil."[74] (Conversely, declining
faith will degrade an orisha's status.) Fifth, it is actually possible for a
mortal to possess an existing orisha. Sixth, mortals who possess orisha

typically possess ones having personalities similar overall to their own or a personality attribute the mortal wishes to acquire for his own purposes.

So how could Killmonger possibly dwell with the Orisha? Yoruba theologian E. Bolaji Idowu speaks of how "certain ancestors have found their way into the [Yoruba] pantheon ... by becoming identified with some earlier divinities."[75] There is strong support for this strategy of associative uplift toward orisha-hood and the Orisha Gate in *Black Panther* comic books. First, many of Wakanda's orisha were human beings before the founding of the country. As a D'Jalia spirit-sage tells it, when proto-Wakandan settlers fought the indigenous monstrous Originators for the land, the humans were no match. But "[t]hen heroes rose among them. And on faith, heroes ascended to gods. Kokou, the Ever-Burning. Mujaji, the Life-Giver. And the most fearsome ... Bast."[76] Second, Idowu mentions the possibility of ascension via an "excessive veneration by the people," meaning the near-religious zeal invested in persons so esteemed by their followers.[77] Even contemporary characters, such as Storm, have been augmented to orisha-like levels by such devotion. Third, while it seems the geographical range for such empowerment-from-faith is limited to within Wakanda, being born Wakandan does not seem to be a requirement for enhancement. Again, this is what happened to Storm, who is half Kenyan, half African American in comics.

To dwell with the Orisha, Killmonger would have to become an orisha. But which orisha would best suit his subjectivity, his quasi-historical self-actualization? If Killmonger could somehow convert the respect of his hardcore supporters in the movie, the Rhino Tribe, into true reverence for him, Killmonger could possibly possess or displace Kokou, Wakanda's Yoruba god of war. Overshadowed by Bast and the other better-known Egyptian orisha, Kokou of Wakanda is more like *Ela*, a god in Yoruba religion, in that they both represent a "spiritual principle which was struggling for expression but did not quite succeed in doing so before it was overwhelmed."[78] But Kokou is still feared as the "Ever-Burning" orisha, holding the reputation of being the most ferocious god in the actual country of Benin's version of Yoruba religion. Given Killmonger's aggressive nature, personally and militarily, combined with Kokou's relatively low standing among the Wakandan orisha, Kokou is a prime candidate for a hostile takeover by Killmonger's fighting spirit.

Yet a stronger argument could be made for Killmonger adopting the guise of a different Yoruba god. Given Killmonger's African American ancestry on his mother's side, his demonstrated affinity toward West African cultures and histories, his allusion to the transatlantic slave trade in his final request, and the resonance that request in the movie has with D'Yshalah in his comic book mini-series, Killmonger arguably would have adopted the persona of *Olokun*, the Yoruba ocean god/goddess. West African worshipers of Olokun prayed to him/her not only for protection of their bodies but also to safeguard their wealth and status.[79] But he/she likely meant even more than that to many who suffered on and survived

after the slave ships to the Americas.[80] To them and some of their present-day descendants, Olokun can represent both immortality and
extinction.[81] Olokun epitomizes "the inexhaustibility, the opaque more-
ness, of human experience ... the uncertainty accompanying the human
endeavor to access and manifest immateriality," religious studies scholar
Marcus Harvey argues.[82] Killmonger's chances of actualizing his destiny
would increase dramatically if he achieved deification as this god.

Out of all the afterlives, the realm of the orisha is the one Killmonger
would prefer most. Killmonger would have dreaded residing in oblivion.
To fade into nothingness? Unthinkable. But theoretically, only D'Yshalah
would hold any chance of not only sustaining Killmonger's subjectivity but
possibly enhancing it. Ironically, the afterlife that threatens most that no
one will remember the name "Killmonger" is actually the best afterlife to
make his name feared and power felt.

"Can You Believe That? A Kid from Oakland ... Believing in Fairytales!"

Olokun is not presently a member of the Wakandan pantheon. However,
getting to the point theoretically where the ascension of Killmonger as
either the orisa Kokou or Olukun is plausible within comic books and the
2018 film demonstrates the potential of Coates's and Coogler's conceptual
decolonization project. The ontological and cosmological problems of the
half African, half African American Killmonger drive the project through
West African Akan and Yoruba metaphysics yet also move it progressively
toward Africa's transatlantic diasporan thought and concerns.

Yet the mobilization of "our own indigenous conceptual schemes in our
philosophical meditations" across cultures should be "judicious," Wiredu
would warn.[83] Dr. Voodoo in the comics counseled T'Challa similarly
when the king once sought to interpret the silence of Wakanda's gods
through Haitian gods who speak to the mage. Through Legba, Dr. Voodoo's
patron god, Voodoo probably could have done so since Legba is "Guardian
of the Eternal Crossroads" in comics and known to be fluent in all mortal
and divine languages in actual Vodou religion. Yet the doctor urges
T'Challa to tread carefully metaphysically: "The Loa and your Orisha
work in different spheres. There are tales of alliance – but also of war."[84]
Similarly, whether in its deconstructive "negative" mode or its constructive
"positive" mode,[85] conceptual decolonization is what African American
philosopher Leonard Harris would probably characterize synthetically as
a "philosophy born of struggle" methodology against life-delimiting
thought targeting Black people especially.[86] Regarding the application of
African thought to both Black people and philosophy, Harris advises that
"[t]here are lots of different and conflicting ... values that can be derived
from Africa. The ones that should be used depends on the warrant of the

values, whether African or not."[87] Hence, Killmonger would not fear conflict between Western, Egyptian, Akan, Yoruba, and African diasporan theories. Rather, he would demand that conceptual clarity and effective utility – if not morality[88] – determine whether an intercultural contest of ideas is worthy of his attention and Wakanda's.

For the idea of Killmonger living after death to be persuasive metaphysically, the removal of problematic Western philosophies of culture and mind and their replacement with African philosophies of substance, subjectivity, and setting is paramount. The very least Erik Stevens would demand from any philosophy of existence, African or otherwise, is a fighting chance to live. The very least a man called "Killmonger" would demand from such philosophy is that it help him fight for his destiny. For Erik "Killmonger" Stevens would never choose "death over bondage" while there was any chance to live that destiny, in the Here and Now, after death.

Notes

1. The Hamitic Hypothesis developed from the Old Testament story of Noah cursing his son Ham to be a slave of his siblings. By the sixth century, the curse had also become racialized to mean the "blackening" of Ham's skin and "staining" of his descendants. Egyptians were considered part of this maligned lineage along with other Africans. However, with the birth of Egyptology in the early nineteenth century, many Europeans could not reconcile the fact that a "Negroid" Egyptian population could have created a world-class civilization, much less one predating their own "Caucasoid" ancient Greece. Tortured logics were employed to "whiten" Egypt racially and recuperate it fundamentally as a Western civilization. Evidence of sophistication among darker African peoples was then attributed to hypothesized cultural and/or biological intermixing with the lighter, allegedly intellectually and morally superior North African society. See Edith R. Sanders, "The Hamitic Hypothesis: Its Origin and Functions in Time Perspective," The Journal of African History 10 (1969), 521–532.
2. "Wakandan History," Marvel Fandom Database, at https://marvel. fandom.com/wiki/Wakandan_History#:~:text=10%2C000%20years%20 ago%2C%20Wakanda%20was%20home%20to%20a,later%20be%20 known%20as%20vibranium%20crashed%20to%20Earth.
3. *Fall of the Hulks: Alpha* #1 (2010).
4. *Fantastic Four* #607 (2012).
5. *Fantastic Four* #607 (2012).
6. *Fantastic Four* #607 (2012).
7. *Fantastic Four* #607 (2012).
8. *Fantastic Four* #608 (2012).
9. *Fantastic Four* #608 (2012).
10. See Charles Bonnet and Dominique Valbelle, *The Nubian Pharaohs: Black Kings on the Nile* (Cairo, Egypt: American University in Cairo Press, 2007).

11. See Steve Vinson, "Demotic: The History, Development and Techniques of Ancient Egypt's Popular Script," American Research Center in Egypt, at https://www.arce.org/resource/demotic-history-development-and-techniques-ancient-egypts-popular-script.

12. This points to the tendency nowadays for the hypothesis not to be pursued as much out of racial animus as what Akan philosopher Kwazi Wiredu would characterize as "the unexamined assimilation in our thought ... of conceptual frameworks ... that have an impact on African life and thought." Kwasi Wiredu, "The Need for Conceptual Decolonization in African Philosophy," in Kwasi Wiredu ed., *Cultural Universals and Particulars: An African Perspective* (Bloomington, IN: Indiana University Press, 1996), 136.

13. *Fantastic Four* #607 (2012).

14. Wakanda is shown to be located between Sudan and Ethiopia in actual Africa. In Coates's comic, it is between where Uganda and Tanzania would be in the real world. See Ken Jennings, "Finding Wakanda's Real-Life Location," *Conde Nest Traveler*, February 26, 2018, at https://www.cntraveler.com/story/finding-wakandas-real-life-location.

15. Jennings.

16. Jennings.

17. *Black Panther* #15 (2016).

18. *Black Panther* #15 (2016).

19. See "Ghekre," Marvel Fandom Database, at https://marvel.fandom.com/wiki/Ghekre_(Earth-616).

20. Even nigh-Ancestral spirits are not spared conceptual decolonization. In the comics, T'Challa's sister Shuri became a Black Panther queen of Wakanda. After she "died" in battle and went to an afterlife, she casually asserted to her griot spirit guide that it was vibranium, the space metal upon which Wakandan technology is based, that "guided us out of our savage years." The griot rebukes her: "'Savage'? Do I seem savage to you?" "Wakanda was great before it had things. And its secrets are older than any vaunted metal." See *Black Panther* #3 (2016).

21. Kwasi Wiredu, "Toward Decolonizing African Philosophy and Religion," *African Studies Quarterly* 1 (1998), 17.

22. Wiredu, 17.

23. The museum curator identifies a mask as originating from the "Bobo Ashanti tribe. Present-day Ghana. Nineteenth century." The Ashanti existed then but the Bobo Ashanti is a Rastafarian group that began in the mid-twentieth century. Therefore, I draw rather on theories derived from the metaphysical thought of the actual Ashanti Akan ethnic group.

24. Kwasi Wiredu, "Death and the Afterlife in African Culture," in Kwame Gyekye and Kwasi Wiredu eds., *Person and Community: Ghanaian Philosophical Studies, I* (Washington, DC: The Council for Research in Values and Philosophy, 2010), 141.

25. For an overview of substance dualism theories, see Samuel T. Segun, "Neurophilosophy and the Problem of Consciousness: An Equiphenomenal Perspective," in Jonathan O. Chimakonam et al. eds., *New Conversations on the Problems of Identity, Consciousness and Mind* (Cham, Switzerland: Springer, 2019), 47–49.

26. *Black Panther* #4 (1988).
27. *Black Panther* #4 (1988).
28. *Black Panther* #4 (1988).
29. Kwasi Wiredu, "Toward Decolonizing African Philosophy and Religion," *African Studies Quarterly* 1 (1998), 33.
30. *Black Panther* #4 (1998).
31. *Black Panther* #4 (1998).
32. *Black Panther* #4 (1998).
33. *Black Panther* #4 (1998).
34. For a founding essay, see Kwame Wiredu, "The Concept of Mind with Particular Reference to the Language and Thought of the Akans," in Guttorm Fløistad ed., *Contemporary Philosophy: A New Survey*, vol. 5 (Dordrecht: Springer, 1987), 153–179.
35. Safro Kwame, "Quasi Materialism: A Contemporary African Philosophy of Mind," in Kwasi Wiredu ed., *A Companion to African Philosophy* (Oxford: Blackwell Publishing, 2004), 346.
36. Kwame, 346.
37. Kwame, 346.
38. Kwasi Wiredu, "Conceptual Decolonization as an Imperative in Contemporary African Philosophy: Some Personal Reflections," *Rue Descartes* 36 (2002), 56.
39. Wiredu (2010), 139.
40. Wiredu (2002), 61.
41. In Yoruba personal ontology, Killmonger's entire human being would be called *eniyan*. There are five major physical/metaphysical components to one's eniyan. An individual's physical body and its parts is called *ara*. The life force that animates the body is *emi*. A person's emotional and psychological traits are located in his *okan*, "heart," the pumping organ understood in its more metaphysical sense. *Ipin* is one's destiny, the allotment of fortune and misfortune determined before birth. Finally, there is *ori-inu*, each individual's metaphysical "container" for his destiny as well as his personal identity. See Segun Gbadegesin, *African Philosophy: Traditional Yoruba Philosophy and Contemporary African Realities* (New York: Peter Lang, 1991), chapter 2.
42. With reference to E. Bolaji Idowu, *Olodumare: God in Yoruba Belief* (London: Longmans, Green and Co., 1995), I prefer Idowu's selection of the *ipin* as roughly the "ori's portion of destiny" (p. 171) than Gbadegesin use of the term *kadara* for destiny for the following reasons: First, Gbadegesin uses the term only occasionally, usually preferring the English word "destiny." Second, according to Yoruba religious studies scholar Oluwatoyin Gbadamosi, the word kadara may actually be derived from Arabic. This may or may not qualify it as being a case of conceptual colonization on Yoruba traditional thought. Third, kadara suggests a sense of destiny that is less responsive to lasting intervention by persons. See Oluwatoyin Gbadamosi, "Ori and Neuroscience: A Contextualization of the Yoruba Idea of Causality in the Age of Modern Science," *Africology: The Journal of Pan African Studies* 12 (2018), 10.
43. Leke Adeofe, "Personal Identity in African Metaphysics," in Lee M. Brown ed., *African Philosophy: New and Traditional Perspectives* (New York: Oxford University Press, 2004), 78–80.
44. Adeofe, 78–80.

45. What would fit neatly alongside these non-metaphysical factors in a desti-ny's manifestation/self-actualization would be the right application of *opolo* ("brains"), *okan* ("heart," as in psycho-emotional drive), and *ifun* ("intes-tines," as in having courage or "guts").

46. Wiredu (2010), 147.

47. Idowu, 198.

48. John S. Mbiti, *African Religions and Philosophy* (Oxford: Heinemann, 1969), 154.

49. A. David Lewis, "The Ancestral Lands of Black Panther and Killmonger Unburied," *Journal of Religion & Film* 22 (2018), at https://digitalcommons. unomaha.edu/jrf/vol22/iss1/39.

50. Lewis, 4–5.

51. For Yoruba example, see Bosede A. Adebowale, "Reincarnation in Plato and Yoruba Traditional Belief," *Yoruba: Journal of Yoruba Studies Association of Nigeria* 7 (2012), 12.

52. John S. Mbiti, *Introduction to African Religion* (London: Heinmann, 1975), 119.

53. *Black Panther* #8 (2016).

54. *Black Panther* #8 (2016).

55. Meyer Fortes, "Some Reflections on Ancestor Worship in Africa," in M. Fortes and G. Dieterlen eds., *African Systems of Thought* (London: Oxford Univer-sity Press, 1965), 122.

56. *Black Panther* #12 (2016).

57. *Black Panther* #2 (2016).

58. *Black Panther* #8 (2016).

59. Wiredu (2010), 145.

60. Wiredu (2010), 147.

61. Mbiti (1969), 32.

62. Mbiti (1969), 33.

63. Mbiti (1969), 103.

64. *Killmonger* #5 (2019).

65. *Killmonger* #1 (2018).

66. Wiredu (2010), 137.

67. Mbiti (1975), 33.

68. Mbiti (1975), 34.

69. Mbiti (1969), 103.

70. There is at least one other plane in Wakandan cosmology that may be a godly realm: *Kummandla*. In the comics, it is the "realm of … the disciples of the Older Gods." Kummandla was "forged in the deep past of Wakanda" and is "an extension of that spirit," one which predates the rise of the orisha. See *Black Panther* #14 (2016). However, though acolytes of the Elder Gods are said to reside there, there is little indication that a physical person becomes more than mortal there or that dead people's subjectivities dwell there. There-fore, this "afterlife" would not suit Killmonger.

71. Mbiti (1969), 34.

72. Idowu, 19.

73. Karin Barber, "How Man Makes God in West Africa: Yoruba Attitude Towards the 'Orisha'," *Africa* 51 (1981), 724–745.

74. *Black Panther* #13 (2017).

75. Idowu, 69.
76. *Black Panther* #13 (2017).
77. Idowu, 69.
78. Idowu, 101.
79. Marcus Harvey, "Engaging the Orisa: An Exploration of the Yoruba Concepts of Ibeji and Olokun as Theoretical Principles in Black theology," *Black Theology: An International Journal* 6 (2008), 74.
80. According to Yoruba scholars Gary Edwards and John Mason, "Olokun holds the key to the mysteries about the history of the cross-Atlantic passage … In this sense, one has only to think about the millions of captive Africans who were lost during that passage, and who entered the kingdom of Olokun carrying cultural and ancestral links with them." See *Black Gods: Orisa Studies in the New World* (Brooklyn, NY: Yoruba Theological Archministry, 1985), 61.
81. Harvey, 73–74.
82. Harvey, 74.
83. Wiredu (1996), 136.
84. *Black Panther* #23 (2021).
85. Wiredu (1996), 136.
86. See Leonard Harris, *A Philosophy of Struggle: The Leonard Harris Reader*, ed., Lee A. McBride, III (New York: Bloomsbury Publishing, 2020), especially chapter 1.
87. Azuka Nzegwu, "Interview with Professor Leonard Harris," *Journal of African Philosophy* 17 (2017), 149.
88. It does not seem that one needs to be virtuous to reside in the Wakandan afterlife(s). Neither N'Jobu's involvement in the theft of vibranium and complicity in the killing of Wakandans during the act nor T'Chaka's abandonment of his nephew Erik as a juvenile prevented either from entering an afterlife. Ostensibly, neither would Killmonger's capital crimes. For more on this point, see Lewis (2018), 3.

15

Wakandan Resources
The Epistemological Reality of *Black Panther's* Fiction

Ruby Komic

Members of marginalized communities experience a lack of representation of their unique life experience in popular fictional media – and if they do see themselves represented, it is often as a stereotype, caricature, or minor character. *Black Panther* broke this mold by offering abundant, nuanced, and non-stereotypical representation of Black experience. Yet, while some lauded *Black Panther* for its portrayal of Black culture, some also criticized the film's depiction.

For example, actor Anthony Mackie saw *Black Panther's* nearly all-Black cast and production crew as being a form of racism. As Mackie stated, in a co-interview with actor Daveed Diggs:

> "I've done several Marvel movies where every producer, every director, every stunt person, every costume designer, every PA, every single person has been white. But then when you do Black Panther, you have a Black Director, Black producer, you have a Black costume designer, you have a Black stunt choreographer. And I'm like, that's more racist than anything else. Because if you only can hire Black people for the Black movie, are you saying they're not good enough when you have a mostly white cast?"[1]

Certainly, with *Black Panther* being released in 2018, two years after the election of Donald Trump, in the midst of the Black Lives Matter movement (which, at the time, hadn't experienced the aftermath that resulted from the killing of George Floyd), and to a media climate sorely lacking representation from people of color, the issue of racism is virtually inescapable, presenting a sort of paradox. On one hand, *Black Panther* is celebrated for its presentation of Black culture and for its use of Black professionals on screen and behind the camera. On the other hand, it is criticized for these very same things.

Of course, *Black Panther* is fiction. There is no Wakanda or vibranium, and Shuri's lab (with all its futuristic gadgets) doesn't exist. Yet, we feel

Black Panther and Philosophy: What Can Wakanda Offer the World?, First Edition. Edited by Edwardo Pérez and Timothy E. Brown.
© 2022 John Wiley & Sons, Inc. Published 2022 by John Wiley & Sons, Inc.

emotional about *Black Panther*, don't we? Indeed, how many people have crossed their arms and said "Wakanda Forever!"? And, with a film like *Black Panther* (that, at times, seems to directly reflect, if not respond to, its contemporary moment) it is difficult to separate or distinguish between the characters and issues of the film and the people and issues of the real world. For Black audiences, *Black Panther* offered a film they could identify with and feel a sense of ownership and pride in, especially if we view the film as a resource that helps remedy the inequality in fictional representations of the Black experience. Similarly, *Black Panther* also offers a way of interpreting the real world through its fictional representations of Black people and Black society.

Philosophically, this offers an interesting version of what is called the Paradox of Fiction, which results from three conditions: (i) we have emotional responses to fiction that are genuine and rational; (ii) in order for our emotional responses to be genuine and rational we must believe the fiction; but (iii) no one really believes the fiction.

Most solutions attempt to resolve the paradox by denying or modifying one of the three conditions. But what if we approach this in a different way? What if we suggest that our emotional response to *Black Panther* is rooted in the film's (knowingly) fictional representation of our real world? In other words, we know *Black Panther* is fictional, yet we also know that the issue of racism is real. So, our interpretation of *Black Panther* depends on our knowledge of both the fictional elements of the story and the issues of the real world the story represents. Put another way, our interpretation (our emotional response) is rooted in an epistemology that requires both fictional and real knowledge. Let's see how this works.

"The Illusions of Division Threaten Our Very Existence."

Fictional works such as *Black Panther* offer viewers a unique type of what Gaile Pohlhaus calls an *epistemic resource*: a resource that individuals draw upon in order to know.[2] Pohlhaus tells us that epistemic resources are collectively held and maintained by an epistemic community, a community of knowers (which given the internet, can be very large).[3] Above all, our epistemic resources need to "answer to our experiences."[4] Pohlhaus lists three potential kinds of epistemic resources: (i) language to express experience; (ii) concepts used to understand; and (iii) criteria to judge the usefulness of a resource.[5] Pohlhaus acknowledges, though, that there may be other kinds of resources beyond these three.[6] For our purposes, we need to answer two questions about fictions and epistemic resources: (i) Do the resources we gain from fictions like *Black Panther* answer to experience? And, (ii) What kind of epistemic resource are they, if they are not language, concepts, and criteria?

When we consume a fictional work, it is possible to learn from and use elements of the work to better interpret the world. Not every aspect of a fictional work is going to be answerable to or directly reflect our experiences in the real world. I have not personally met a Klingon warrior, for example, attended Hogwarts School of Witchcraft and Wizardry, or wielded one of Okoye's spears. Fiction is enjoyable because it can reach beyond what is possible of the real world, and is not confined by it, like everything Shuri creates in her lab. But fiction also contains elements that are salient to us in the real world, that correlate to what we experience or what we know, like Killmonger's Oakland upbringing and his understanding of slavery and oppression. Given this, we can understand *Black Panther* as providing viewers with *epistemic resources*, because it gave (and continues to give) many people new conceptual tools to understand and communicate about Black and particularly African American culture and experience, whether the viewer is Black or is not. Thus, the film serves as an important addition to the epistemic resources that we all share and collectively maintain.

Even if it's just the moral of the story – such as the racial politics of *X-Men*, or the allegory of American liberalism in *Star Trek: The Original Series* – fictional works like *Black Panther* can add to our understanding of real-world phenomena even if they don't directly represent them. In this sense, fictions *do* seem to answer to our experiences. We draw upon them in order to better understand and interpret the world, and therefore gain epistemic resources. The question of what *kind* of resources fictions offer – if not language, concepts, and criteria – however, requires a longer response.

"The Real Question Is: What Are Those?"

Fictions are tied up with the imagination; a fiction asks us to use our imagination to mentally represent to ourselves what the fiction is describing or showing.[7] It asks that we employ a "suspension of disbelief," treating the fiction as though it's true and allowing ourselves to be immersed in it. Often, we know that what we subsequently imagine really could be (or could have been), if circumstances in the real world were different. Fictions in this sense ask us to imaginatively entertain *possibilities*, particularly possibilities pertaining to oneself.[8]

This is what Catriona Mackenzie calls "imagining oneself otherwise."[9] She argues that the cultural imagery that constantly surrounds us – including popular fictions – informs our imagination through constructing a repertoire of imagery upon which we draw when we want to imagine something.[10] The subsequent imaginings have *affective* power: products of our imagination are highly evocative, causing emotional reaction and deep engagement with their content.[11] Mackenzie argues that we use imaginative practices to develop our identity and self-conception, through what we imagine of ourselves.[12]

For example, *Black Panther* asks us to imagine a world in which an African nation (Wakanda) did not suffer invasion, colonization, enslavement, and plundering of its resources by a white Western nation. It further asks us to imagine that, given the ability to self-determine, this country uses its rich natural resources to further develop itself and promote its people, becoming the richest, healthiest, and most technologically advanced nation in the world. Importantly, *Black Panther* also asks us to imagine that this nation was able to maintain close connection to and honor its cultural traditions, unfettered by Western interference. People in the real world where there is no Wakanda can therefore imagine what might have been, or what could be, had there been an alternate world history. Black audience members have the opportunity to unite themselves around Wakandan identity, building the film's positive representation of Black identity into their self-conception. The affectivity of fiction-based imaginings makes this possible.

The hypothetical nation of Wakanda also gives audience members of other racial groups a different or new perspective on Black identity, which can aid their interpretations of the real world. That is, the film challenges racist stereotypes of Black people and culture, suggesting that the absence of a Wakanda-like nation in the real world is due to Western interference rather than some inherent problem in Black societies. Through the imaginative engagement with fiction, and the affective power of the imaginings, we glean new meanings, significance, and understanding of things in the real world. The epistemic resources we gain from fictions are not language, concepts, or criteria, but another sort of resource – *a narrative meaning-making practice* that involves imagining what the fiction tasks us with imagining. With resources like *Black Panther* improving our collection of epistemic resources, we are able to go forth and interpret the world *better* than we would have before.

Black Panther is a good epistemic resource by Pohlhaus's definition because the film offers nuanced representation of Black culture, experiences, attitudes, and possibilities, unlike stereotypical representations, and therefore improves our interpretations of the world. *Black Panther* also reflects aspects of reality and is answerable to experience, despite being fiction, because of the team of majority Black creators who constructed the fiction. Therefore, when the film is used as a tool through which to interpret the world, the interpretation is less likely to be inaccurate or incorrect because of faulty resources. Fictions like *Black Panther* frame aspects of the real world into their own narrative (like Oakland in 1991 or the history of slavery), and when we consume such a fiction we are able to use that framing to better interpret and understand those aspects of the world that the fiction represents. In that sense, consuming films like *Black Panther* is an epistemic activity as well as an imaginative one. It is an activity of adding to our epistemic resources, both personally in one's own mind, and as a collective of people who now have that resource available

to them. Imaginative engagement in the fiction is not merely about enter-
taining possibilities or building one's self-conception, it is also about supporting our ability to interpret the world well.

So, let's consider exactly what framing and representations *Black
Panther* offers to its audience. That way we can see how it's not just a good
epistemic resource, it's also an example of how an audience's interpretation requires real and fictional knowledge.

"What Can a Nation of Farmers Offer the Rest of the World?"

First and foremost, *Black Panther* challenges the stereotypical depictions
of Black people, nations, and culture. Its characters offer abundant and
aspirational imaginative possibilities for Black members of the audience.
Few other popular fictions represent a Black man as a respected king of a
wealthy nation, or Black female characters as able to influence the narrative beyond being a love interest, let alone as revered warriors like the
Dora Milaje. Shuri's character offers a rare representation of a young
Black woman as a technological genius and inventor (arguably more
capable than Bruce Banner and Tony Stark), afforded the resources and
freedom to pursue her interests.

That these representations transgress stereotypes does not mean they
are impossible in the real world. Black people are well aware that their
community members are capable of the excellence that the characters
display. But in an oppressive culture that largely limits the fictional representation of Black people to stereotypes, *Black Panther* provides legitimacy and feasibility to imagining this excellence of oneself. That is, *Black
Panther* makes it easier for a Black viewer to imagine that they could be
king, or a warrior woman, or a tech genius, because they can use the depictions in the film as a reference point that says, "Here, imagine this!" We
can see that *Black Panther* has exactly this effect in the social media posts
about young Black girls dressing up as Dora Milaje and children roleplay-
ing as King T'Challa that flooded the internet after the film's release.[13]

So *Black Panther* allows the audience members who identify with it to
imagine a range of possibilities for themselves. But it has another
function: to represent Black and African American experience to
everyone. The film offers imaginative possibilities, but it also tries to
reflect current reality through fictional representation. The depiction of
Black women in the film is especially notable, as even though T'Challa
is the protagonist, he is flanked by powerful Black women who are different in their motivations and values, and who drive the narrative forward in their own ways. Even their visual depiction is significant.
Okoye's head is close-shaved throughout the film, and in the one instance that she wears a wig, she is vocal in her displeasure and throws

the wig at an opponent. Calling the wig a "ridiculous thing" flies in the face of Western demands of how Black women should perform femininity and beauty. Similarly, Nakia and Shuri maintain their natural hair, styled in ways designed to accentuate its qualities, not stymie its abundance. After decades of not seeing Black women with natural hair on screen, the recent cultural return to natural hair in defiance of white supremacy's expectations is reflected and validated in the fictional characters.

Importantly, the representation that the film offers, and that Black and African American people can identify with, isn't one-dimensional, but plural and nuanced. Usually, Black representation in film is limited to one, maybe two characters. In *Black Panther*, the vast majority of characters are Black (and played by Black actors) which means the characters can have narratives that are not driven by their relations to white characters and whiteness. "Nearly every touch, every relationship, and every plot point [that] exists is to build connection between Black characters."[14]

For example, the ideological tension between T'Challa and Killmonger reflects the disagreement between those who have been able to live largely free of systemic oppression, and those who have suffered it. Killmonger's alienation from his Wakandan origins mirrors many Black American's experience of being caught between two cultures: African heritage and American present. T'Challa, on the other hand, has never been removed from his ancestral home. T'Challa, though a Black man, has not experienced first-hand the racial oppression to which Black people are subjected in the United States, unlike Killmonger. In this sense, Killmonger's narrative reflects the real-world struggle of being Black in the United States, depicting rage at the injustices incurred, and a desire to secure reparations.[15]

Nakia has a similar tension with T'Challa and Okoye. Nakia has experienced much of the world outside Wakanda. Though she does not experience structural oppression in the way Killmonger has, the suffering and oppression of Black populations outside Wakanda troubles her deeply. We first see her undercover on a mission to stop the kidnapping and forced sexual slavery of African women – a real-world problem – and the film reiterates that she is well-traveled. She says to T'Challa, "I've seen too many in need just to turn a blind eye. I can't be happy here knowing that there's people out there who have nothing."

Nakia is offered the queenship at T'Challa's side, but she believes the role and Wakanda's traditions would restrict her ability to help the rest of the world. Urging T'Challa to open Wakanda to the world and share its resources, she says "We could provide aid and access to technology and refuge to those who need it." Though Killmonger is the antagonist, Nakia approximates his outlook – that Wakanda in its wealth should allow access to its resources in order to lift people oppressed in other parts of the world.

Similarly, after T'Challa loses the duel with Killmonger, Nakia challenges Okoye's decision to stay and serve the new king. When Nakia suggests a plan to overthrow Killmonger, Okoye is taken aback, believing her
duty is to the institutions of her country and therefore the throne. Nakia,
however, believes that she can best serve her country by ensuring its better
future, even if doing so contravenes tradition and law. When Okoye tells
her, "Serve your country," Nakia responds, "No, I *save* my country." This
exchange reflects a political dilemma in the real world: often, oppressed
populations such as Black Americans have to break the law or conventions
in order to effectively resist their oppression. Some find this an uncrossable
boundary, but others believe society's laws are inherently corrupt because
of the unjust system that created them.

Black Panther does more than one thing, representationally. Like all fictional works, it is open to varying interpretations of its content, and the
accounts of what *Black Panther* does for its audience are not unanimous.
Significantly, the film combines real and fictional elements to inspire dif-
fering reactions. For example, the tension between T'Challa and Killmonger
left some Black audience members struggling to empathize with the story's
hero over its villain. Steven Thrasher for *Esquire* wrote, "I couldn't get
myself to root against its antagonist ... [and] I found its ending political
message far more conservative than the revolutionary possibilities teased
by anything with 'Black' and 'Panther' in the title."[16] While Killmonger is
positioned as the antagonist, his aspiration to liberate Black people globally, and the sense of injustice he feels, often approximates the experience
of Black people in the real world better than T'Challa's attitude of preserving peace. Moreover, Killmonger is the main African American
character in the film. Though his heritage is Wakandan, his character
shares the cultural and national background of many of the film's viewers,
whereas T'Challa has always been rich, powerful, and physically *safe*.
Killmonger has experienced the same precariousness in life as many of the
film's Black audience members, "searching for an intact Black body, only
to be largely rejected."[17] Some Black moviegoers therefore found themselves rooting for the 'villain', because he was a closer representation of
themselves.

T'Challa's characterization might be further criticized for upholding the
white colonialist value of passivity and peacefulness in Black people,
designed to minimize Black retaliation to injustice. Black anger, particularly Black women's anger, is culturally demonized as less valid and justified than white anger.[18] In this respect, the ultimate victory of T'Challa's
peaceful ideology is less revolutionary than some Black audience members
would have liked. Moreover, Agent Ross's deterministic account of
Killmonger – that he is doomed to reproduce the destructive habits of his
training and country – could be interpreted as a pessimistic representation
of radical Black politics. Killmonger's efforts to secure resources to liberate
Black populations isn't equivalent to the United States' methods of

destabilizing foreign powers for its own gain. Suggesting otherwise through Killmonger's narrative glosses over the initial motivation of his actions: the profound oppression of Black people and culture by Western powers.

Varying interpretations do not mean that *Black Panther* does a poor representational job. Quite the contrary, *Black Panther* is a film that can elucidate a multitude of Black peoples' experiences and perspectives. The variety of interpretation allows for nuanced discussion about real-world issues through the lens of the film – a practice of using the epistemic resources *Black Panther* gives to viewers. Epistemic resources do not need to serve a particular viewpoint, and in fact they should not stray towards only one understanding of the world. To be valuable, an epistemic resource needs to add to our tools of understanding in some meaningful way. *Black Panther* does this, partly because it can have conflicting interpretations.

So, even though *Black Panther* is a good epistemic resource, we, as audience members and knowers, have been ill-served by the fictions that came before it, which gave us faulty, stereotypical resources to understand and interpret Black and African American experience. In turn, Black and African American people have been ill-served by previous fictions, as their experience and realities have suffered misinterpretation and stereotyping partially through the fictions in our cultural repertoire. Therein, I suggest, lies an injustice of an epistemic nature.

"We Must Right These Wrongs."

Just as epistemic resources help us to better interpret the world, the absence of certain resources can lead to poor interpretation or misunderstanding of aspects of the world. Importantly, *Black Panther* was released to a cultural climate in which the representation of Blackness in fiction was severely restricted, and largely remains so, as Anthony Mackie noted. Where *Black Panther* improves our epistemic resources, minimal and stereotypical Black representation worsens them, and as such perpetuates the social and structural oppression of Black people and communities.

When racism and sexism lead to poor or scant epistemic resources suited to interpreting the world, what Miranda Fricker calls an "epistemic injustice" is committed.[19] This kind of injustice targets those subject to it in their capacity as knowers along the same lines as social identity prejudices, such as racism, sexism, ableism, and so on.[20] Marginalized knowers who are victims of epistemic injustice find it difficult to be believed when they should be, or to make their experiences salient to others through language and culture.[21] As I've described, one way to make experiences salient to others is to produce fictions like *Black Panther*, which represent experiences and offer the epistemic resources to allow knowers to correctly interpret experience. The historic lack of adequate resources for interpreting and understanding Black culture, possibilities, and experience, leads to these aspects of living as a Black person in the world becoming obscured or poorly understood by other people. Moreover, because the resources available to understand Black lives are largely stereotypical or derivative, so too is much subsequent understanding of Black culture and experience.

The right kind of fiction can help alleviate this sort of epistemic injustice by providing better epistemic resources for interpreting the world and allowing marginalized individuals to articulate their experiences through the fiction, for others to understand. *Black Panther* in this sense is a case of epistemic *justice*. It provides plentiful and rare representation which was produced by a majority Black creative team. It uses the fictional medium of film to contribute to our epistemic resources and improve collective understanding of Black people's experience and possibilities. While all the work to alleviate the epistemic injustice done to Black and African American populations is certainly not complete, *Black Panther* and fictions like it are part of the remedy. One can only imagine, given all that's transpired in the real world since *Black Panther*'s release, what elements the *Black Panther* sequel will incorporate with regard to real and fictional knowledge. Will it continue to seek epistemic justice? Will it show a world (not just the Wakandan nation) where Black lives matter? Will we see the effects of Shuri's and Nakia's outreach efforts? And how will the sequel deal with Chadwick Boseman's/T'Challa's death? Indeed, this returns us to the paradox of fiction. We know Chadwick is gone and we know his depiction of T'Challa is too. Yet the Black Panther, whoever it ends up being, must live on, especially in our imaginations.

Notes

1. BreAnna Bell, "Actors on actors: Anthony Mackie & Daveed Diggs (Full Conversation)," *Variety*, June 28, 2020, at https://variety.com/video/actors-on-actors-anthony-mackie-daveed-diggs-full-conversation/#!.
2. Gaile Pohlhaus, Jr., "Relational knowing and epistemic injustice: Toward a theory of willful hermeneutical ignorance," *Hypatia* 27 (2012), 716.
3. Pohlhaus (2012), 716.
4. Pohlhaus (2012), 718.
5. Pohlhaus (2012), 718.
6. Gaile Pohlhaus, Jr., "Varieties of Epistemic Injustice," in Ian James Kidd, José Medina, and Gail Pohlhaus, Jr. eds., *The Routledge Handbook of Epistemic Injustice* (New York: Routledge, 2017), 16.
7. Kendall Walton, *Mimesis as Make-Believe* (Cambridge, MA: Harvard University Press, 1990), 19.
8. Catriona Mackenzie, "Imagining Oneself Otherwise," in Catriona Mackenzie and Natalia Stoljar eds., *Relational Autonomy: Feminist Perspectives on Autonomy, Agency, and the Social Self* (Oxford: Oxford University Press, 2000), 132.

9. Mackenzie, 126.
10. Mackenzie, 126.
11. Mackenzie, 126.
12. Mackenzie, 133.
13. Walter Thompson-Hernández, "'Black Panther' cosplayers: 'We're helping people see us as heroes,'" *The New York Times*, February 15, 2018, at https://www.nytimes.com/2018/02/15/style/black-panther-movie-cosplay.html.
14. Steven Thrasher, "There is much to celebrate – and much to question – about Marvel's *Black Panther*," *Esquire*, February 20, 2018, at https://www.esquire.com/entertainment/movies/a18241993/black-panther-review-politics-killmonger.
15. Thrasher.
16. Thrasher.
17. Thrasher.
18. bell hooks, *Killing Rage: Ending Racism* (New York: Henry Holt and Company, 1995), 14.
19. Miranda Fricker, *Epistemic Injustice: Power and the Ethics of Knowing* (New York: Oxford University Press, 2007), 1.
20. Fricker, 4.
21. Fricker, 155.

PART IV
Vibranium

16

When Tech Meets Tradition
How Wakandan Technology Transcends Anti-Blackness

Timothy E. Brown

Black Panther was more empowering for me than I thought it would be. Here we had a mainstream film about an ultra-advanced African nation, set in Marvel's mostly white cinematic universe. And there I was, watching this Africanfuturist film on opening day, in Seattle's famous Cinerama theatre, a Black nerd surrounded by white nerds. It was surreal to think that this audience would accept or even embrace stories that center on Africa or Africans. As I have written elsewhere,[1] if the film didn't live up to their expectations – as a watershed moment for Black representation in futurist blockbuster films[2] – I would be responsible for explaining to my white friends what happened.

After all, the unfortunate truth is that science fiction often excludes Black people. What's more is that even when we are included, it isn't clear how Black people *arrive* in the future. Representations of us seem distinctly "post-racial," disconnected from the messy histories and lived traumas of colonialism, diaspora, and the transatlantic slave trade. This disconnect is troubling. Representations of the future will inspire the next generations of scientists, engineers, and designers who will shape our future – Star Trek's communicators and Personal Access Display Devices (PADDs) are today's smartphones and tablets. But it's not clear if Black Americans ever receive the kind of reconciliation and support they deserve.[3] As more technologists and scholars push us to transcend humanity's current limitations, to become "posthuman," several questions remain. Will Black people be included in this transhumanist future? What role would they play if they were, and what form and flavor would our cultures take?

Black Panther and Philosophy: What Can Wakanda Offer the World?, First Edition. Edited by Edwardo Pérez and Timothy E. Brown.

Black Panther, even with the deep problems in how it represents Black American men,[4] grapples with messy histories directly, in plain sight of white audiences. The motivations and struggles of the characters Shuri and Erik "Killmonger" Stevens, in particular, show us how *Black Panther*'s blend (or collision) of Africanfuturism and Afrofuturism is meant to teach us how our memories of the past (as painful as they are) must connect with our visions of the future. In this way, *Black Panther* is an introduction to how Africanfuturism pushes back against the more naïve transhumanist visions in a way that allows us to at least begin to imagine a future that has confronted its past, filled with technologies that we are a part of.

Are There Black People in the (Transhumanist) Future?

In 2017, the artist Alisha Wormsley installed the words "THERE ARE BLACK PEOPLE IN THE FUTURE" on a billboard in Pittsburgh's East Liberty neighborhood. Wormsley's installation was just the most recent iteration of artist Jon Rubin's *The Last Billboard* project, featuring a rotating series of artists sharing similarly impactful (or otherwise cryptic) messages. These simple words, especially, are both reassuring and affirming. After all, our past and current technologies exclude or actively target Blacks, and media representations of the future so often either exclude Blacks or push us to the margins. These words were also, apparently, controversial. Eve Picker, the landlord who owned the building and the billboard space, was "contacted by a number of people in the local community who said that they found the message offensive and divisive."[5] This, she concluded, was against the tenants' lease agreement "that states the billboard cannot be used for items 'that are distasteful, offensive, erotic, [or] political,'" and so she forced the project to take the message down from the billboard. Fortunately, an outpouring of public support in response, across social media and in Picker's email inbox, pushed her to reverse her decision.

But why were these words so controversial in the first place? Why would anyone take them to be offensive? Perhaps this follows a similar logic to the way that the simple phrase "Black Lives Matter" seems like a kind of favoritism of Black lives over white lives – such that some whites feel compelled to respond, "All Lives Matter." The very idea that Black people will play a role in humanity's progress, or even the idea that Black people will exist in the future, should be a truism. Yes, there are Black people in the future, and we need to say as much because it seems that people have forgotten. Instead, it is construed as polemical – perhaps as a type of "reverse racism," perhaps as a form of "attention seeking," or perhaps as just an unnecessary claim.

Black Panther presents a vision of a distinctly African future that not only affirms that there are in fact Black people in the future, but also gives us a glimpse of *how* Black people make it to the future and what kind of home we make there. Further, *Black Panther* demonstrates how humanity must grapple with past traumas and ameliorate present harms if it has any chance at building such a future. The promises of enthusiastic technology "thoughtleaders" and "transhumanists," like Elon Musk and Jeff Bezos, seem out of touch with communities of color entirely – the details of how we will reconcile many of the harms of the past are lost as noise beneath loud signals warning about colonizing space through commercial space-flight,[6] getting along with AI,[7] and extending our minds through brain–computer interfaces.[8]

What is transhumanism, and what does it transcend? According to an early version of the Transhumanist's Principles, transhumanists "strive to remove the evolved limits of our biological and intellectual inheritance, the physical limits of our environment, and the cultural and historical limits of society that constrain individual and collective progress."[9] The goal of many stripes of transhumanism, then, is (at the very least) two-fold: to overcome sickness and death, and to overcome humanity's physical and cognitive limitations through enhancement.

Let's look at a few claims and projects transhumanist thinkers have proposed. In "The Fable of the Dragon Tyrant," philosopher and self-proclaimed transhumanist Nick Bostrom characterizes death as a seemingly invincible dragon, terrorizing the world.[10] He cautions against accepting death and becoming complacent in our collective attempts to thwart it. If it is at all possible to extend life, we have a moral obligation to do so. Bioethicist Julian Savulescu – perhaps infamously – argues that we have a moral obligation to select for the best possible children if presented with the means to.[11] That is: when a person produces and selects a fetus to implant at an in vitro fertilization clinic, or when a person uses prenatal genetic tests to screen for so-called birth defects like Down syndrome, they ought to select for the fewest genetic defects. A number of disability rights scholars and advocates, Adrienne Asch most chiefly, argue that using prenatal genetic tests to identify "defects" in (and ultimately to abort) fetuses expresses a discriminatory attitude toward people with disabilities.[12] The philosopher Ingmar Persson (along with Savulescu) argues that we collectively do not have the moral capacities necessary to meet global challenges like climate change, poverty, or a global pandemic.[13] He and Savulescu argue that we should "morally enhance" ourselves – or use biomedical means of improving capacities for moral reasoning and decision-making. This might take the form of drugs that may increase empathy, reduce anger, dampen fear, in the hopes that we become more responsive to pressing moral issues. I have argued elsewhere that the push to morally enhance will likely burden Black people directly by reframing their warranted feelings of distrust, suspicion, and anger as moral deficiencies.[14]

A number of scholars, however, remind us that race and racism are embedded in our technologies. The aforementioned transhumanist projects fail without dealing with these. Kate Crawford, for example, remarks that artificial intelligence (AI) and machine learning (ML) has a "white guy problem."[15] Heralds of "the singularity" – or the moment when AI surpasses human intelligence – are all too often white men, and the technologies that would bring about the singularity are often created by teams of white men.[16] The technologies produced by these teams – in all likelihood inadvertently, but still perniciously – consistently malfunction for Black people. Technologists Joy Buolamwini and Timnit Gebru, in their *Gender Shades* project, tested facial recognition software from Face++, IBM, and Microsoft.[17] They found that this software misidentified Black women as Black men. Buolamwini created a spoken-word poem, "AI, Ain't I a Woman," to accompany a slideshow of facial recognition software misidentifying famous Black women, like Shirley Chisholm, Michelle Obama, and – yes – Sojourner Truth herself.[18] This artistic project links the experiences of Black women who fought for both suffrage and abolition simultaneously to the experiences of Black women fighting against technologies that erase their existence.

This is only the tip of the iceberg. Ruha Benjamin describes how our technologies coalesce to support anti-Blackness and white supremacy – sometimes inadvertently, oftentimes explicitly.[19] These technologies create what she calls "the New Jim Code" or technologies that make our inequities worse, all while seeming more objective or equitable than the systems they replace. The term "New Jim Code" is a reference to Michelle Alexander's *The New Jim Crow*[20] where she argues that classifying or coding Blacks as "criminals" has become a means of justifying discrimination, disenfranchisement, and a new form of slavery through prison labor. Alexander's term is, in turn, a reference to "Jim Crow," the ubiquitous and garish minstrel show caricature that stood as the symbol for early twentieth-century racial segregation law and severe disenfranchisement in the Southern United States. The New Jim Code, Benjamin argues, hides these inequities inside what Benjamin calls *anti-blackboxes*; the technologies seem race-neutral, but how they work is opaque and results in harms against people of color. Further, Benjamin, along with several others,[21] invites us to think of race *as* a technology "designed to separate, stratify, and sanctify the many forms of injustice experienced by racialized groups."[22] We can hardly think about chattel slavery in the antebellum South, for example, without thinking about the theories, techniques, and tools used to keep the slave trade running: from ships to carry slaves across the Atlantic, to chains to hold slaves in place, to pseudoscientific arguments meant to establish that whites are superior to Blacks (or that there are distinct races in the first place).

It is hard to imagine how it's possible to advance (or even transcend) humanity through the use of technology unless we acknowledge the histories, current practices, and possible futures of *technologized racism*. Without acknowledging these realities – that Blacks experience, but so many people of color do as well – transhumanists' promises and goals fall flat. After all, how can Black people get excited about the singularity when racist codes are embedded in the algorithms? How can Black people get excited about "transcending cultural bias" when it will likely mean leaving their culture behind? *Black Panther*, both the film and the more recent runs of the comics, does not ask us to ignore technology's possibility to harm or empower Black people. It does not ask us to abandon our identities and worries to understand it. On the contrary, *Black Panther* gives us opportunities to consider possibilities of the future through past traumas and harms we've experienced.

"You Savages Didn't Deserve It!"

Erik "Killmonger" Stevens pays a visit to the African artifact section of a museum. The museum director – a white woman – approaches him, clearly suspicious of his presence there, and makes an attempt to educate him on the origins of each of these artifacts. He, of course, doesn't need this education, nor is all of her information correct. Killmonger knows that one of these artifacts is not like the others – it is a Wakandan artifact made of vibranium, the most valuable material on Earth, and he's going to take it for himself. The museum director was already suspicious of Killmonger, or in his words, "You got all this security watching me ever since I walked in." Even a stopped clock tells the time twice a day.

The interaction between this museum director and Killmonger illustrates how visions of the future can be rooted in visions of the past, and how our distorted (read: anti-Black) visions of the past can distort (read: whitewash) our visions of the future. The museum director wouldn't even entertain the possibility that an old African farming tool was anything more than an artifact from a primitive time, made by primitive people. Her expression said it all: this primitive tool couldn't possibly be made from the most powerful material in the world; this suspicious-looking Black man couldn't know more about Africa than she does. Killmonger's dispute with the museum director, then, was not just a dispute over the facts, but a dispute over the authenticity of the artifact. In this moment, their dispute became a dispute over what can count as authentically African. We might think of Killmonger the same way, as a castaway artifact of Wakanda, possessed by foreigners.

Paul C. Taylor draws our attention to how disputes over provenance and authenticity arise when we evaluate African art, and how these disputes are driven by an interest in African history.[23] Some African artists participate in the artistic practices of modern Europe. They create art for the *artworld* through installations, galleries, collections. Others, however, create what Taylor calls "workshop" art, "anonymous masks, carved figurines, and the like"[24] – and these might be extensions of traditional artisanal practices, or they might be attempts to pass off modern-day objects as genuine historical artifacts. The more "traditional" African artworks – those artifacts displayed by museums for their anthropological or ethnographic significance – are sought after for their authenticity. No one wants a knockoff, do they?

They are also deeply politicized. Museums and the people who visit them may value traditional African art/artifacts because of what Taylor calls "aesthetic Africanism" – building on author Toni Morrison's language[25] – where "modern societies imagined themselves as modern in part by distinguishing themselves from the pre-modern, which they then located in societies with unfamiliar modes of social organization and different orientations to the world of technology."[26] Modern societies look even more modern when compared with supposedly pre-modern societies. In many cases our collective fascination with traditional African art reifies the expectation that African cultures are primitive, and it engenders an incredulous attitude about the intelligence of Africans broadly.

This incredulity is a common theme throughout the film. Take, for example, the moment Ulysses Klaue – Wakanda's public enemy #1 – reveals to Agent Ross that Wakanda is not just the nation of "shepherds, textiles, and cool outfits" he thinks it is. Instead, Wakanda is a technologically advanced nation with a mine of vibranium. "It's all a front," Klaue insists, "Explorers searched for it for centuries. El Dorado. The Golden City. They thought they could find it in South America, but it was in Africa the whole time. A technological marvel. All because it was built on a mound of the most valuable metal known to man – Isipho they call it. The gift. Vibranium." Ross, of course, questions his story, "That's a nice fairy tale but Wakanda is a third-world country and you stole all of their vibranium." Agent Ross, of course, has seen alien invasions and superhero civil wars; he also knows that T'Challa is the Black Panther. Yet he still, somehow, finds it hard to believe that Wakanda is anything more than a "third-world country."

Even Klaue, who has seen Wakanda with his own eyes, who knows how Wakandans use vibranium, is incredulous. In his face-off with T'Challa in South Korea, Klaue fires a shot using his prosthetic arm, a weapon made of stolen vibranium. T'Challa effortlessly absorbs the blow with his newly designed Black Panther suit and asks, "Where did you get this weapon?" Without hesitation, Klaue responds, "You savages didn't deserve it!" In his face-off with Killmonger in the scrapyard, Klaue admonishes his opponent, "You really wanna go to Wakanda? They're savages." Pointing to the symbol carved into his neck, a branding he received after stealing vibranium from Wakanda, he continues, "This is what they do to people like us." The incredulity of these white characters talking about Wakanda is a representation of the world's collective incredulity about African progress, about Black progress globally. This incredulity, this form of *Africanism*, is an attempt to confine Africa to its past and keep Black people (more globally) out of the future.

The Future Must Have Roots and Branches

In making the distinction between Afrofuturism and Africanfuturism, Nnedi Okorafor writes: "Africanfuturism is concerned with visions of the future, is interested in technology, leaves the earth, skews optimistic, is centered on and predominantly written by people of African descent (black people) and it is rooted first and foremost in Africa. It's less concerned with 'what could have been' and more concerned with 'what is and can/will be'. It acknowledges, grapples with and carries 'what has been.'"[27] We can see Killmonger in this description[28]: his ambition is to force both a global reckoning with anti-Blackness and an internal reckoning within Wakanda, to destroy both colonialism and Wakanda simultaneously, to force everyone to grapple with what is and has been. We also see Shuri more centrally in this description.

Shuri pushes the boundaries of everything, pleading with her brother that "just because something works doesn't mean it cannot be improved upon." And Shuri's imagination reaches far enough to influence so many aspects of Wakandan life. We see many examples in the film: a new panther suit that absorbs and reflects kinetic energy; kimoya beads that make it possible to drive cars remotely, provide range-unlimited communication, and stabilize otherwise fatal wounds; and mining carts that can transport vibranium more safely than before. Shuri, however, approaches her work with an open skepticism about Wakanda's rituals and traditions. Lord M'Baku – the "great gorilla," leader of the Jabari Tribe – protests leaving Wakanda's technological advancements in the hands of a girl who "scoffs at tradition." He has a point. She's the one who flips off her brother (the incoming king) in jest in front of their mother, the newly widowed queen. She's the one who demands that everyone just "wrap it up and go home" at T'Challa's coronation, just before the Jabari challenge T'Challa to ritual combat for the throne. She's the one who takes responsibility for Bucky Barnes, the winter soldier, the first "white boy she [fixed]" before Agent Ross – these outsiders are a threat to Wakandan interests. Shuri, however, grows immensely by the end of the film. She witnesses, through Killmonger's coup and attempted worldwide insurrection, what impact her technologies could have on the state of Blacks globally. That is, she learns the stakes of leading and fighting for Wakanda – of what her attempts to transcend could mean for Wakanda, for humanity, and for the universe (looking ahead to *Avengers: Infinity War*).

We have yet to see how much Shuri will grow in Marvel's Cinematic Universe, but in recent comics – both Ta-Nehisi Coates's *Black Panther* and Nnedi Okorafor's *Shuri* – we've already seen Shuri grow even more. Shuri takes up the mantle of Black Panther in T'Challa's absence, and when Thanos and his Black Order invade Wakanda, Shuri staves them off at the (at least temporary) cost of her own life. Her spirit takes a journey to D'Jalia – the Ancestral Plane where Wakanda's collective memory is housed – where her ancestors show her what Wakanda was like before the vibranium meteorite hit, before Wakanda's technology blossomed. They train her, and they bestow powers upon her: the ability to enter and exit D'Jalia at will, the power to hear ancient spirits that advise her (whether or not she wants their advice), and the power to transform into and travel as a flock of birds. Her ancestors give her the name "Ancient Future," a name that reflects both her greatest strength and also the weakness she must overcome to become the technical and spiritual leader Wakanda needs. Even if Shuri is stubborn to a fault, even if she wants to rely on her ability to make vibranium do as she wants it to, even if she wants to transcend the traditions of her culture, she knows (and must accept) that her knowledge and skills are rooted in and connected with traditions she has only yet begun to understand. Shuri – Wakanda's Ancient Future – unifies Wakanda's memories with its vision of and hopes for the future.

Technological advancement in Wakanda, then, is not just the result of ongoing attempts to transcend Wakanda's traditions: even given Shuri's rebellious attitude, even when Shuri grows tired of her ancestors butting into her affairs. Instead, the wisdom of Wakanda's ancestors – in the D'Jalia, passed down from monarch to monarch – is what allows Wakanda to move forward. This, it turns out, is central to the goals of Africanfuturist works like Coates's *Black Panther* and Okorafor's *Shuri*. The entire point is for characters like Shuri to confront characters like Killmonger: to make sense of how Shuri's technologies can exist in (or will fit into) a world made up of current and former colonies who need her technologies to lift them up. Wakanda doesn't just somehow pop into existence in the future, with no context or connections to its past. It stretches up like the branches of an old tree, but it can only stretch its furthest when it is well nourished through a network of deep roots.

Blackness as a Pathway to the Future

Media studies scholar Beth Coleman invites us to think of race as a "prosthesis," or "as a technology [that] adds functionality to the subject, helps form location, and provides information."[29] She likens this to the way a blind person might use a cane to feel their way around without sight, to interact with their surroundings. Embracing Blackness could help us find a way toward a more just future, to help develop more equitable technologies. With every new technology released – be it an AI-driven photo app or a self-driving car – we should ask, "How will this device impact Black people? Will it ignore them? Will it target them?" In these moments, Blackness becomes a probe used to stress test technologies.

African/Afrofuturist works like *Black Panther* help us calibrate our walking canes, in a way. Instead of taking it for granted that there will be Black people in the future, Killmonger's fight for liberation forces us to confront the possibility that we won't make it. Instead of pushing for progress for the sake of progress, Shuri's experiences (both of coming back from the dead, and of her fight against Killmonger) illustrate just how important it is to figure out how to leverage our turbulent past to give our technologies context, purpose, meaning. Wakanda and its people, then, can be a yardstick by which we measure the futures we dream up.

Notes

1. Timothy E. Brown, "Black Panther," *The Philosophers' Magazine* 81 (2018), 108–109.
2. Jacob Robbins, "'Black Panther' is a watershed moment in pop culture," *The Eagle*, February 16, 2018, at https://www.theeagleonline.com/blog/silver-screen/2018/02/black-panther-watershed-moment-in-pop-culture.
3. In the pilot episode of *Star Trek: The Next Generation*, "Encounter at Far-point," the omnipotent (but fickle) being named Q places Captain Jean-Luc Picard and his crew on trial for the crimes of humanity. At the very beginning of this trial, Lieutenant Commander Data claims that "in the year 2036, the new United Nations declared that no Earth citizen could be made to answer for the crimes of his race or forbears." While it is eminently important to protect individuals from being persecuted for harms caused by their forbears, any protections must also be accompanied by acknowledgment of the past harms of those forbears, as well as restitution or reparations to those harmed.
4. Chris Lebron, "'Black Panther' is not the movie we deserve," *Boston Review*, February 17, 2018, at http://bostonreview.net/race/christopher-lebron-black-panther.
5. Melissa Rayworth, "'There are Black people in the future' sign can go back up, says landlord, and ELDI speaks up," *NEXTpittsburgh*, April 5, 2018, at https://nextpittsburgh.com/latest-news/removal-of-east-liberty-billboard-sparks-reactions-across-the-internet.
6. Elon Musk, "Making humans a multi-planetary species," *New Space* 5 (2017), 46–61.
7. Elon Musk, "I hope artificial intelligence is nice to us," *New Perspectives Quarterly* 31 (2014), 51–55.
8. Sarah Marsh, "Neurotechnology, Elon Musk and the goal of human enhancement," *The Guardian*, January 1, 2018, at https://www.theguardian.com/technology/2018/jan/01/elon-musk-neurotechnology-human-enhancement-brain-computer-interfaces.
9. Alexander Chislenko, "Transhumanist Principles 1.0a," 1996, at http://www.aleph.se/Trans/Cultural/Philosophy/Transhumanist_Principles.html.
10. Nick Bostrom, "The fable of the Dragon Tyrant," *Journal of Medical Ethics* 31 (2005), 273–277.

11. Julian Savulescu, "Procreative beneficence: Why we should select the best children," *Bioethics* 15 (2001), 413–426.

12. See Erik Parens and Adrienne Asch eds., *Prenatal Testing and Disability Rights* (Washington, DC: Georgetown University Press, 2000) – esp., Adrienne Asch, "Why I Haven't Changed My Mind about Prenatal Diagnosis: Reflections and Refinements," 234–258.

13. Ingmar Persson and Julian Savulescu, *Unfit for the Future: The Need for Moral Enhancement* (Oxford: Oxford University Press, 2012).

14. Timothy E. Brown, "Moral bioenhancement as a potential means of oppression," *The Neuroethics Blog*, March 24, 2020, at http://www.theneuroethicsblog. com/2020/03/moral-bioenhancement-as-potential-means.html.

15. Kate Crawford, "Artificial intelligence's white guy problem," *The New York Times*, June 25, 2016, at https://www.nytimes.com/2016/06/26/opinion/ sunday/artificial-intelligences-white-guy-problem.html.

16. Roli Varma, "US science and engineering workforce: Underrepresentation of women and minorities," *American Behavioral Scientist* 62 (2018), 692–697.

17. Joy Buolamwini and Timnit Gebru, "Gender shades: Intersectional accuracy disparities in commercial gender classification," *Proceedings of the 1st Conference on Fairness, Accountability and Transparency*, PMLR 81 (2018), 77–91.

18. Joy Buolamwini, "AI, Ain't I a Woman?" YouTube video, June 28, 2018, at https://www.youtube.com/watch?v=QxuyfWoVV98.

19. Ruha Benjamin, *Race after Technology* (Hoboken: John Wiley & Sons, 2019).

20. Michelle Alexander, "The New Jim Crow," *Ohio State Journal of Criminal Law* 9 (2011), 7; Michelle Alexander, *The New Jim Crow: Mass Incarceration in the Age of Colorblindness* (New York: New Press, 2010).

21. See Beth Coleman, "Race as technology," *Camera Obscura: Feminism, Culture, and Media Studies* 24 (2009), 177–207; Holly Jones and Nicholaos Jones, "Race as technology: From posthuman cyborg to human industry," *Ilha Do Desterro* 70 (2017), 39–51.

22. Benjamin, 19.

23. Paul C. Taylor, *Black is Beautiful: A Philosophy of Black Aesthetics* (Oxford: Wiley Blackwell, 2016).

24. Taylor, 140.

25. Toni Morrison, *Playing in the Dark: Whiteness and the Literary Imagination* (New York: Vintage, 2020).

26. Taylor, 141.

27. Nnedi Okorafor, "Africanfuturism defined," *Nnedi's Wahala Zone Blog*, October 19, 2019, at http://nnedi.blogspot.com/2019/10/africanfuturism-defined.html.

28. This, perhaps, would be more Afrofuturist than Africanfuturist on Nnedi Okorafor's view, since Killmonger's reckoning centers the struggles of Black Americans.

29. Coleman, 194.

17

Vibranium Dreams and Afrofuturist Visions
Technology, Nature, and Culture

Alessio Gerola

SHURI: If you're going to take on Klaue, you'll need the best the Design Group has to offer. Exhibit A. Old tech.

T'CHALLA: Old?

SHURI: Functional, but old. Eh, people are shooting at me, wait, let me put on my helmet.

T'CHALLA: Enough.

SHURI: Now look at these [...] Oooh! The entire suit sits within the teeth of the necklace. Strike it.

T'CHALLA: Anywhere?

SHURI: Mhm. [...] Not that hard genius!

T'CHALLA: You told me to strike it, you didn't say how hard.

SHURI: I invite you to my lab, and you just kick things around.

T'CHALLA: Maybe you should make it a little stronger, eh? Wait a minute.

SHURI: The nanites absorb the kinetic energy and hold it in place for redistribution.

T'CHALLA: Very nice.

SHURI: Now strike it again, in the same spot.

Technology clearly plays a central role in *Black Panther*. From futuristic combat suits to flying ships, from maglev trains to powerful weapons to Shuri's lab, technological prowess is one of the things that distinguishes Wakanda from the rest of the world. And, as all of these examples illustrate, all of Wakanda's futuristic power comes from the substance known as vibranium, one of the most coveted materials in the Marvel Universe. In the films, Captain America's shield is the most iconic object made of vibranium. In the comics, vibranium appears in various weapons and suits belonging to an eclectic array of characters: Misty Knight's arm, Warpath's daggers, Echo's

Black Panther and Philosophy: What Can Wakanda Offer the World?, First Edition. Edited by Edwardo Pérez and Timothy E. Brown.

staff, and Doctor Doom's Doombots – including the Doctor Doom-created Trans-Human Robot, designed to protect Wakanda's vibranium mines.

As the film's prologue explains, vibranium (called isipho in Wakandan, which means "the gift") came from a meteorite that landed on the African continent millions of years ago. In *Black Panther*, we see an array of uses for vibranium. It's not just an object or weapon, it's a material with the capacity to absorb, store, and emit large quantities of kinetic energy (as Shuri demonstrates to T'Challa), and it has mystical and healing powers (as Agent Ross learned). Vibranium structures the Wakandan way of life, but is vibranium the essence of Wakandan prosperity? Does Wakanda's power really come from an alien substance? Or is there something else hidden beneath the Vibranium Mound?

Vibranium Vibes

To understand why vibranium is not the whole story of Wakanda's technology, we need to understand vibranium's role in Wakanda's culture. Fundamental disagreements about vibranium's existence and use drive the film's plot, but the mythology and history of vibranium are even more essential to understanding how and why characters like Klaue, Killmonger, T'Challa, and Shuri treat vibranium the way they do.

At the dawn of Wakanda's history, five tribes waged war against each other to gain control of vibranium. When Bashenga emerged as the first Black Panther by eating the Heart-Shaped Herb, coming to physically incorporate vibranium, four tribes pledged allegiance to the new king. Their peaceful cooperation led to a flourishing technological society, which isolated itself from the rest of the world in order to protect its stability and resources. The fifth tribe however, the Jabari, withdrew to the mountains and shunned the use of vibranium altogether, adhering to a more traditional lifestyle. According to the Jabari, vibranium-enabled technological progress makes the other tribes neglect Wakanda's original traditions. This is one disagreement regarding the use of vibranium the film illustrates, especially through the perspectives of M'Baku and Shuri.

M'Baku, as the current leader of the Jabari, sees the people of the Golden City as devoid of traditional values. In contrast to the Jabari, Shuri, the leader of Wakanda's design lab, embodies the technological ingenuity and excitement that the country of Wakanda represents as a vibranium-based futuristic society. As M'Baku says during his challenge ceremony: "We have watched with disgust as your technological advancements have been overseen by a child ... who scoffs at tradition!" (It's a fair point, given how Shuri complains about her ritual outfit). M'Baku and Shuri represent a deep-seated contrast between traditionalism on one side and technological progress and innovation on the other. Compared to Shuri, even T'Challa is more of a traditionalist, as the scene in her lab illustrates (not just with the panther suits, but also with T'Challa's sandals).

A second disagreement regards the issue of whether vibranium-based technology should be shared. We see this through the different philosophies of Nakia and Killmonger. Nakia is a spy who is first encountered thwarting the plans of human traffickers. Her humanitarian calling makes her wish that Wakanda would share their technical innovations to help the less fortunate rise from poverty and exploitation. Killmonger's goal is similar – he wants to use vibranium to change the world – but his position is more extreme, given that he wants to use vibrainum weapons to empower all subjugated people, giving them the means to overthrow their oppressors. Of course, while Nakia's position would actually help people (and it's what T'Challa ends up choosing to do), Killmonger's position would cause worldwide upheaval and violent revolution. Or, as Killmonger puts it, "The world's gonna start over." Certainly, the perspectives of Nakia and Killmonger highlight differences not just in philosophy but also in the social and political uses of technology. One central question in *Black Panther* is: what role should technology play with regard to aiding impoverished and/or oppressed peoples? Is addressing basic needs (including health issues) enough? Or should groups be armed so that they can gain control of their destinies? Or, would arming them make things worse? At what point does technology like Wakanda's become more of a problem than a solution?

The third and perhaps main disagreement about vibranium in the movie revolves around T'Challa's own inner struggle. At the beginning, the newly appointed king strives to uphold the historically isolationist values of Wakanda, agreeing with his father, T'Chaka, that hiding vibranium from the world is in the best interests of the country. However, the turning point occurs after T'Challa confronts his father's mistakes through Killmonger's revenge, which leads the king to forcefully reject his father's and his ancestors' choice ("You were wrong! All of you were wrong! To turn your backs on the rest of the world! We let the fear of our discovery stop us from doing what is right!"). Vibranium is not a treasure to hide anymore, but an isipho, a gift to be shared. T'Chaka and T'Challa thus form a third pair of opposing ideologies about the identity of Wakanda's technological culture: traditionally isolationist and self-caring on one side, and an open society willing to cooperate with the rest of the world on the other.

M'Baku and Shuri, Nakia and Killmonger, T'Chaka and T'Challa: Three pairs that represent as many different disagreements about technological power. Tradition against technological innovation, humanitarian aid against armed revolution, isolation and self-protection against openness and mutual help. What's significant is that these themes are found in our real-world debates about emerging technologies, such as gene editing and Artificial Intelligence (AI). Let's examine this further.

Is Vibranium Just an Instrument?

The chief concern throughout the film is what philosophers would call the *normative* status of vibranium technology, that is, what we *ought to* do with it, what its value is for us. If gene editing gives us the power to remove a hereditary illness, should we make use of it? If it gives us the power to determine a future child's level of intelligence or ability at sports, should we make use of it? In other words, through the different disagreements outlined in the previous section, *Black Panther* tries to make us think about the benefits and risks of employing vibranium – and by extension any advanced technology – to different ends. This boils down the underlying motive of all the disagreements to a single cause.

Essentially, vibranium enables incredibly advanced applications in medical, transportation, communication, and military technology. But if we examine it closely, the scientific details of vibranium's nature remain quite irrelevant to its functioning in powering various gizmos. Vibranium, from a narrative point of view, simply represents the power of possibilities and the disagreements that arise about the "great responsibilities" that follow from such "great powers."

Precisely because the narrative importance of vibranium is due to its exceptional power, the film frames vibranium through an *instrumentalist* view of technology. Technological instrumentalism views technology as a neutral instrument designed to achieve a given goal. Technology is simply a means to an end, and it is the value of that end that establishes the normative status – the value – of the means. For an instrumentalist, a given technology does not influence which goals we ultimately opt to pursue and which ones we don't. To put it concretely, guns are neither good nor bad according to an instrumentalist; they are just neutral tools that can be used for good or bad purposes. Similarly, for the characters in *Black Panther*, vibranium is neither good nor bad, it is just a marvelous material that enables incredibly advanced technology. The question, then, becomes how such advanced technology should be used.

This is why different characters treat vibranium differently, as an instrument – to wage war, to heal, to make life better. It's a tool that makes wishes come true (especially in Shuri's lab). Accordingly, vibranium and its debate mirrors the instrumentalist treatment of technology in transhumanism, a view that considers the integration of technology and biology as a way to overcome natural human limitations and (possibly) achieve superhuman status. For example, transhumanists may believe that, thanks to advances in gene editing, humanity will be able to stop aging, or that, by connecting with AI, we will reach superintelligence. The concrete technologies that would enable us to achieve these goals, and especially their social consequences and side effects, seem to disappear as we consider the consequences of these grandiose goals. By transcending its current limits through technology, silicon- or vibranium-based, humanity will realize the transhumanist dreams of technological transcendence. The movie's implicit treatment of technology, in other words, does not seem to be very different from transhumanism, in that both treat technologies as mere tools to realize any goal.

Technology and Culture

If vibranium plays the role of a mere instrument, then it seems puzzling how vibranium could also be the reason for Wakanda's prosperity. Why is this? Basically, because the story ignores how the particularities of vibranium-based technologies have influenced the cultural and political institutions of Wakanda. That is, the precise ways in which vibranium is extracted and used to manufacture products do not seem to bear any significant influence on the cultural and sociopolitical organization of Wakanda – the material itself and its actual properties did not affect the history of the country. This level of technological concreteness simply does not matter when we try to explain why Wakanda developed into the utopia it is through vibranium, because, as we have seen, vibranium is a transparent symbol of technological transcendence.

Technologies in the real world, on the other hand, invariably produce social and political consequences that are not always anticipated, and they often shape the way in which a society is structured. The textbook example about how artifacts influence politics is Langdon Winner's idea of the politics of artifacts, most famously presented in his description of the bridges designed by Robert Moses in New York.[1] These bridges were allegedly built on purpose to be too low for buses to drive underneath, thus preventing public transports used by the majority of the low-income population from reaching affluent residential and recreational areas. In this way, the bridges exerted an indirect social effect that selected who could reach a certain location and who couldn't. Technologies can also lead to changes in our values. For an obvious example just think about how mobile phones changed our work-related habits, as we are now expected to be available anywhere at any time. Returning to Wakanda, there is no hint to be found about how vibranium technologies might have influenced the history and culture of Wakanda as an advanced but peaceful and enlightened country.

Of course, vibranium did provide the motivation for Wakanda to isolate, as past kings wanted to protect its power and did not want to deal with the constant warfare that would have ensued as other nations tried to grab it for themselves. Still, Wakanda would have had the power to subdue any invader and conquer any other nation. The Wakandan Empire that Killmonger intended to bring about had always been a real possibility. So why didn't it materialize? If we just look at the metal itself, we find no answer.

In spite of its futuristic level of technology Wakanda is neither a technocracy, where a minor elite governs thanks to its exclusive access to technological power, nor is it an imperialist state that aims to dominate the world through its technical superiority. Vibranium could make Wakanda the greatest military power on Earth, but Wakandans seem wise and enlightened enough not to wage war on the rest of the world. *Black Panther* presents Wakanda as a peaceful, isolationist nation, where traditional culture and advanced technology harmoniously coexist – and this kind of prosperity cannot be simply the result of vibranium's incredible powers.

The reason, as we have seen, is that technological instrumentalism separates culture from technology. Nakia makes this clear when she insists that Wakanda could share its technology without essentially changing its way of life because it is "strong enough." If vibranium is just an instrument, sharing its power with other nations would not change Wakanda's culture, and Wakandans would be able to use the metal in the peaceful ways they always had. This seems naive and unrealistic, though. If another country gained access to vibranium weapons, we can imagine what the consequences might be for international relations. The truth is that technology, politics, and culture are always inextricably interrelated, and it's almost impossible to understand one without the others. If we are looking for an explanation of Wakanda's prosperity, then the most promising point to look at is the relation of its inhabitants with their technology.

Wakandan Technological Culture

If vibranium is just an instrument that stands as a symbol for any goals, working as a narrative device to move the characters into action,[2] then the secret of Wakanda's prosperous society must lie in the harmonious relations that its inhabitants developed between technology, nature, and culture. Wakanda's depiction as an independent African technological utopia where people live in harmony with nature and among themselves offers a celebration both of the fruits of technology and of traditional African cultures. By imagining what an African techno-utopia might look like, the movie tries to reimagine the relations between technology and culture. With this focus, the movie fits squarely within *Afrofuturism*. The term refers to science fiction and other works of art composed by authors of the African diaspora that imaginatively address issues at the intersection of science, technology, and Black futures.[3] By reframing technology through the cultural lens of diasporic experiences, Afrofuturist artworks often provide a great opportunity for reflection on common implicit assumptions about technology, and offer an inspiration for cultural critique. Through this blend of traditional cultures and technology, the *Black Panther* movie works as a powerfully imaginative thought experiment that explores the technological and cultural ramifications of an enlightened technologically advanced Afrofuturistic civilization.

So how does *Black Panther* achieve that? Perhaps ironically, it's vibranium's transparency that enables the imaginative explorations of *Black Panther*'s Afrofuturist design. By standing as a symbol for any goal, vibranium is not simply the material that Wakanda's technology is made of, it is the starting point of an experiment in speculative world building that leaves the field open for imagining futuristic technologies that blend in seamlessly with traditional designs. It is in this way that *Black Panther* provides sources of inspiration for ways to rethink how we non-Wakandans relate to technology ourselves.

Let's explore some of the lines along which *Black Panther* redraws the relations between technology and culture. The aesthetics of *Black Panther* blends traditional African designs with futuristic technologies. What is the cultural role of technology in Wakanda? In the Golden City, technology seems to be mainly about living a comfortable life while celebrating traditional African aesthetics through architecture, vehicles, and fashion. Organic architecture inspired many of the buildings we see in the Wakandan capital, which use wood and display design in the form of natural shapes and traditional African architecture (such as the famous Mosque of Timbuktu). Many of the flying ships are biomimetic in design, meaning that they resemble (mimesis) living creatures (bios), such as dragonflies and birds. Wakanda also features a large number of wearable technologies, such as the omnipresent kimoyo beads and the vibranium shields of the Border Tribe inspired by the Basotho blankets of Lesotho. Aside from clothing and accessories, technology is also embedded within intangible environments such as the holograms with which T'Challa, Shuri, and Ross interact at different points in the movie.

All the above examples point at two main features of Wakandan technology: first, the large consideration granted to the natural world and to the world of cultural symbols, which work as reminders of the fact that advanced technology does not entail the replacement of traditional values; and second, the materialization of these designs into concrete forms firmly roots futuristic technology into traditional shapes. A case in point of the second is represented by the remarkable absence of AI, a fact which bespeaks the concrete embeddedness of Wakandan technology. As an illustration, consider how Tony Stark, the American tycoon, imbues his Iron Man suit with the immaterial artificial intelligence Jarvis. By contrast, T'Challa's suit is embedded in a traditional-looking collar decorated with panther fangs, literally enveloping the King of Wakanda in vibranium – the substance that spiritually and materially constitutes his country.

Vibranium has a cultural and spiritual role that is more prominent than its strictly technological properties. Vibranium is a metal with a deep biological and cultural importance for Wakanda, and not just because the Great Mound, where it is currently mined, is a consecrated place. In the times following the meteorite's impact, vibranium influenced both flora and fauna. It originated the Heart-Shaped Herb that gave rise to the first Black Panther and his religious cult and political rule. In the comics, vibranium also altered the White Gorilla flesh, sacred to the Jabari. Vibranium forms the ground, the vegetal and animal life of Wakanda, and links this world to its people through their technologies.

It is true, though, that in all this technological spirituality vibranium itself tends to remain a transparent idol. However, there is still a Wakandan tribe that adopts a more cautious approach to technology, to the point of rejecting vibranium entirely. The Jabari shun the power of vibranium as they contend it contrasts with traditional Wakandan ways of life. Instead they opt to make use of wood-based technology, which they employ to reach remarkable levels of comfort. (Some speculate, though, that it consists of a particularly hardened variety of wood that has been influenced by vibranium). By rejecting vibranium on a cultural basis, the Jabari display the awareness, in contrast to Nakia, that technological change is impossible without cultural change. For the Jabari, adopting vibranium would mean an alteration of their lifestyle. They do not reject technology itself, just a particular form of it that they do not approve of. Here vibranium stops being a mere transparent tool, and it becomes the active object of reflection on the relations between culture and technology. The initial attitude of the Jabari towards vibranium was of utter rejection, but they are open to change. When M'Baku later joins the Tribal Council and the rest of Wakandan society, the Jabari come to embrace change and accept a compromise between traditional ways and vibranium technology.

What the World Can Learn from Wakanda's Afrofuturism

Wakanda is not only technologically advanced, it is also peaceful and almost utopian. If other countries had vibranium, it's quite likely we would have used it to make superpowerful weapons to try to conquer each other. Vibranium, however, did not provoke Wakanda into becoming an empire. So why did they restrain themselves, with such power at their disposal? Because, along with technological power, they possess the wisdom of how to employ it. They have developed a harmonious relationship with the technology created from vibranium, and they see it as a means of cultural expression rather than as a means of oppression. To achieve this wisdom, it is not enough to treat vibranium as a mere means to an end. We need to understand how artifacts and technology influence us; we need to use them in ways that do not betray but rather express traditions. By blending tradition and innovation, Wakandans understand that advanced technology must come with the wisdom to know not just how to use it, but also how to relate to it in shaping society and culture.

In light of this wisdom, it is then a little puzzling how, when Wakanda decides to open itself to the world, its rulers seem to think that their technological gifts will flow without altering Wakanda along with the rest of the world. As we have seen, from a narrative point of view, vibranium is just a place-holder for technological marvels, which the movie beautifully employs to reimagine the relation between humans and technology. These Afrofuturist visions open our minds to a harmonious coexistence with technologies, where they do not replace but rather integrate with and innovate traditional beliefs and our connection to nature. If Wakanda were to usher the world to a new stage of development it would not achieve it by exporting vibranium, as the movie would have us believe, but rather by inspiring us to think about how technology, nature, and culture can harmoniously coexist.

Notes

1. Langdon Winner, "Do artifacts have politics?" *Daedalus* 109 (1980), 121–136.
2. In narrative theory, such a literary device is sometimes called a MacGuffin, an object whose main purpose is to motivate the characters into action, but whose nature and characteristics have no or little further consequences on the actual story. For example, the Ark in *Raiders of the Lost Ark* might be considered a MacGuffin.
3. Ytasha L. Womack, *Afrofuturism: The World of Black Sci-Fi and Fantasy Culture* (Chicago, IL: Lawrence Hill Books, 2013), 8 (ebook edition).

18

Black Panther's Afrofuturism
Reconnecting Neural and Cultural Pathways

Michael J. Gormley, Benjamin D. Wendorf, and Ryan Solinsky

Black Panther presents an African cultural tapestry. Just think, for example, of the dress, makeup, and bodily marks borrowed from across a spectrum of different African cultures. In addition, there are references to *orishas*, the deities of West African religions, and there are narratives of loss and forced migration from African societies. The wide breadth of these African elements fit *Black Panther* well within Afrofuturism, a genre defined by its use and placement of people of African descent in the past, present, and future of society.[1] Beyond these cultural elements, as we'll see, *Black Panther*'s Afrofuturism employs water imagery and spinal cord injury as potent symbols of disconnection and reconnection.

Past and Future

Consider *Black Panther*'s opening: a child in Oakland asks his father to tell him a story – "Baba?" "Yes, my son." "Tell me a story." – much like a child in Africa would have centuries before. The past of Afrofuturism can be seen as two distinct and sometimes overlapping trends: African folklore and storytelling, preserved by enslaved Africans, and the African Diaspora's new engagement in the emerging literary genre of science fiction. The past is crucial for shared African cultural identity, in addition to its common usage in science fiction to explain how the setting of the story came to be.[2]

Black Panther and Philosophy: What Can Wakanda Offer the World?, First Edition. Edited by Edwardo Pérez and Timothy E. Brown.

Historically, Africans actively resisted enslavement throughout the Middle Passage, and they used a variety of cultural tools to explain, endure, and subvert their oppressive circumstances.[3] This resistance included utilizing West and Central African rhythmic structures and instruments to recreate African songs and influence the European and Christian songs they encountered. It also included bringing together complex literary and philosophical traditions, including proverbs, poems of the prolific *jelimuso* (the so-called griot tradition), and localized folklore taught to children as an element of community child raising as well as for establishing and maintaining social mores.[4]

This oral, sometimes written, tradition included fantastic and supernatural tales of bodily transformation, talking animals, and superhuman abilities. Put through the trauma of enslavement, African peoples in the Americas turned this tradition towards managing a new set of circumstances, and new narratives emerged. One of the most widespread and compelling examples of a new narrative directly addressed the struggle for cultural preservation. Africans wanted to stay connected, or reconnect, with the African continent. Thus emerged "Flying African" tales.[5] In these stories, the main characters had endured the Middle Passage and were experiencing extreme hardship or severe punishment in the Americas. In response, they abruptly rose up, levitated, and flew back to their homes in Africa.

The Flying African tales are more than just escapism; they are a source of hope. To fly is to connect, and return – a crucial skill affirming identity. Unsurprisingly, *Black Panther*'s Afrofuturism reimagines antebellum slavery society's flight fantasy as a powerful science fiction, T'Challa's Royal Talon Flyer. Indeed, *Black Panther* draws from a long tradition of Afrofuturist literature that is influenced by a desire to remedy the injuries of the past and reconnect people of African descent with the continent from which they've been severed.

People of African Descent in Science Fiction

From Afrofuturism's roots in the nineteenth century, people of African descent – authors like Charles W. Chesnutt, M.P. Shiell, Sutton E. Griggs, and George Schuyler – sought to engage science fiction literature, though they were frequently rebuffed by discrimination in publishing opportunities. In the early 1960s, Samuel Delany was among the first Afrofuturist authors, and his work opened doors for other African American writers in science fiction. More than any other writer of the time, Delany took readers to far-off planets and galaxies and wove complex, multicultural societies, placing people of African descent squarely in the center of future worlds and narratives, often as protagonists or crucial characters. This wasn't accomplished without a fight on Delany's part. Despite his widespread success by the late 1960s, his award-winning novel *Nova*, whose protagonist Lorq von Ray was half-Senegalese, was initially rejected as a serial publication. The publisher who rejected the work told a white author that "a technologically advanced black civilization is a social and a biological impossibility."[6] Less than coincidentally, by this time Jack Kirby and Stan Lee had recognized a growing demand for Black characters in their own work, having added the Afrofuturist leader and progenitor of the Black Panther narrative, T'Challa, to their Marvel Comics series in 1966.

In addition to Delany, we should note Octavia E. Butler, who profoundly influenced a new direction for Afrofuturism from the mid-1970s onward. Her works contained no less otherworldly or futuristic detail than did Delany's, but they more often grounded the narrative in the past, present, and future of Earth. Works like *Kindred* (1978) and the Parable series (1990s) were cautionary and prescriptive stories tied to the African American experience in the United States. Butler's Patternist series (1970s and 1980s) gives Afrofuturism a wide historical arc, tying ancient Egyptian societies to future worlds of people of African descent. More recently, Caribbean Afrofuturists like Nalo Hopkinson and Africanfuturists like Nnedi Okorafor have brought knowledge of African and Caribbean culture and folklore into the genre. These authors have added anti-colonialism to Butler's focus on racism and enslavement and have shifted Afrofuturism out of North America and into the Atlantic World.

It's no surprise, then, that a Black Panther story woven into the literary history of Afrofuturism includes themes of technological advancement, anti-colonialism, and reconnection. The narratives of T'Challa, Shuri, and Wakanda have been continuously remolded and expanded upon since the 1960s by artists who have been inspired by other Afrofuturist works.

Spinal Cord Injuries and Afrofuturist Reconnections

Wakanda's transformative neurotechnology is highlighted after Agent Ross suffers a spinal cord injury at the hands of Killmonger. When Ross remarks that "bullet wounds don't just magically heal overnight," Shuri notes that they do in Wakanda. Recovery from spinal cord injury not only highlights Wakandan tech, it also elegantly paints an Afrofuturist backdrop.

In the past, the spinal cord was thought of as a cable, with groups of wires (nerves) from the central processing unit (the brain) running down and out to the rest of the body. Severing of this central cable thus leads to varying degrees of muscle paralysis and loss of sensation, depending on which bundles of nerves are damaged. While this simplified physiologic construct served as one of the cornerstones of medicine's understanding since the time of the Egyptians,[7] in the past 50 years it has proven increasingly incorrect.

A better way to think of the spinal cord is as a minicomputer, processing sensory signals and distributing reflex outputs without need for detailed central processing in the brain. After a spinal cord injury, in the absence of descending signals from the brain, the spinal cord continues to modulate sensory information and tries to initiate reflexive movements. Nerves that fire together, wire together, and new connections can be extremely helpful in reconnecting and amplifying any signal that may be quietly whispering from the brain. However, with the loss of the overseeing central signal, this unregulated neural tissue can form functionally deleterious new connections. These new connections are likely culprits for many pathologic secondary complications of spinal cord injury, from nerve pain and muscle spasms, to bizarre losses of blood pressure control causing individuals to pass out or suffer hypertensive strokes.

Perhaps surprisingly, spinal cord injury illustrates the Afrofuturist threads that are entwined throughout *Black Panther*. Disconnected from established traditions, and often victims of repression if they practiced them in the Americas, African peoples suffered social and psychological trauma. Their forceful disconnection from the African continent required them to innovate and find creative ways to reconnect to their past.

The technology Shuri employs to heal Agent Ross is likely similar to the approach she took with Vision in *Avengers: Infinity War* when the Mind Stone needed to be removed. With Vision, Shuri intricately maps all of the neural connections he has formed to the Infinity Stone, then tries to reconnect them in the absence of the stone (allowing it to be safely removed and destroyed by Scarlet Witch). With Agent Ross, Shuri likely employed a similar, albeit less complicated, approach to heal his spinal cord injury. This glimpse into futuristic tech has wider implications beyond spinal cord injury, as it informs healing the African Diaspora. In a beautifully Afrofuturist way, the analogy of spinal cord injury in *Black Panther* offers a way forward, rebuilding vital connections to what was lost.

Black Panther's Afrofuturism: Flying Wakandans

Reading *Black* Panther as a progressive model of Afrofuturism illuminates the Wakandan leadership ritual, which features vibrant representations of diverse Wakandan subcultures and connects the people of Wakanda to their ancestors and land. Circulating in this scene are notions of Wakanda as a storied and diverse population that has maintained deep and potent rituals extending back to the first Black Panther and the country's unification. Naturally, T'Challa shows up to this ancient rite in essentially a "Bugatti spaceship," his Royal Talon Flyer. This spectacle serves as a profoundly Afrofuturist depiction of the Flying African folklore tradition.

Black Panther's Afrofuturism argues for a productive blend of tradition and modernity connecting the deep African history of Wakanda with its futuristic technology. Consider how T'Challa approaches the site aboard his Royal Talon Flyer, maintaining reverential focus and wielding an iklwa and shield, shoulders and chest adorned with painted panther spots. Technological additions to ancient rituals do not necessarily "scoff at tradition" or disrupt their power. A ritual's essence can remain intact among modern or futuristic processes. T'Challa perpetuates Wakanda by connecting the rituals of the past with the technologies of the present. In this way, there is resonance between Flying African folklore and Wakandan ritual.

The Flying African myth further resonates with an important turn in Afrofuturism's literary tradition. The genre spent much of its formative years in space, but these days Afrofuturist stories are returning to Earth, usually the African continent.[8] The first scene of the film allegorizes this return in the origin story of Wakanda: "Millions of years ago, a meteorite made of vibranium, the strongest substance in the universe, struck the continent of Africa, affecting the plant life around it," extending out like nerves or rivers. Luminous and blue, vibranium connects with the surrounding environment and organisms. In *Black Panther*'s Afrofuturism, Flying African folklore appears as science fiction motifs, first a space metal and then a futuristic aircraft, to establish agency in a post-colonial, global world.

Outside Wakanda, approaches to reconstructing neural connections severed through spinal cord injury seem clumsy and disjointed. The Wakandan approach stands in Stark (pun intended) contrast to those seen elsewhere in the Marvel Universe. In *Captain America: Civil War*, Colonel Rhodes suffers a similar spinal cord injury when his flying War Machine suit crashes to the ground, resulting in complete paraplegia. However, after traditional intensive rehabilitation, Rhodey regains his ability to walk not through some deeper healing or intrinsic neurologic reconnection, but by donning a robotic exoskeleton created by Tony Stark.[9] The fragility of this solution is on full display in the final battle in *Avengers: Endgame*, when Rhodey's exoskeleton suit is crushed by the rubble from Thanos's assault. Still broken, he pulls his paralyzed body through the water and debris to save his injured friends; his mind has reconciled trauma and can still act independent from technology.

Black Panther's Afrofuturism: The Duality of Water and Violence

Preceding T'Challa in the leadership ritual, delegations from Wakandan provinces, aboard river barges, approach the waterfall under which ritual combat for kingship is held. During this vibrant scene of ceremonial dance and music, the Dora Milaje stomp their vibranium spears to open a triad of drains that redirect water from the falls. Critically, diverting the river illustrates control over Wakandan identity, especially as technology detaches the ritual from seasonal chronology. The Wakandan origin story opening the film shows that combat has always produced unifying Wakandan leadership. The quelled river is the quelled internal strife of the provinces, presently manifest as ceremonial individuality moving literally and metaphorically toward unified Wakanda. The ritual combat then, like the story and drains, turns destructive violence to productive violence. The controlled river and controlled violence represent the, at least partial, reconciliation of continental African populations to water.

T'Challa triumphs in his first ritual combat, applying a rear triangle choke to M'Baku while hanging over the edge of the quelled falls. T'Challa seems not to notice his precarious position, raising his arm in triumph. He has rightful command of Wakanda, and the land itself poses no risk or danger. The symbolic connections and literal pathways of the river could not harm him, for they are indistinguishable from Wakanda and its king. T'Challa is able to channel M'Baku's destructive violence by imbuing their shared ritual with productive violence – and this process culminates in the Jabari standing with and as part of Wakanda in the final battle of *Avengers: Infinity War*.

The arrival of Killmonger brings a confrontation that cannot be redirected: a confrontation with deep, dark water that swallows and erases with silent violence. Killmonger is not a product of internally connective African rivers. Rather, Killmonger relates to Wakanda as someone separated by an ocean that cannot be flown around or redirected. His arrival in Wakanda signals the oceanic water that silences and entombs. In the film's first ritual combat, the waterfall is harmless, inconsequentially trickling by T'Challa – perhaps cinematographically stressful and foreshadowing, but water is just not a problem for geographically and philosophically insular Wakanda. In the second ritual combat, Killmonger throws a lacerated and immobile T'Challa over the falls into a deep and dark erasure, body and sound consumed by roiling water.

Killmonger brings to Wakanda the pain born of transatlantic African identity, and he remains disconnected from a productive global future by the oceanic trauma of the forced African Diaspora. Even after his defeat, Killmonger refuses T'Challa's offer to convert the destructive violence of the combat ritual into a healing process: "So you can just lock me up? Nah. Just bury me in the ocean with my ancestors that jumped from the ships 'cause they knew death was better than bondage."

Agency in Water

T'Challa witnesses how his father's isolationist philosophy offers nothing to African people elsewhere. The ability to control internal pathways is a confined and hidden sort of strength, critical to constructing agency, but it provides no connection with surrounding systems. T'Challa also sees the destructive violence born of the disconnect from home and attempting to maneuver a global space that provides no facility for connecting internal self with external circumstance. The power that oceans hold in the Diaspora cannot be diverted or worked around. The trauma of the forced African Diaspora is a persistent pain. As King of Wakanda, T'Challa must create an identity that has mobility in(to) the future by connecting Wakanda, the people of the Diaspora, and the world.

Black Panther restructures water and the philosophies it conveys as snow. In this image of water lies *Black Panther*'s purpose: to provide a method for connecting present African populations with ancestral Africa across the traumatic fracture of the forced African Diaspora to create a healed global future. M'Baku packs snow around T'Challa's lacerated and comatose body as he awaits the vibranium-infused Heart-Shaped Herb, shifting the ancestral connection from an insular Wakandan context to a watery, Diasporic, one. Unlike deep water, snow does not drown a person. Instead, it keeps the body alive so T'Challa may interrogate the past and act differently in the present with generational strength. Healed, T'Challa sits up and the snow falls away. While there is something to the Heart-Shaped Herb's meteoric powers, Afrofuturism becomes subtler, more presently tangible.[10] Wakanda's global presence is in Wakandan International Outreach Centres, built upon and converting trauma, and the Science Information Exchange offers knowledge – subtle and potent developments of *Black Panther*'s Afrofuturism. Consider that way the film positions spinal cord injury and repair among these storied Afrofuturist motifs to provide a notion of healing to the concept of return and connection.

Ultimately, *Black Panther* develops Afrofuturism's flight and water motifs as connecting African continental past, through the forced Diaspora, to a global future. By including this imagery, the film facilitates the reconciliation of persistent Diasporic trauma in global culture.

Okorafor, the Singularity

The *Black Panther* film is not alone in drawing together Flying Africans, agency in response to Diasporic water, and reconciliation with spinal cord injuries. The prolific and powerful Africanfuturist writer Nnedi Okorafor similarly constructs Wakanda with her *Black Panther*, *Wakanda Forever*, and *Shuri* comics. In addition, her autobiographical *Broken Places and Outer Spaces* details her process of relearning to walk after surgery for scoliosis left her paralyzed.[11]

Nnedi Okorafor is a singularity, a human and literary nexus of this chapter's themes and a critical point of connection between our reading of *Black Panther* and Afro-/Africanfuturism.[12] Okorafor fashions Shuri as a Flying African who constructs vibranium nanotech wings to soar about

Wakanda.[13] As in Coogler's Afrofuturistic *Black Panther*, technological flight does not disconnect one from culture. Instead, Shuri is deemed "Ancient Future" by the "empowered spirits bouncing about [her] mind"[14] and is a literal mediator between these ancestors and Wakanda's technofuturist identity. Okorafor similarly empowers the Dora Milaje to represent an already reconciled relationship to oceanic water as they fight Hydro-Man on the ocean floor.[15] Underwater, the Dora Milaje casually apply rebreathers and fight agilely with spears. They then freeze Hydro-Man solid, quipping that "we even have a weapon for nonsense like you."[16] In Okorafor's writing, the ocean poses no threat. The deep, entombing water is already reconciled and does not require further attention.

Okorafor promisingly closes her autobiography with words that are fitting for closing this chapter: "There's a strange feeling that I get before I go into the ocean. It happens at the point just before the ability to walk stops mattering and the ability to swim begins to matter. This is especially true when it's windy, motion not only in the water, but also in the air. The hypnotic ripples on the surface of the water, the swirling of the air, and the sinking and suction of the sand beneath my feet take my balance away. Before I can get to the point where I am swimming, I have to fall ... Before I fall, I throw myself in the water. Then I am flying."[17]

Notes

1. For deeper definition and analysis of Afrofuturism, see Alondra Nelson, "Introduction: Future texts," *Social Text* 20 (2002), 1–16, and Reynaldo Anderson and Charles E. Jones eds., *Afrofuturism 2.0: The Rise of Astro-Blackness* (Lanham, MD: Lexington Books, 2015).
2. Nelson, 2–8.
3. Great works on African examples of resistance include Sylviane Diouf ed., *Fighting the Slave Trade: West African Strategies* (Athens, OH: Ohio University Press, 2003); there are many hundreds more to choose from for African American examples, the earliest perhaps being W.E.B. Du Bois's *The Souls of Black Folk* (Chicago: A.C. McClurg & Co., 1903).
4. A seminal work on this subject, primarily focused on African folklore, is Jan Vansina's *Oral Tradition as History* (Madison, WI: University of Wisconsin Press, 1985).
5. Some great examples of the Flying African tales are found in Henry Louis Gates and Maria Tatar eds., *The Annotated African American Folktales* (New York: W.W. Norton & Company, 2017).
6. Gates and Tatar, 387.
7. The Smith papyrus is the first to refer to spinal cord injury as a "condition not to be treated," due likely to the physician's life being at risk if they were unable to heal a given malady.
8. Although there are important discussions differentiating between African and African American Afrofuturism, Black Panther likely falls into the latter category, though the differentiations lie outside the scope of this chapter.

9. Similar robotic exoskeletons are far from science fiction, and have been used for individuals with paralysis since 2011.
10. Killmonger's defeat happens by literally turning off vibranium.
11. If you prefer your biographies fictional, check out Okorafor's Venom story.
12. This chapter, focused on the analysis and impact of *Black Panther*, does not make distinctions between the many exciting and varied forms that constitute the African science fiction and fantasy genre, utilizing Afrofuturism as a collective term constituted by the permutations within the genre. We are arguing that Coogler's *Black Panther* is a text that draws into the total genre (certainly, to some of its subcategories) the spinal cord injury motif. Splitting those hairs is outside the scope of this argument and book. That said, Okorafor is an Africanfuturist. So in short, check out *Lagoon* (London: Hodder & Stoughton, 2004) and call Okorafor an Africanfuturist.
13. Nnedi Okorafor, *Shuri: The Search for Black Panther* (New York: Marvel Comics, 2019).
14. Nnedi Okorafor, *Broken Places and Outer Spaces* (New York: TED Books, 2019), 71.
15. Arguably the worst place to fight a villain composed of water.
16. Nnedi Okorafor, *Wakanda Forever* (New York: Marvel Comics, 2018).
17. Okorafor (2019), 92.

19

Wakanda and the Dilemma of Racial Utopianism

Juan M. Floyd-Thomas

In February 2018 numerous pundits and commentators rained on the collective parade of countless *Black Panther* fans, remarking that Wakanda was totally fictional and not a real African nation. In response, I hurled my disgust and dismay into the Twitterverse: "By the way, to all those who feel compelled to mention #Wakanda is a fictional place, thanks a lot – now do the same thing whenever you mention Gotham, Metropolis, Asgard, Camelot, Olympus, Oz, and Westeros!" Surprisingly, my tweet struck a nerve that sent waves to 1000+ folks who viscerally resonated with the statement I launched into the social media cosmos. My painfully obvious observation was a sincere, succinct pushback against a looming cultural prejudice that not only rejects the notion of attainable utopia but openly mocks the vision of an Afrocentric one as infinitely laughable. But, this dream has never been a laughing matter.

This dismissive perspective certainly forgets that the idea of an Afrofuturist utopia has been a mainstay in African American intellectual history long before Stan Lee and Jack Kirby's creation of Wakanda, most notably in the Harlem Renaissance. It also glosses over the significance of *Black Panther*'s depiction of Wakanda, which, as I see it, advances a complex notion of what I call "racial utopianism."

While borrowing cues from Thomas More's eponymous source, the concept of racial utopia is hardly a chocolate-covered version of the perfect social, legal, apolitical system depicted in that sixteenth-century English text. Instead, the ideology of "racial utopianism" has a more organic and ultimately pragmatic philosophical and aesthetic concern, emerging from the exigent circumstances and passionate longings of African diasporic peoples, than does the Eurocentric manifestation of utopianism. Such freedom quests have been the fact of Black life since the antebellum period. But, as Toni Morrison once stated, "All paradises, all utopias are designed by who is not there, by the people who are not allowed in."[1] This dynamic is what makes Wakanda's utopia so compelling.

Black Panther and Philosophy: What Can Wakanda Offer the World?, First Edition. Edited by Edwardo Pérez and Timothy E. Brown.

Seeking both relief and ultimate release from various modes of white supremacy, the quest for a veritable "promised land" is a yearning for the chance to live in an ideal society where each Black person could freely live to his or her fullest human potential. Since 1619, America has never realized that vision of itself as a society. But, in the Marvel Cinematic Universe (MCU), Wakanda is exactly the place where Black people can flourish. Yet, this creates a dilemma. On one hand, the Wakandan utopia provides a visionary example of how an ideal African nation could be realized – as if in response to Morrison, *Black Panther*'s Wakanda was designed by Ryan Coogler and company. On the other hand, Wakanda's utopia also serves as an implicit indictment of colonialism, suggesting that a Black utopia is only possible because Wakanda existed in strict isolation. Is this the case? Is Wakanda too far-fetched? Is it even worth dreaming about? What does Wakanda's utopian vision mean in the "real world"?

"This Never Gets Old."

Originally created by Stan Lee and Jack Kirby in 1966, Wakanda's utopian underpinnings are realized through the depiction of an idealistic vision of human society as a vibranium-powered Afrofuturistic version of Plato's *Republic*. In his history of Marvel Comics, Sean Howe notes Wakanda "reflected a growing interest in the collision of ancient civilizations and futuristic technologies."[2] They intentionally crafted T'Challa's homeland to exemplify its superior technological prowess as well as its truly enlightened views of human nature, cultural heritage, and equal opportunity. Even though white authors and artists like Stan Lee, Jack Kirby, Don McGregor, and Rich Buckler among others were crucial to the genesis of the title character and the evolving Wakanda mythology, it has been the influence of Black writers such as Christopher Priest, Reginald Hudlin, and Ta-Nehisi Coates that has shaped the contemporary vision of Wakanda that we know and love.

In its evolution from printed page to silver screen, historian Jelani Cobb contends that *Black Panther* "exists in an invented nation in Africa, a continent that has been grappling with invented versions of itself ever since white men first declared it the 'dark continent' and set about plundering its people and resources. The fantasy of Africa as a place bereft of history was politically useful, justifying imperialism."[3] From imperialistic wars to power-hungry insurgents to megalomaniacal supervillains to machinations by secret governmental agencies, the various struggles illustrated in the pages of the *Black Panther* comic books resonate with the larger narratives of race, slavery, and imperialism in modern world history, potentially undermining the very notion of human progress for which *Black Panther* is so famous.

Within the MCU, Wakanda's existence and significance was revealed several years before *Black Panther*'s release. Beginning with *Iron Man 2* (2010), Wakanda flickers on a world map. Later, in *Avengers: Age of Ultron* (2015), there is an entire sequence devoted to introducing Wakanda as a resource for the extremely rare, valuable element, vibranium, through the failed machinations of Ulysses Klaue. However, it is in *Captain America: Civil War* (2016) that we see a glimpse of Wakanda in the film's final scene, after Steve Rogers has taken his friend Bucky Barnes to Wakanda for refuge and recovery in T'Challa's care. Finally, in *Black Panther* and *Avengers: Infinity War*, we get a fuller picture of Wakanda's utopian society – from the force field that protects Wakanda from the outside world to Shuri's lab to the everyday streets that T'Challa and Nakia walk through. What is significant for the MCU's version of Wakanda is that it is isolated and insulated within their utopia, existing apart from the stigmatized perception of the "Dark Continent" Cobb notes.

Certainly, Wakandans are aware of the outside world's history of racism, slavery, and colonialism (thus the epithet "colonizer" is uttered with a particularly dismissive tone), but their knowledge isn't firsthand because they literally exist within their idyllic bubble. Nakia is an exception to this and so is Killmonger's father, N'Jobu, both having spent a significant amount of time outside of Wakanda (which made them sympathetic to non-Wakandans). Still, to Morrison's point, we must ask how (or why) Wakanda's utopia came into existence? As Killmonger observes to the Wakandan council, "y'all sittin' up here comfortable." So, is Wakanda a utopia because of who is not allowed inside – not just colonizers but also other people of African descent, too? Put another way, is it possible to expand Wakanda's utopia beyond its own borders?

"The Sun Will Never Set on the Wakandan Empire."

One of the ways we can examine colonialism is through the film's two main antagonists, Ulysses Klaue and Erik "Killmonger" Stephens. Klaue, a murderous European mercenary and arms smuggler, represents the film's more obvious and conventional villain. Much like his role in the *Black Panther* comic books, Klaue embodies a long history of European imperialism especially in the ways he callously violates African countries' national sovereignty, wantonly murdering their peoples, and literally robbing their most precious resources. In the MCU films, Klaue steals a cache of vibranium with N'Jobu's help – this is what gets explained in *Black Panther* and it's an act that influences several storylines seen in *Avengers: Age of Ultron*, *Captain America: Civil War*, and *Black Panther*, as well as offering key subtext for Disney+'s MCU television series such as *WandaVision, The Falcon and The Winter Soldier*, and *What If...?*. In *Black Panther*, we see

Klaue and Killmonger steal vibranium when they rob the Museum of Great Britain, and the filmmakers use this scene to signify the impact of colonial theft of the African continent based on the obscured legends and stolen legacies – Killmonger even broaches this matter with the museum curator just before she collapses and dies after unwittingly drinking a poisoned beverage. By the film's end, however, Killmonger, not Klaue, emerges as the true villain in his own right, representing the outrage of African Americans and confronting both the historic and contemporary abuses suffered in America and elsewhere across the globe.

What is especially fascinating about Killmonger's villainy in the film is his scheme to literally weaponize Wakanda, thereby totally reorienting the utopia. Indeed, the key solution to the problems Killmonger sees – his painful past as well as the oppression of Blacks around the world – is vibranium, which is clearly an "ideal" substance capable of just about anything imaginable. Once Killmonger's arrival on Wakandan soil is finally detected, it is Agent Ross who quickly recognizes the looming menace that Killmonger represents to the entire nation. Unlike his backstory in the comics, the cinematic incarnation of Killmonger (his code name as a CIA covert operative responsible for innumerable killings done in the name of American empire) is a product of US imperialism. So, Killmonger's takeover of Wakanda is highly symbolic of America's foreign infiltration and overthrow of independent African nations in order to destabilize and dominate them. This subversion of Wakanda's isolationist posture certainly would have happened if Killmonger had successfully flooded the globe with Wakandan undercover spies and high-tech weaponry. In the sixth episode of the first season of the *What If...? Disney+ series* --"What If... Killmonger Rescued Tony Stark?"--we get a glimpse at the sort of regime that might have been produced under Killmonger's reign.

We must also consider that Killmonger represents both sides of the utopian coin. He's Wakandan royalty by virtue of birthright, yet the film depicts him as being *apart from* rather than *a part of* Wakanda. Ultimately, as the film takes great pains to articulate, he was more like the "colonizers" than he ever was a Wakandan. As Killmonger sees it, the roughly 2 billion people of African descent who routinely face oppression, poverty, and adversity worldwide are owed the Wakandan technological and military might necessary to liberate them all. He believed that sending Wakanda's advanced weaponry, as opposed to its vast wealth, advanced technology, and cultural expertise, around the world was the key to saving the African diaspora. As such, Killmonger's idea of waging war and killing all those who stand against them is a wicked mode of retributive justice that should not be endorsed. And, to paraphrase T'Challa, it is not the role or duty of Wakanda (or any nation for that matter) to unilaterally play judge, jury, and executioner. However, when one looks at the bigger picture, T'Challa's and Killmonger's respective worldviews diverge because the former is defined by equity while the latter is rooted in vengeance. So, which embodies the freedom quest of "racial utopianism"? And, even if Killmonger's goal is to help the oppressed, can a utopia be rooted in vengeance?

"This Time, We're on Top."

These sorts of questions and issues take on a different dimension when we consider that *Black Panther*, while fictional, was written and filmed in the midst of the #BlackLivesMatter movement. Director Ryan Coogler clearly chose 1992 Oakland as the backdrop for the movie's prologue to illustrate the identity crisis of Black America's political consciousness. As the Black Panther Party's birthplace in the 1960s, Oakland is significant for being a hotbed of Black nationalist movements and political unrest. A generation later, the 1992 Los Angeles uprisings contextualized the film's narrative, situating Killmonger's early childhood in an urban neighborhood during a violent, turbulent era in which police brutality, gang warfare, drug abuse, and homicide were at a high point. Additionally, the filmmakers depict the "rachet" ghettocentric and righteous Afrocentric aspects of Black political consciousness of the early 1990s by juxtaposing hip hop icons Too Short and Public Enemy, two polar opposites on this political spectrum.

The film also takes great pains to establish the fact that Killmonger and T'Challa are cousins; this family bond is notable because it is not represented in the comics. T'Challa's steadiness is the product of a loving, stable, and empowering environment, whereas Killmonger's fury might not have been so prevalent had he not lost his family and sense of home. Clearly, Coogler's narrative decision to give the film's hero and villain a shared regal ancestry is significant – for Black Lives Matter activism, for colonialism, and for utopian visions, illustrating not just the opposite sides of these issues but, more significantly, that the opposing sides of these issues are inextricably linked. It is also important to recognize that Killmonger was raised simultaneously as a royal heir and a traumatized orphan of a murdered father and a vanished mother dealing with his misplaced grief, pain, and rage at the world. This dilemma reinforces these dualities – he's a prince and a pauper, a colonizer and a colonized, an insider and an outsider to a utopian dreamworld.

From this, we can also recognize that Wakanda's isolationism was never based on their hatred of other nations and people, but instead these measures were meant to safeguard Wakandans (as T'Challa and T'Chaka argue) and their powerful, precious resources from the "colonizers" around the world. What happened over the course of its history when Wakanda went into self-imposed seclusion was that its vanishing from the world stage was very much to the detriment of all other oppressed peoples in the African diaspora (as both Killmonger and Nakia observe in drastically different ways). This realization is a key source of Killmonger's deep-seated anger towards Wakandans. Inasmuch as Killmonger hates how white supremacy oppresses Black people on a world-historical basis, he also feels that he's been wounded and betrayed by the people of his own ancestral homeland. But, rather than seeing Wakanda as a model of "racial utopianism," Killmonger considers it as the basis of a dystopian empire.

"What Do You Know about Wakanda?"

Killmonger's outrage is compelling because he raises valid points. When Killmonger takes the throne and begins implementing his global take-over plan, he proclaims "the Sun will never set on the Wakandan Empire." In light of this declaration, a great realization occurs: in this superhero epic, characters are not quarreling about whether or not white supremacy exists but rather how best to attack and abolish it. Put another way, Jelani Cobb contends "there is a great deal that differentiates *Black Panther* from other efforts in the superhero genre. The film is not about world domination by an alien invasion or a mad cabal of villains but about the implications of a version of Western domination that has been with us so long that it has become as ambient as the air."[4] For this reason, the impact of watching this ideological conflict play out in the midst of this mainstream MCU movie (remember Marvel Studio films are still Disney productions after all[5]) is a truly remarkable feat.

Of course, much more than DC, Marvel (despite its Disney ownership) wants to engage audiences in discussions relevant to our contemporary real world. *Civil War* asks if heroes like the Avengers should govern themselves, and if they are heroes or vigilantes. *Infinity War* questions depletion of natural resources and decimation of the planet. *Endgame* as well as *The Falcon and the Winter Soldier* ask whether or not "The Blip" – a mass extinction-level event of cosmic proportions – was actually a good thing, and also delves into the psychology of "survivor's guilt" and the consequences of coming back after a five-year absence (which *WandaVision* and *Spider Man: Far From Home* also contemplate). Certainly, *Thor: Ragnarok*, *Loki*, and *Captain Marvel* also dive into comparable psychological and philosophical themes. Yet, *Black Panther*'s engagement with white supremacy and colonialism and its presentation of a Black utopian society resonate perhaps more directly and pointedly with con-temporaneous issues surrounding the film's release than any other MCU film.

If we read Killmonger's death through a Black Lives Matter lens, for example, we can see how his and T'Challa's perspectives offer a point/counterpoint that resonates with the killing of Black people. On one hand,

T'Challa offers hope, telling Killmonger, "Maybe we can still heal you." But Killmonger asks "Why? So you can just lock me up?" He tells T'Challa "Just bury me in the ocean with my ancestors that jumped from the ships' cause they knew death was better than bondage." As a commentary on Black lives (particularly the lives of Black men), T'Challa's perspective is one that looks for a way to heal. Is he offering a utopian vision where the wounds of Black people can be healed? If so, why doesn't Killmonger say yes? This is what makes Killmonger's perspective interesting. Blacks in twenty-first-century America might not be in literal bondage but are suffering in the form of voter suppression, racial profiling, institutional racism, mass incarceration, political underrepresentation, economic injustice, and the outright killing of Black people. So, does Killmonger's decision to die reject the possibility of Wakanda's ability to heal either his wounded body or his broken psyche? Or is he embracing the historical tragedy and trauma that shapes the modern Black experience instead because it is more familar? Indeed, Killmonger's perspective reflects social theorist Paul Gilroy's concept of the "Black Atlantic," which frames the African diaspora as a global identity centered upon expropriation, exile, and exodus of African peoples across the Atlantic Ocean for roughly 500 years.[6] This imagined community helps constitute the paradox of what I call a "landless nationalism" for African Americans, for whom Killmonger serves as a surprisingly strong and sympathetic avatar. It also illustrates Killmonger's point, which T'Challa respects: that utopian solutions aren't all the same. Certainly, Killmonger's identity as an African American resonates as a man without a country within the global diaspora and not with T'Challa's/Wakandan utopia.

"You Know, You Really Shouldn't Trust the Wakandans."

Audiences might be enthralled with the film's overall vision of racial utopianism, but this enthusiastic reaction and interpretation isn't universal. Thus, it is important to demonstrate the negative images and racist ideas the filmmakers were fighting against with this movie. In a 2019 interview with IndieWire in which he was asked his general opinions about the MCU movies, former member of the legendary Monty Python comedy ensemble and acclaimed film director Terry Gilliam took direct aim at *Black Panther* by saying:

> I hated *Black Panther*. It makes me crazy. It gives young black kids the idea that this is something to believe in. Bullshit. It's utter bullshit. I think the people who made it have never been to Africa […] They went and got some stylist for some African pattern fabrics and things. But I just I hated that movie, partly because the media were going on about the importance of bullshit.[7]

But, just in case one thinks that Gilliam's derogatory rant was an isolated outburst by a politically incorrect Hollywood provocateur, let us see examples of this racist outlook at work in the American political sphere.

Deeply angered that United Nations delegates from the African nation of Tanzania did not align themselves with the declared US position of recognizing Taiwan as an independent nation-state, then-California governor and future US president Ronald Reagan vented his outrage to President Richard Nixon during an October 1971 phone conversation. While expressing his complaint about that matter, Reagan then let Nixon know his utter disgust at the delegation: "To see those, those monkeys from those African countries – damn them, they're still uncomfortable wearing shoes!" On the audio recording of their telephone exchange, Nixon merely joked and laughed with Reagan about their shared disdain for the Africans.[8] Several decades later, in a closed-door meeting in the Oval Office with a bipartisan group of US Senators on January 9, 2018, President Donald Trump claimed in his typically brusque, crude fashion that African, Caribbean, and Latin American immigrants were coming from "shithole countries."[9] White supremacy has perpetually misrepresented the African continent as the land of debt, drought, disease, death, and disorder, a repugnant viewpoint perfectly captured by Trump's "shithole countries" comment.

Thus, the timing of *Black Panther*'s cinematic debut (roughly a month after this incident) unveiled Wakanda as a wondrous rejection of Trump's horribly racist utterance, rebuking the starkly crude and cruel white supremacist outlook of Trump's "Make America Great Again" followers (who, by the way, clearly envision their own version of America as a white racial utopia). For example, during the film's mid-credit scene, T'Challa delivers a stirring address to the United Nations assembly that seems to take direct aim against Trumpism. The King of Wakanda announces that his nation will no longer isolate itself from the world. When inevitably one of the delegates ignorantly asks what Wakanda can even give the world, the scene ends wordlessly with T'Challa's wry smile, and viewers know that T'Challa is about to blow the minds of all the UN delegates with evidence of Wakanda's secrets. Furthermore, having successfully reunited his divided nation and resolved to end his homeland's centuries of isolation, T'Challa reminds the gathered diplomats and the viewers that it is wiser to build bridges than walls.

In a broad sense, as much as T'Challa's speech served as a great "mic drop" moment to the selfish and simplistic models of racism, authoritarianism, and isolationism that have been encapsulated in Trumpism, his message also serves as an unadulterated summation of the value of a liberal world order in which the collective security of humanity could be ensured in an open and orderly atmosphere that promotes human dignity, national unity, and global solidarity.

"More Unites Us than Divides Us."

Taken together, these dimensions of how Wakanda is portrayed offer an example of "racial utopianism" in *Black Panther* not merely as a model of greater diversity and representation in contemporary Hollywood entertainment but also as a blueprint for engaging more substantive reflection on critical and challenging issues within human society and culture worldwide. When imagining the future of the world as we know it, the moral and philosophical underpinnings of Wakanda present a fantastic (albeit fictional) place where Black people could live fully and free from white supremacy, sexism, poverty, and oppression, without the looming specters of geopolitical instability, exploitation, humiliation, and misery perennially haunting them from cradle to grave.

If folks ever wondered what levels of innovation, ingenuity, wealth, well-being, and collective goodwill people of African descent could cultivate if they had never been subjugated to the forces of colonialism, slavery, lynching, Jim and Jane Crow racial segregation, mass incarceration, and second-class citizenship, Wakanda is our best example yet. As a wondrous illustration of a racial utopia, Wakanda allows us to focus more on the advantages of this kind of self-definition and self-determination, while never turning our collective gaze away from the risks and ravages of racism, sexism, colonialism, authoritarianism, militarism, and isolationism. Accordingly, through Killmonger, we are also cautioned against a dangerous dystopia – because weaponizing vibranium on a global scale to effect mass genocide in order to end white supremacy is, well, extreme. Yet, we are also shown two examples of related yet vastly divergent worldviews, one being a utopian realm framed through the diasporic dreams of freedom and the other wrought by centuries of hardship.

Thus, the cinematic depiction of Wakanda in *Black Panther* remains a dilemma of sorts, laying bare the perils as well as promises of racial utopianism by asking the film's audience if it is possible to make Black excellence a reality, while also asking what Black excellence means. Therefore, based on the cinematic examples offered in *Black Panther* as well as our shared history, the more thoughtful and meaningful question would be: "What would a Black utopia really look like?" Although Wakanda is not absolutely perfect, it has helped millions of people to envision even better, brighter possibilities.

Notes

1. Toni Morrison, "PBS news hour: Conversation with Elizabeth Farnsworth," March 9, 1998, at https://www.pbs.org/newshour/show/toni-morrison.
2. Sean Howe, *Marvel Comics: The Untold Story* (New York: Harper Perennial, 2012), 86.

3. Jelani Cobb, "Black Panther and the invention of Africa," *The New Yorker*, February 18, 2018, at https://www.newyorker.com/news/daily-comment/black-panther-and-the-invention-of-africa.

4. Cobb.

5. Indeed, a film like *Black Panther* (or any of the MCU films) would be dramatically different if it were filmed like Amazon's *The Boys* or HBO's *Watchmen*.

6. Paul Gilroy, *The Black Atlantic* (Cambridge, MA: Harvard University Press, 1993).

7. Ryan Lattanzio, "Terry Gilliam on Marvel movies' dangerous lie and the 'Don Quixote' producer he compares to Trump," IndieWire, December 20, 2019, at https://www.indiewire.com/2019/12/terry-gilliam-marvel-movies-don-quixote-interview-1202197447.

8. Tim Naftali, "Ronald Reagan's long-hidden racist conversation with Richard Nixon," *The Atlantic*, July 30, 2019, at https://www.theatlantic.com/ideas/archive/2019/07/ronald-reagans-racist-conversation-richard-nixon/595102.

9. Ryan Teague Beckwith, "President Trump called El Salvador, Haiti 'shithole countries': Report," *Time*, January 11, 2018, at https://time.com/5100058/donald-trump-shithole-countries.

20

The Value of Vibranium

Edwardo Pérez

KLAUE: What do you actually know about Wakanda?

ROSS: Uh, shepherds, textiles, cool outfits.

KLAUE: It's all a front. Explorers searched for it for centuries. El Dorado. The golden city. They thought they would find it in South America, but it was in Africa the whole time. A technological marvel all because it was built on a mound of the most valuable metal known to man. Isipho, they call it. The gift. Vibranium.

ROSS: Vibranium, yeah, strongest metal on earth.

KLAUE: It's not just a metal, they sew it into their clothes. It powers their city, their tech, their weapons.

ROSS: Weapons?

KLAUE: Yeah, makes my arm-canon look like a leaf-blower.

ROSS: That's a nice fairy tale but Wakanda is a third-world country and you stole all their vibranium.

KLAUE: I stole all of it? I took a tiny piece of it. They have a mountain full of it. They've been mining it for thousands of years. And they still haven't scratched the surface. I'm the only outsider who's seen it and gotten out of their alive. If you don't believe me, you ask your friend what his suit is made of … what his claws are made of …

Agent Ross's interrogation of Ulysses Klaue doesn't just explain the significance of vibranium, it frames vibranium as "the most valuable metal known to man," which, in turn, establishes what ends up being a moral dilemma for T'Challa – when Agent Ross gets shot and, later, when T'Challa learns the truth about his father's past. The scene also adds to the fabled mystery that the larger Marvel Cinematic Universe (MCU) narrative weaves throughout the other films.

We're first introduced to vibranium in *Captain America: The First Avenger* when Howard Stark is showing Steve Rogers some options for shields. When Steve sees the iconic (though unpainted) shield and asks about it, Howard replies that it's made of vibranium, the rarest metal on Earth. In *Avengers: Age of Ultron* we first hear the name Wakanda (which Bruce Banner can barely pronounce) when the Avengers team is investigating

Black Panther and Philosophy: What Can Wakanda Offer the World?, First Edition. Edited by Edwardo Pérez and Timothy E. Brown.

Ulysses Klaue and we get a hint about vibranium's possibilities and origin. In *Captain America: Civil War*, T'Challa makes his first appearance as Black Panther and we get a better idea (but still just a glimpse) of what vibranium can do besides make shields. Indeed, it's not until *Black Panther* that we get to see the full extent of vibranium's uses and its value exactly as Klaue describes to Agent Ross – from the metal's mythological appearance on Earth to the ways it permeates nearly every aspect of Wakandan society to Shuri's lab, where she can test new sneakers, fit the Black Panther suit into a necklace, and fix the spinal injuries of colonizers with ease.

Although the metal's uses are fictional, the concept and presence of vibranium in *Black Panther* and the depiction of Wakanda in the larger MCU narrative present some philosophical issues with regard to vibranium's value. What makes vibranium "the most valuable metal known to man"? Is vibranium a commodity? Is it the defining cultural feature of a particular society? Or, does all of humanity have a right to vibranium? How do we measure and understand the value of vibranium?

"Guns, so Primitive."

According to Karl Marx (1818–1883), a *commodity* is something that fulfills a human want. This is a broad definition. It suggests not just that anything can be commodified, but that commodification is relative (in a "one man's trash is another man's treasure" kind of way) and that a commodity's value depends on its ability to satisfy a given want or need. Or, put another way, the value of the *commodity* depends on its use, which can be further understood through what Marx calls *use value*, a value based on an object's utility, and *exchange value*, a value based on the quantitative worth of an object, which can be traded and which can fluctuate (like in a free market). *Black Panther* illustrates many uses for vibranium. It's not just a metal, as Klaue explains to Agent Ross, and its uses seem to be limited only by one's imagination. As Ultron, referring to Captain America's shield, quipped in *Age of Ultron*, "the most versatile substance on the planet and they use it to make a frisbee, typical of humans, they scratch the surface." Of course, Ultron never met Shuri, whose imagination seems unlimited. Ultron did, however, work with Klaue, who certainly views vibranium as a commodity.

For Klaue, vibranium is a tool that gives him power – in his artificial arm, in the money he makes from selling vibranium weapons on the black market, and in the alpha-male power he derives from his arm and his wealth (like when he struts into the underground bar in Korea). Klaue's overall narrative suggests that he prizes vibranium's *exchange value* more than its *use value*, because Klaue isn't interested in using vibranium for anything other than obtaining money and power. In *Age of Ultron*, Ultron transfers billions of dollars into Klaue's bank accounts in exchange for vibranium – and it's significant that Ultron and Klaue view vibranium differently. For Ultron, it's the "rock he's going to build his church on," while for Klaue, it's simply a substance "worth billions," which he uses to further his cause in *Black Panther*. Indeed, Klaue certainly benefits from the *use value* his vibranium arm provides. Yet, his motivation remains money and power. We can see this in the way Klaue treats Killmonger as an object that has *exchange value*. To be fair, Killmonger does the same with Klaue, killing Klaue and exchanging him in Wakanda for an opportunity to challenge T'Challa. In contrast to Klaue, Wakandans utilize vibranium for its *use value* not its *exchange value*.

Wakandans don't trade vibranium, so it's not a commodity with *exchange value* for them, though it's easy to imagine what sort of economy they'd have if vibranium was exported throughout the world. Instead, Wakandans value vibranium for its *use value*, structuring every aspect of their society around vibranium – to the extent that Wakanda might not be able to function without vibranium. It's also easy to imagine what would happen to Wakanda if they were to commodify vibranium and eventually deplete their supply, given the likely demand of global consumption, which brings us to capitalism.

Marxism views capitalism as being dependent on the buying, selling, and trading of goods at the market. It's how a capitalist society relates to the world at large and it's why things like precious metals and weapons are typically commodified. Wakanda has elements of capitalism (and democratic socialism), but it's also a monarchy. Though there is a ruling class (there are kings and princesses), and a division of Wakandans into haves and have-nots, the have-nots still have access to vibranium. And, the structure of Wakandan society isn't necessarily class-based, it's tribal. Each tribe performs a function and is treated equally, enjoying the benefits of vibranium – and, when the time comes, every tribe is able to challenge for the throne, preventing power from becoming hereditary or dynastic.

While vibranium's *use value* is important to Wakandans and its *exchange value* is important to villains like Klaue, another way to understand the value of vibranium is to examine its cultural value.

"Nah, I'm Just Feeling It."

KILLMONGER: Now tell me about this one.
CURATOR: Also from Benin, seventh century. The Fula tribe, I believe.
KILLMONGER: Nah.
CURATOR: I beg your pardon?
KILLMONGER: It was taken by British soldiers in Benin, but it's from Wakanda, and it's made out of vibranium. Don't trip, I'm gonna take it off your hands for you.
CURATOR: These items aren't for sale.
KILLMONGER: How do you think your ancestors got these? Do you think they paid a fair price? Or did they take it, like they took everything else?

The Museum of Great Britain makes for an interesting setting, as Killmonger (looking professorial with glasses) schools the Curator on the history of West African artifacts. It's a stark contrast to Killmonger's later, more physically violent, persona. Yet, it highlights the value of culture, which, for Killmonger, fuels his motivation – and, it hints at the moral dilemma surrounding the issue of cultural heritage and the use of vibranium that eventually drives the film. If a culture (like Wakanda) values something it deems unique to its cultural identity (like vibranium) does that culture have the sole right to the thing it values? Put another way, if another culture (say, American) were to adopt the thing of value (begin using vibranium), would this be considered a cultural theft or cultural appropriation of Wakandan society? How are we to understand value when it comes to culture? And, how are we to understand vibranium's value with regard to Wakanda's cultural identity and cultural heritage?

Killmonger would argue that Wakanda is obligated to aid every Black-skinned person in the world by virtue of being Black-skinned (he says as much when he arrives in Wakanda). For Killmonger, Wakandan culture isn't Wakandan, it's African. Taking this further, Killmonger also maintains that if all life originated in Africa, then Wakanda (clearly the most advanced African society) isn't just obligated to save the world, it's justified in ruling the world. What's significant is that Killmonger wants to appropriate Wakandan culture and vibranium for himself – and, to be fair, he does technically have a birthright, which grants him cultural heritage. Yet, Killmonger was raised in Oakland, California, as an American named Eric Stevens, and it's this perspective (as an oppressed African American) that drives Killmonger's desire to use vibranium to wage war on the world. It's also how he rules as king, not as a Wakandan, but as an African American, which is what ultimately leads Okoye to fight against him rather than defend him. This is a contrast to Klaue, who doesn't value vibranium for its cultural value and who doesn't try to appropriate Wakandan culture. Yet, in stealing vibranium, Klaue raises an interesting issue with regard to culture: can a culture claim ownership of a substance just because that substance is found on their land? Can something like vibranium be considered *cultural property* of Wakanda? After all, vibranium isn't a naturally occurring substance native to Wakanda, it comes from space. So, who really owns it?

Of course, most Wakandans seem to view vibranium as *cultural property* – otherwise, they wouldn't have erected a shield to hide Wakanda from the rest of the world and they wouldn't have pursued Klaue so vigorously. After all, it's not like Klaue stole a crown jewel from the Tower of London, something irreplaceable and indicative of England's cultural heritage. To be fair, though, the artifact Klaue and Killmonger stole was indicative of African heritage, even if it was mislabeled as being from Benin instead of Wakanda. As Klaue points out, there's a mound of vibranium with plenty to spare. Sure, Wakanda is the only place vibranium exists on earth and it represents Wakanda's heritage, but does that necessarily mean vibranium is Wakandan property? Does vibranium belong to Wakanda or to Earth? Is it something only Wakandans can enjoy or should humanity also benefit? Who has the stronger claim to vibranium?

For a *cultural nationalist*, an item like vibranium would be considered the *cultural property* of Wakanda, as its value is integral to Wakandan society. Without vibranium, Wakanda wouldn't be Wakanda. Vibranium defines Wakanda's history and cultural heritage, structuring their way of life and their religion. Given what we see of Wakanda in *Black Panther*, this position seems correct. It's Killmonger's position at the museum and it's initially a position T'Challa argues, as he says to Nakia early in the film, "If anyone found out what we truly are, what we possess, we could lose our way of life." Yet, at the end of *Black Panther*, T'Challa holds a position that fits a *cultural internationalist* perspective, one that sees specific cultures contributing to the overall human culture, giving everyone a compelling interest in a *cultural property* such as vibranium. Consider his speech:

> Wakanda will no longer watch from the shadows. We cannot. We must not. We will work to be an example of how we, as brothers and sisters on this earth, should treat each other. Now, more than ever, the illusions of division threaten our very existence. We all know the truth: more connects us than separates us. But in times of crisis we build bridges, while the foolish build barriers. We must find a way to look after one another, as if we were one single tribe.

So, does T'Challa really change his mind? Does vibranium belong to humanity's "one single tribe" more than it belongs to Wakanda? One thread that runs through science fiction movies (from *Close Encounters of the Third Kind* to *Arrival* and, of course, *Superman*) depicts extraterrestrial visitation as an event that transforms humanity. In *Black Panther*, though, the object carrying vibranium never transformed humanity, it transformed Wakanda. Is this why T'Challa changes his mind? Should Wakanda have treated the arrival of vibranium as a global (humanity-transforming) event rather than a local (community-transforming) one?

"Who are You?"

T'CHALLA: Our weapons will not be used to wage war on the world. It is not our way to be judge, jury, and executioner for people who are not our own.

KILLMONGER: Not your own? But didn't life start here, on this continent? So ain't all people your people?

T'CHALLA: I'm not king of all people. I am king of Wakanda and it is my responsibility to make sure our people are safe and that vibranium does not fall into the hands of a person like you.

T'Challa may initially claim he isn't king of all people, but his actions throughout the film suggest his philosophy has always been more concerned with the greater good rather than just with Wakanda. For example, T'Challa spares M'Baku's life, saves Agent Ross's life, and offers to save Killmonger's life – and he spares Helmut Zero's life in *Civil War* and calls all of Wakanda to war (even lowering the defense shield) to help save Vision's life in *Avengers: Infinity War*. In all of these instances, T'Challa is concerned about the consequences of his actions and what they mean for the larger world, not just for Wakanda. In fact, many of these decisions place Wakanda directly in danger – a means he hopes will justify the ends. For a deontologist like Immanuel Kant (1724–1804), T'Challa, as king, would be wrong in every one of these situations because he's bound by duty to put Wakanda first. As Kant maintains, we should act by principled reason and apply that reason to all contexts. Or, as he formulates his categorical imperative, we should act in such a manner that our actions could become universal law. So, what does that mean for T'Challa? If his decisions place Wakanda in danger, should he have decided differently? Should he have let Agent Ross die in order to protect Wakanda?

Utilitarianism, on the other hand, seeks to make moral decisions based on finding the outcome that provides the greatest good. Jeremey Bentham (1747–1832) defines this greatest good as the greatest happiness for the greatest number of people. Bentham believes we should calculate (as best we can) the pains and pleasures (or, in his equation, the goods and evils) that could reasonably result from making a certain moral decision. In deciding to share vibranium, it seems that T'Challa decided that the benefits of vibranium (medical and technological) outweighed the risks (weaponizing it and misusing it). Likewise, saving Agent Ross and sparing M'Baku's life also proved to be decisions where the benefits outweighed the risks, especially considering the roles Agent Ross and M'Baku end up playing in saving Wakanda from Killmonger. What's paramount is that T'Challa's actions match a utilitarian philosophy. He may initially profess to be bound by duty to Wakanda, but as his speech at the United Nations shows, his concern extends to humanity, perhaps more than it does to Wakandans, as he sees the proper use of vibranium as a responsibility to the world and not just to his people.

Of course, it's worth noting that T'Challa is also motivated by a need to redeem the mistakes of his father and the kings that came before them. Consider his speech in the Ancestral Plane, delivered to his father, T'Chaka, and his ancestors:

> You were wrong! All of you were wrong! To turn your backs on the rest of the world! We let the fear of discovery stop us from doing what is right! No more! I cannot stay here with you. I cannot rest while [Killmonger] sits on the throne. He is a monster of our own making. I must take the mantle back. I must! I must right these wrongs.

T'Challa isn't just pissed, he's ashamed of his father's and ancestors' actions. Thus, his decision to share vibranium with the world also represents a chance for atonement as much as it represents an opportunity to help the world.

"What Can a Nation of Farmers Offer the Rest of the World?"

ROSS: Is this Wakanda?
SHURI: No, it's Kansas.
ROSS: How long ago was Korea?
SHURI: Yesterday.
ROSS: I don't think so. Bullet wounds don't just magically heal overnight.
SHURI: They do here. But not by magic, by technology.

Black Panther ultimately envisions a world that values learning more than killing and embraces the future rather than longing for the past, equalizing all of us through mutual benefit rather than mutually assured destruction. More pointedly, in T'Challa's ideal world, though we might need weapons (and Black Panther suits) to protect ourselves, what we really need is technology that makes life better for everyone. In such a world, tomorrow matters more than yesterday. It might be a utopian fantasy (and Wakanda certainly looks like a utopian heaven, especially Shuri's lab), but after years of dystopian nightmares, it's a refreshing change to consider a narrative and a hero more oriented toward peace than destruction, more willing to build than destroy.

This is what makes the final scene of the film so moving. By buying the buildings in Oakland and committing Wakanda to outreach and exchange programs (starting with the colonized), T'Challa is able to begin redeeming his ancestors, atoning for his father's crime, and even fulfilling Killmonger's dream, which might be vibranium's greatest value – not money, not power, not culture, not even morality, but simply uniting humanity in the realization that we really are one tribe living on one planet.

PART V
Black Lives Matter

21

Dismantling the Master's House with the Master's Tools

Thanayi M. Jackson

I have to admit, whenever I see Michael B. Jordan, I still see Wallace from HBO's *The Wire*. Well, at least I did. After seeing *Black Panther*, I am convinced that Wallace did not actually die in that Baltimore row, but rather was transported to a parallel dimension, a multiverse Earth, where he manifested as N'Jadaka in an Oakland 'hood.

In *The Wire*, 15-year-old Wallace is trapped in a cycle of poverty attributable to the legacy of slavery and Jim Crow. The lost child of colonialism. The unfortunate son of capitalism. He is a child drug dealer in one of America's colonized cities. But, I'm telling you, in *Black Panther* Wallace is Resurrected. In *Black Panther*, N'Jadaka overcomes. Propelled by his own genius, he is an MIT graduate: a master of the technology and science that has been historically co-opted by manifest destiny. Science and technology were (and continue to be) *the* historical justification for colonialism, imperialism, and globalism. In the name of progress, white supremacy builds hierarchies on top of racial and ethnic distinctions. Propelled by his own vengeance, N'Jadaka transforms into Erik Killmonger, CIA operative: a master of the weapons wielded by a colonial global empire, who wields these weapons himself in a quest to destroy the system that has oppressed people of color since ships set sail for the Caribbean over 500 years ago.

Killmonger may know how colonizers think, but is his quest really possible? Can the master's house be destroyed with the master's own weapons? For example, if T'Challa (and Shuri and Okoye and Agent Ross and everyone else who battled at the end of *Black Panther*) hadn't stopped Killmonger, would Killmonger's plan have worked? Could white supremacy have been pulled apart? Would the world have started over, as Killmonger put it, with Black people on top?

Black Panther and Philosophy: What Can Wakanda Offer the World?, First Edition. Edited by Edwardo Pérez and Timothy E. Brown.
© 2022 John Wiley & Sons, Inc. Published 2022 by John Wiley & Sons, Inc.

The Master's Tools

To understand Killmonger's perspective, it is helpful to continue the comparison between Killmonger and Wallace – not just because Michael B. Jordan rocks both rolls, but because understanding the similarities between Killmonger and Wallace's environments will give us insights for making sense of Killmonger's plan. For example, both N'Jadaka and Wallace are orphans of Africa reared by America's ghettos. Wallace lives in a vacant row house, the sole provider for his seven younger siblings. He sells drugs to survive. He is inevitably drawn into the brutality of the job, but his humanity is his weakness. After giving his bosses a tip on the location of a rival, he cannot psychologically handle it when the boy is monstrously murdered. He becomes mindful of his complicity in an underworld normalized to him since birth. Realizing his inevitable role in the death and suffering he lives every day, his self-awareness is Kafkaesque and he is overwhelmed to the point of dysfunction. He sinks into depression: sleep, sorrow, solitude. He turns to heroin. He is in despair. This becomes the death of him.

Killmonger is also self-aware. A CIA operative, Killmonger, too, is complicit in the cycle of drugs and poverty that murders boys like Wallace. But, significantly, Killmonger acts like a colonizer. As he says: "I trained. I lied. I killed just to get here. I killed in America, Afghanistan, Iraq. I took life from my own brothers and sisters right here on this continent – and all this death just so I could kill you." Another way to understand Killmonger's actions is to see him not just as someone who thinks like a colonizer but also as someone who knows how to wield the tools of a colonizer.

So, if Killmonger is a supervillain (say, before he drinks the Heart-Shaped Herb) then his superpower is his ability to wield the master's tools, isn't it? If so, then perhaps Killmonger (not T'Challa) is the superhero we deserve. Philosopher Audre Lorde (1934–1992) taught us that this is impossible.[1] But, at least in the Marvel Cinematic Universe (MCU), superpowers (and, in *Black Panther*, vibranium) make the impossible possible. To be clear, Lorde, a Black lesbian feminist, was critiquing white feminism, suggesting that it failed to dismantle white supremacy (and she was doing this in the 1970s). Yet, her famous words – "For the master's tools will never dismantle the master's house" – get reinterpreted through Killmonger, who has mastered the art of global colonial capitalism. And, having mastered the masters' tools, Killmonger sets out to dismantle the house and give it *all* back! "Don't trip," he tells the museum curator, "Imma take it off your hands for you."

The Master's House

The museum scene is our introduction to Killmonger. There he stands, right pose, wrong clothes, in a London museum surrounded by Africa's stolen history. It's a colonial stage straight from the master's toolbox.

That's the thing about museums, they have the power to validate historical evils by presenting material culture through a narrative of primitivity. In this story, treasures of the past are not stolen but saved from those without the intellectual or technological ability to appreciate such masterpieces.[2] Not this time. Killmonger is armed with the Black gaze and he quickly dismantles the museum as a site of colonial oppression. He focuses in on the diversity of African culture. Each piece, a brief history of colonialism.

What's significant about the museum scene is that Killmonger not only outplays the curator with his superior knowledge of the artifacts, he also outplays the colonizer mentality. The curator may have called for security, but they'd been tracking him since he arrived. Not because he's a supervillain, his superpowers are invisible and they can't recognize their tools in his hands. They're not focused on his intellect or his ability, they're focused only on what they see: a Black man. Thus, they're blind to the hammer of colonialism he wields over them – ultraviolence – as he and Klaue murder the museum guards and take back history.

WOW! I am the Diaspora's side-eyed satisfaction. I cheer! But, while I'm still riding high on this freedom dream, I am interrupted and sent back to Wakanda for a straight-up coronation. OK, maybe I'm just not getting in the spirit here, but Wakanda is literally a monarchy with a throne determined by patriarchal blood right and brute might. Sure, this bout was a good fight. T'Challa wins, the people cheer, he is crowned king, and trumpets blow. I mean, don't get me wrong, I'm feeling Wakanda. I am. Monarchy or no, it feels good to know that Wakanda is the most powerful nation on Earth. It feels superhuman to see a powerful Black nation as a superpower. Black Power! I choose to revel in it because of everything it represents (and maybe because I want to see a reckoning). And yet, Wakanda is the master's house too, right? Or, at least it's in the neighborhood, no? I defer to bell hooks' explanation of Audre Lorde's theory in an interview justifying why she called Beyoncé a terrorist. As hooks states:

> I think it's fantasy that we can recoup the violating image and use it. I used to get so tired of people quoting Audre Lorde, the master's tools will never dismantle the master's house, but that was exactly what she meant, that you are not going to destroy this imperialist, white supremacist, capitalist patriarchy by creating your own version of it. Even if it serves you to make lots and lots of money.[3]

Is hooks right? If lots of money won't tear down the master's house, what about a mountain of vibranium?

Certainly, most of the world is as confused as the French Ambassador in thinking that a third-world looking nation like Wakanda has anything to offer. This is because Wakanda has everyone fooled. In the reality of the MCU, they are ultra-first world, the most powerful nation on Earth and they're ruled by a king with superpowers. They have all the weapons and all the technology. They could take over the world in a second, but they don't, and by that fact they claim to not be part of the problem of colonialism. Even Wakanda, whose power is greater than all the tools of the master's house put together, doesn't dismantle it. And as we watch, we take pride in their power even though it does not include us. Wakanda sits on the world council but does nothing about colonial oppression. And that's the rub. They don't dismantle the master's house because they're living in it, too, aren't they? Why does colonialism even exist alongside a Wakanda? What does decolonization look like in this world? What does it look like in any world?

Wakanda's House

Wakanda has but won't share, not with Oakland. And furthermore, Wakanda don't want you. No, really. Try to go to Wakanda. Border Tribe will yoke you up! N'Jadaka's father warned him, and despite Killmonger's rightful claim to challenge the throne, when he comes for the crown he is immediately opposed, not because of his brutality, but because he is not one of "us." Oh, indeed. In Wakanda, "us" are Wakandans. Nation. Wakanda has the privilege to not care about global anti-Blackness, to not recognize Diasporic struggle because they have all the weapons, all the power.[4] Black Power. "Y'all sittin' up here comfortable," Killmonger tells the council. "Must feel good. It's about two billion people all over the world that looks like us, but their lives are a lot harder. Wakanda has the tools to liberate 'em all."

T'Challa does not want to use Wakanda's weapons to wage war on the world because, as he claims, "it is not our way to be judge, jury, and executioner for people who are not our own." And he's right, isn't he? The master's tools cannot tear down the master's house. And also, Wakanda don't want you. Killmonger may protest, "Not your own?" and he may rhetorically ask "But didn't life start right here on this continent? So ain't all people your people?" But T'Challa and the Wakanda council ain't having none of it from a boy from the 'hood. To Ramonda, Killmonger is a "Charlatan." Thus, as T'Challa explains, vibranium can never "fall into the hands of a person like you." Because Wakanda is a master's house with master's rules.

So, N'Jadaka's/Erik Stevens's/Killmonger's superpowers are born of the Diaspora. His superpower is linked to American Black radicalism and the historical Black Panthers.[5] The director and co-writer Ryan Coogler, an Oakland native, drives this connection home as he grounds us in our Civil Rights lore. The Oakland setting, the Black is beautiful leather, and ooohhhh, yes, the rhetoric. It was late-twentieth-century Oakland, home of the Black Panther Party for Self Defense, that radicalized Killmonger's father when he was stationed there on a War Dog assignment in 1992. As Zuri tells T'Challa, "The hardships he saw there radicalized your uncle," and as N'Jobu himself tells us:

I observed for as long as I could! Their leaders have been assassinated, communities flooded with drugs and weapons, they are overly policed and incarcerated. All over the planet our people suffer because they don't have the tools to fight back. With vibranium weapons they could overthrow every country and Wakanda could rule them all … the right way.

Again, what does decolonization look like in this world? In any world? When N'Jadaka stumbles upon his father's journal, I imagine it reads like the revolutionary ideology of Huey Newton. We must unify the dispersed colonies of colonialism, scattered all over the world, and bound by legislated disparity. We must dismantle capitalism that hides as nationalism and hoards the planet's finite resources using superweapons, using war. We must dismantle first- and third-world distinctions through a redistribution of power![6]

What's significant is that Killmonger's (and his father's) perspective is compelling. They might be the "villains" of the movie (because they're Black revolutionaries?) but they have a point, don't they? I mean, maybe it's Michael B. Jordan's charisma, but was I the only one rooting for Killmonger to tear it all down?

Killmonger's House

I envision young Erik Stevens's transformation to supervillain happening on that Oakland basketball court as he's looking up, watching Wakandan planes fly away over the projects. He's looking at the master's house. He sees how it is built and with which tools. He sees its simplicity. The Black gaze. He is not lost at all. As he tells the spirit of his father, "Well, maybe your home is the one that's lost. That's why they can't find us." Indeed.

After reclaiming the throne, Killmonger is transported back to his Oakland home. He visits his father and he is again reborn. Ultraviolence at full power, hell-bent on (self)destruction. It's telling that one of his first acts is to order the burning of the Heart-Shaped Herbs. In the scene, it seems as if Killmonger just wants to ensure there'd be no chance someone could succeed him. But is that really why he wants the herbs destroyed? Nah. He doesn't think he'll live to be king forever, that's not his superpower. He's a revolutionary superprodigy. He means no-more-kings – after him, of course. And that's a good thing, right? Yet, Killmonger's speech to the council embodies Audre Lorde's warning:

You know, where I'm from when Black folks started revolutions, they never had the firepower or the resources to fight their oppressors. Where was Wakanda? Hmm? Yeah, all that ends today. We got spies embedded in every nation on Earth. Already in place. I know how colonizers think. So, we're gonna use their own strategy against 'em. We're gonna send vibranium weapons out to our War Dogs. They'll arm oppressed people all over the world so they can finally rise up and kill those in power, and their children, and anyone else who takes their side. It's time they know the truth about us. We're warriors! This world's gonna start over, and this time, we're on top!

Will this work? After all, Killmonger is in the master's house and he has access to the master's tools. Is he still a revolutionary prodigy or is he a new master?

Killmonger's reckoning is not Black utopia. It is Black nihilism. He wants to see the world burn. To hell with the aftermath. But he also wants the colonizer to know why he set them ablaze. He will destabilize first-world nations using the same formula they have used to create the Third World. Agent Ross was unphased when Nakia told him Killmonger burned the Heart-Shaped Herb. As Ross reasons, "Of course he did. That's what he was trained to do. His unit used to work with the CIA to destabilize foreign countries. You get control of government, the military [...]" So, Killmonger doesn't just know how colonizers think, he knows how masters think, and Wakanda is no longer the master's house, it's Killmonger's house.

Killmonger may boast during his final battle with T'Challa, claiming "I learn from my enemies. Beat them at their own game," but as T'Challa sees it, "You have become them! You will destroy the world, Wakanda included." T'Challa's right, isn't he? I mean, that's literally Killmonger's plan. But is this really what he set out to do?

It's a shame that most of Killmonger's backstory is not revealed in *Black Panther*. I mean, what happened to the little boy after he found his father dead, another Black leader murdered in Oakland? I imagine him as Wallace again. Wallace could have gone to MIT. Hardworking, smart, compassionate, dreamer – so human, with the right knowledge in the wrong place, trapped by systemic forces beyond his control. Ahhhh, the master's house.

Of course, when Wallace tried to use the master's tools, it was just as Audre Lorde told us. The game was killing him. It was doubtful he would make it to adulthood. But, convinced that street strength was the path to money and manhood, he's drawn back in. He returns to the pit, declares himself in the game for life, a man, and is promptly executed beneath a watching 2Pac poster by his lifelong friends … other children.[7] The cycle continues unbroken. The master's tools cannot tear down the master's house, not for Wallace and, ultimately, not for Killmonger.

Mastering the Master's Tools

Mastery of the master's tools is a superpower born of the blood of all the Wallaces and Erik Stevenses of the world. Killmonger promises to tear it all down and I am totally here for it. Hey, this is why I comic. But, it's a slippery slope. I, too, am aware. I, too, know the master's tools. When Killmonger murders his lover, the only Black American woman in the film, I gasp.[8] Bang. Dang. She is a pawn, as disposable as he. Make no mistake. He is not good. He is the culmination of all the hate in all the masters' houses from the Caribbean to the castle. It is not liberation. It is war, destruction, ultraviolence. It is the end.

Ultimately Killmonger loses because the master's house is too strong. And yet, T'Challa, seemingly inspired by Killmonger's history, asks his father "Why didn't you bring the boy home? Why, papa?" T'Chaka doesn't have a good answer and T'Challa proceeds to admonish his father and their ancestors:

> You were wrong! All of you were wrong! To turn your backs on the rest of the world! We let the fear of our discovery stop us from doing what is right! No more! I cannot stay here with you. I cannot rest while he sits on the throne. He is a monster of our own making. I must take the mantle back. I must! I must right these wrongs.

By the way, where was Prince N'Jobu? Why wasn't he in the Ancestral Plane? Or was his spirit confined to haunt the Oakland apartment he was killed in? In any case, while T'Challa might be right – the wrongs need correcting – it's worth asking if he's going about it the right way. After all, his process apparently includes making minor concessions to M'Baku, whose environmental pleas have gone unheard for generations, and joining with the CIA to bring down the Black revolution. So, yeah, the master's house and the master's tools are slippery.

In Killmonger's final scene we can see his superpowers slipping away with the sunset. What he once recognized as a superpower now seems to him a fairy tale. As he says to T'Challa, "My pop said Wakanda was the most beautiful thing he'd ever seen. He promised he was gonna show it to me one day. You believe that? Kid from Oakland, running around believing in fairy tales."

It's enough to push T'Challa to do more than just yell at his dead ancestors.

You see, in response to Killmonger, T'Challa is seemingly reborn again. Neo-T'Challa is prepared to share Wakanda's technology with the rest of the world, starting with Oakland, even though they're still colonized by the United States, leaving me wondering how exactly that's supposed to work. I mean, I'm sure sharing Wakandan technology with the United States will be fine and all, but what about the militarization of local police forces? What about Black Lives Matter? What about gentrification? On top of that, Wakandans are already acting all Ultra-First again with Shuri talking about Coachella (and in *Infinity War*, Okoye wants a Starbucks? In Wakanda?).

Ultimately, Killmonger is a supervillain. He can't win. But, could his superpowers dismantle the master's house? ...or just refurbish?

Notes

1. Audre Lorde, "The Master's Tools Will Never Dismantle the Master's House," in Cherríe Moraga and Gloria Anzaldúa, eds., *This Bridge Called My Back: Writings by Radical Women of Color* (New York: Kitchen Table Press, 1983), 94–101.

2. The museum scene engaged an ongoing dialogue regarding the museum's role in colonialism. See Mary Carole McCauley, "'Black Panther' raises difficult questions in museum community," *Baltimore Sun*, March 2, 2018, at http://www.baltimoresun.com/entertainment/movies/bs-fe-black-panther-museums-20180227-story.html.

3. bell hooks, "Beyoncé is a terrorist," *Genius*, at https://genius.com/Bell-hooks-beyonce-is-a-terrorist-annotated. Full panel can be viewed online, "Are you still a slave?" at The New School, May 6, 2014, at https://livestream.com/The-NewSchool/Slave. See also Simamkele Dlakavu, "Beyoncé debate: The master's tools won't dismantle master's house," *City Press* (Johannesburg, South Africa), February 14, 2016, at https://www.news24.com/citypress/voices/beyonce-debate-the-masters-tools-wont-dismantle-masters-house-20160214.

4. Except for Nakia, she's a G… in the film at least. Let's not even talk about her chasing T'Challa around in the comics.

5. The Black Panther character may not have originally been named after the Black Panther Party but that's how history works. It is not that history is dismissive of original intent, it is just that history doesn't stop. Imagine a world in which the two were NOT joined by memory. Think about it. They both emerge the same year. Both use the imagery of powerful Black men and proud African heritage. However, that it was not intentional speaks most closely to one of my favorite historical concepts: the cosmic historicity of human thought. The black panther, as a symbol of black power, was in the air of the mid-twentieth-century Civil Rights movement. That's the only way different people in different places doing different things arrive at the same idea. The African American 761st Tank Battalion adopted the black panther as its mascot fighting for double victory against white supremacy during World War II. Student Nonviolent Coordinating Committee (SNCC) activists emblazoned their newsletter with it during the Civil Rights Movement. The Black Panther Party solidified it as a black power symbol, hence why they are the first to come to mind. Historically speaking, they are of the same epistemic murk. That the Black Panther Party for Self Defense and the Black Panther of Wakanda both appear within months of one another in 1966 only heightens philosophical questions about art, life, reflection, and impersonation. It is fate, and 52 years later the Black Panther Party for Self Defense is embedded in the vibranium fabric of the comic. I mean, come on, *Killmonger*, vol. 1, #1 is called "By Any Means!" See Bryan Edward Hill (writer), Juan Ferreyra (pencilist, inker, colorist), Joe Sabino (letterer) "By Any Means," *Killmonger*, vol. 1, #1, December 5, 2018, Marvel Comics.

6. Thinking about Black Panther revolutionary ideology, my thinking on dispersed colonies is most inspired by Huey Newton's concept of intercommunalism, see Huey P. Newton, "Speech Delivered at Boston College: November 18, 1970," in *The Huey P. Newton Reader* (New York: Seven Stories Press, 2002); Huey P. Newton, "Intercommunalism," 1974, reprinted in *Viewpoint Magazine*, June 11, 2018.

7. How come there are no children in Wakanda, only in Oakland?.

8. The only other mention of a Black American woman in the film is Killmonger's mother, who is conspicuously absent.

22

An Impossible Return? (Anti)Colonialism in/of *Black Panther*

Julio C. Covarrubias-Cabeza

Is it possible to reclaim an identity that existed before the moment of colonization? To recover a way of life erased by the racial violence, genocide, and slavery that birthed the modern world? These are recurring questions in the social thought of more than one peoples caught in the wake of European empire. But these were also important questions raised in *Black Panther*. Latent in the film's depiction of the tragic villain, Erik "Killmonger" Stevens, such questions underwrite not only the narrative arc of his doomed quest to (re)claim "Wakanda" as his homeland, but his subjective motivations and desires.

Yet in a film that would not exist save for the horrors of chattel slavery, colonialism, and white supremacy, it is remarkable that these concepts and their cognates are rarely directly invoked – and when *Black Panther* does invoke them, it simultaneously scrambles their true significance. From the opening sequence of *Black Panther*, in which we learn about the origins of Wakanda and of its exceptional position in Africa; to the climax, in which Killmonger cites the horrors of transatlantic slavery to declare his allegiance to the devalued dead; to the denouement, in which King T'Challa decides to formally integrate Wakanda into the world-system and open his kingdom to Western influence: all of these decisive moments in the film make sense only within a context of white global racial violence and colonial domination, though the film manages to never directly confront this reality or contend with the difficult issues its history raises—such as those which will be explored in this chapter.

A specter, we might then say, haunts *Black Panther*: the specter of the colonialism and decolonization. For, as I will argue, the film's narrative coherence both depends on the history of colonial violence, even as it must simultaneously bury that history to maintain its palatability to a white

Black Panther and Philosophy: What Can Wakanda Offer the World?, First Edition. Edited by Edwardo Pérez and Timothy E. Brown.

audience. The place where it buries it, in turn, is in the film's pathological caricatures of the only radical, anti-colonial option it depicts in Erik "Killmonger" Stevens.

Despite its external trappings, this film is thus not about racial liberation. Not only is it straightforwardly racist, as others have already argued.[1] But from the perspective of anti-colonial theory– the rich and heterogeneous traditions of resistance against racism, colonialism, and capitalism that have been practiced and theorized by Black, Brown, and Indigenous peoples the world over – *Black Panther*, is *supremely* colonial.

Anti-Blackness in *Black Panther*

While many have celebrated *Black Panther*, some have also criticized it – such as contemporary philosopher Christopher Lebron, who argues that *Black Panther*'s plot is centrally driven by anti-Black stereotypes about Black Americans, and particularly about Black American men. As Lebron observes, while *Black Panther* is cherished for "its [B]lack star power and its many thoughtful portrayals of strong black women," the film ultimately "depends on a shocking devaluation of [B]lack American men."[2] Even as it positioned itself as *the* "woke" event of the year, its final message is that the greater good must be safeguarded "against the threat *not* of white Americans or Europeans, but a [B]lack American man, the most dangerous person in the world."[3] Lebron thus emphatically suggests that *Black Panther* is quite the opposite of a film about racial liberation.

Let's consider Killmonger's actions: He murders the only Black American woman in the film (his partner and lover, Nightshade). He puts an elderly Wakandan medicine woman in a chokehold when she disagrees with his decision to burn the "Heart-Shaped Herb." He disrespects Ramonda (calling her "Auntie" and treating her as if she doesn't matter), the entire Wakandan council, and all authorities. Counting every kill by scarring his body, Killmonger is portrayed as simultaneously charismatic but crude, radical but reactionary, intelligent but thoughtless, lofty but cruel. He is superior, but inferior. All of this reflects the fact, noted long ago by the Martinican anti-colonial philosopher Frantz Fanon (1925– 1961), that to the European mind "the [B]lack man has a function: to represent shameful feelings, base instincts, and the dark side of the soul."[4] "Deep down in the European unconscious," Fanon explains, "[there] has been hollowed out an excessively black pit where the most immoral instincts and unmentionable desires slumber" and the European "has attempted to repudiate this" by projecting these instincts and desires onto *le Noir*.[5]

But this is not all. It is revealing, Lebron tells us, to compare the fate of Killmonger with Loki, another sympathetic villain in the Marvel Cinematic

Universe. Loki gets multiple opportunities to do the right thing and play the role of the hero, while Killmonger never gets a chance at redemption. Once again, as Fanon observed, those who hold negative views of Black people (consciously or unconsciously) project onto Black peoples' bodies their own worst instincts, their worst fears. No surprise, then, that Killmonger is little more than "a receptacle for tropes of inner-city gangsterism."[6] We see this in how Killmonger is portrayed – he's not a *villain*, he's a *thug*, which is just a contemporary ("politically correct") way of saying the N-word in public discourse. Taking this further, as philosopher Cody Dout suggests, Killmonger isn't just portrayed as the substantive social meaning of the N-word, rather he's a Black man who wants to commit "white genocide" – the historic irrational fear of white people across the political spectrum, from liberals like the eugenicist Madison Grant (1865–1937), to literal neo-Nazis.[7] This is why Killmonger, unlike Loki, *has* to die, and it is why Lebron's assessment is right that *Black Panther* should be seen as just another example in a long tradition of racist film, going as far back as *The Birth of a Nation*.

The philosopher Tommy J. Curry elaborates that, circulating around the image of the Black male, there is the host of racist fears and stereotypes: the idea of the Black male rapist, the abuser, the hypermasculine "beast," the inhuman and subhuman enemy of civilization; that is, the barbarian – no "man" at all, but, in Curry's specialized terminology, a "man-not." "Racist accounts of Black males," he says, "depict them as lesser males who are lazy, unintelligent, aggressive, and violent toward women and children and who abandon their families physically and cannot provide for them economically, while nonetheless requiring coercive legal and extralegal sanctions to control their hyper-masculinity and predatory inclinations." What Curry's work demonstrates is that there is a deeply entrenched cultural inability to see Black men as vulnerable beings that, at the same time, makes us prone to seeing them as pathological perpetrators of harm – despite multiple studies showing that Black men "are by far the most liberal sex-race grouping in America," "are more involved than other males in doing housework, tending to children, and sharing decision making with their female counterparts."[8]

In *Black Panther*'s depiction of Killmonger as the paradigmatic "Black Macho" who covets the power of white patriarchy ("we are going to use their own strategy against 'em"), the film thereby perpetuates the stereotypes of Black men as dangerous "super-predators," the same myths that prevent some people from seeing Black men as vulnerable beings and as victims of gendered and genocidal anti-Black hatred. The theorist William A. Smith has called this latter *anti-Black misandry*: the "exaggerated pathological aversion toward Black males that [like its counterpart in anti-Black misogyny] is created and reinforced in societal, institutional, and individual ideologies, practices, and behaviors."[9] But *Black Panther*'s participation in anti-Black misandry is not accidental. Its portrayal of Killmonger is an important means by which the film is able to discredit radical anti-colonial politics in favor of a politics of reform and accommodation to white power, revealing it to be a supremely colonial, not only racist, film. But to understand this, we need to understand what colonialism and anti-colonial theory are.

Anti-colonial Theory

Anti-colonial theory emerges in situations of colonial domination. But there are different kinds of colonialism, and there are different manifestations of anti-colonial resistance. The image of colonialism that *Black Panther* most directly invokes – stopping short, however, of openly recognizing it – is really just one species of colonizatism. Called *franchise* or *dependent colonialism* by the late Australian anthropologist Patrick Wolfe (1949–2016), this is a form of colonization "primarily established to extract surplus value from indigenous labour."[10] It occurs when a state sponsors, or itself enlists, a relatively small population to subjugate an area with an extant majority population(s) while the minority subsequently come to depend on the labor of the majority. Passing over Wakanda thanks to the cloaking technology they developed using vibranium, the extractive enterprises of franchise colonialism are nevertheless a key factor in how the narrative motivates Wakandan isolationism, the latter being justified "to keep vibranium safe" from colonial powers.

This image of colonialism, conceived as a bygone period in history, has become so familiar that we forget that forms of colonial domination are alive and well today. For the purposes of this discussion, however, we can focus on just those forms the film itself cites.[11] Beside this "classical" form of colonialism, then, there is another type which the film cites, called *neocolonialism*. To understand this form of colonialism, consider that the purpose of invasion in this classical colonialism is largely economic: colonizers want the resources and the labor of the peoples they invade, and this requires access to large pools of cheap or "free" labor. This they can most effectively obtain by subjecting the Native population, or by importing slave labor. In either case, once these populations are enslaved, the *preservation* of their subjection will become a key aim in the administration of any franchise colony. In actual history, as the Peruvian philosopher Anibal Quijano (1930–2018) writes, it was the conjunction of franchise colonial domination with the rise of a global market that gave rise to the *racialized* control of labor after 1492 – since justifying the violent expropriation of Indigenous lands (for resources) and African bodies (for labor) required that they be socially classified so as *to remain* subjected *as* inferior races.[12] Racial domination, at first a structural concomitant of colonial extraction, thus gained an independent, self-propelling momentum that later served to sustain emergent *neocolonial* formations. Race, as Quijano says, thereby has "proven to be more durable and stable than the colonialism in whose matrix it was established."[13] He terms this the *coloniality of power*.

Quijano's account helps us to explain how, in the wake of the formal decolonization of franchise colonies, a new, indirect form of colonial rule – *neocolonialism* – has taken the place of the old. As Kwame Nkrumah (1909–1972), the revolutionary leader and eventual president of Ghana, defined it: "The essence of neo-colonialism is that the State which is subject to it is, in theory, independent and has all the outward trappings of international sovereignty. [But] In reality its economic system and thus its political policy is directed from outside."[14] Deeply shaped by the social relations that franchise colonialism established between the Global North and Global South countries, neocolonial power thus refers to the *international* political, social, and economic system in which, despite a formal acknowledgment of equality, the Global North countries (the economic and political *centers* or *metropoles*) continue – through the cooperation of international finance institutions, transnational corporations, and local elites – to extract the human and natural resources of the Global South (the *peripheries*).[15]

The net effect of this is that the peripheries have become subject to the whims of the centers of global power, the poverty of the periphery being no accident, but a structural consequence of the precise mode in which they are integrated into the global economy. Furthermore, whenever the neocolonies attempt to assert their sovereignty, whenever they balk at the external imposition of trade policy, wealthy nations, like mafia enforcers, step in to make an example of them to the rest of the oppressed. Although the film never openly acknowledges this kind of colonialism *by name*, it is what Killmonger is alluding to when he says that he knows "how colonizers think," because colonial domination was what he enforced as a Black Ops specialist. In fact, it is this backdrop of neocolonialism that undergirds and explains the whole impetus for Killmonger's *global* rather than just *local* revolution. Killmonger's quest to arm the oppressed people of *all* the world makes sense only if there is a global circumstance of neocolonial racial domination.

While much more could be said with regard to theories of colonialism, it is clear from the global aspirations of Killmonger's uprising that he means to abolish all forms of colonization, regardless of the label. "We're gonna send vibranium weapons out to our War Dogs," he says. "They'll arm oppressed people all over the world so they can finally rise up and kill those in power." Doing so, in fact, would follow the internationalist impulses of all forms of Black radicalism. As Kwame Touré (AKA Stokely Carmichael) and Charles V. Hamilton write: "Black Power means that [B]lack people see themselves as part of a new force, sometimes called the 'Third World'; that we see our struggle as closely related to liberation struggles around the world. We must hook up with these struggles."[16] On this view, the Black nation within the white *Amerikan* nation was an *internal colony*. Similarly, in "Why We Are Not Racists," the Black Panther Party wrote that "We do not fight racism with racism. We fight racism with solidarity. We do not fight exploitative capitalism with [B]lack capitalism. We fight capitalism with basic socialism. And we do not fight imperialism with more imperialism. We fight imperialism with *proletarian internationalism*," the latter being the idea that "the revolution" should have global aspirations to be successful if the oppressed are to overthrow the world-system of capitalism.[17] As Killmonger says to the Wakandan elite: "It's about two billion people all over the world that looks like us, but their lives are a lot harder. Wakanda has the tools to liberate 'em all."

It is a mark of the power of this revolutionary vision that, despite *Black Panther*'s attempts to water down, caricature, and libel the radical thought and practice of the descendants of Black captives, its logic yet shines, like a jewel in the gunk, beneath all of the film's convolutions. This is what makes Killmonger an appealing and sympathetic, and ultimately tragic, villain. But now that we've surveyed theories of colonialism, we are positioned to see how colonialism and decolonization were mis-portrayed in *Black Panther*, and why the film's central commitments require that this be the case.

(Anti)Colonialism in/of *Black Panther*

As previously noted, *Black Panther* rarely invokes the concepts of slavery and colonialism. Slavery is only directly cited twice: first, in the imagery of Africans being loaded onto the holds of slaveships in the opening sequence, just in time for the narrator (ostensibly, N'Jobu talking to the young Erik) to say that "the world [outside of Wakanda] descended further into chaos"; second, when Killmonger declares that he would rather die free than live in bondage, just in time to catch the sunset over Wakanda as he unceremoniously takes his own life. In turn, "colonialism" is directly invoked just twice. Intended by the filmmakers, one surmises, to be a crowd pleaser that lends credibility to the idea that the film really is as "woke" as it presents itself, the first time is when Shuri calls Agent Ross a "colonizer" to poke fun at him. The second instance is when Killmonger says that he knows "how colonizers think," and alludes to the strategies of global domination that white capitalist power has executed historically and that Killmonger has learned through his participation in American military agencies.

That colonialism and slavery should be invoked so scarcely, however, is no coincidence. For while the film depends on this history of colonial violence for its narrative coherence, it must also *bury* that history to calm the white colonial shame it elicits. The Black experience of racial horror inhabits what we might describe as the film's "subconscious," since the film relies on it to explain Wakanda's political isolationism and to motivate the marvel of its technological sophistication amidst the perceived wreckage and underdevelopment of the rest of Africa. The facts that might explain this, however, *have to remain* repressed and disavowed in the narrative structure if the film is to maintain its commitment to appeasing white moviegoers and vilifying the radical anti-colonial perspective of the descendants of African peoples. At the same time, these social processes cannot be cited without exposing fundamental antagonisms in the film's structure.

This is evident in the film's treatment of both slavery and colonialism. In the opening sequence, for instance, the film lumps together images of the transatlantic slave trade and colonial wars with those of world wars between global superpowers and the detonation of atomic bombs. In doing so, the distinctive racialized evil of chattel slavery and colonialism is lost to the film's narrative structure, and makes it just another link in the long chain of *humanity*'s moral blunders (*in general*), not that of *white* peoples' (*specifically*). The effect is to absolve European colonizers and their descendants who continue to benefit from the global white power structure of any wrongdoing, since it is human folly *in general* that is at fault for "evil that men do," rather than the specific cultural and social tendencies of Europeans. Yet this is in obvious tension with the second time slavery is directly cited at the climax of the film, since the aesthetic and emotional force of Killmonger's final line of dialogue relies on the *specificity* of the evil of racial slavery, which cannot therefore be just another "human" blunder.

Likewise, in Shuri's crack at Agent Ross as a colonizer, it's not the "wokeness" of the film that it is evidenced. What it instead reveals is that the Wakandans are well aware of the racist international colonial order that exists outside their nation, exposing their reluctance to end racial suffering, despite having the power to do so, and even their willingness to stand with this white colonial order against the oppressed peoples of the world. Even as the Global North continues its neocolonial plunder of the South, Killmonger throws the complicity of the Wakandan leadership in its face: "Y'all sittin' up here comfortable." It is later revealed that, rather than accept Killmonger as their new leader, the Wakandan ruling class would much rather ally with the CIA and go to civil war with their own people – even providing Agent Ross with the weapons and tools by which to kill other Wakanadans.[18]

On the other hand, for it to make any sense at all that Killmonger would use the colonizer's own methods against them, one has to already have a sense of the techniques of regime change that white American power has used to destroy democratic and liberation movements across the world. In point of fact, when describing just how dangerous Killmonger is to T'Challa, Agent Ross admits that there are US agencies dedicated to covertly overthrowing foreign governments. It is noteworthy that *none of the Wakandans present are disturbed by this revelation*; they are more concerned with the potential threat posed by Killmonger. But by this point in the narrative, the film has already gone to great lengths to demonize Erik Stevens. So his invocation of using "the colonizer's methods" merely completes the film's conceptual linkage between Black radicalism and the pathological masculinity of the racist "super-predator" trope. His motivations are thus muddled, and the logic of his mission rendered incoherent, by the film's commitment to portray Black men and Black radicalism as more morally repugnant and wrongheaded than CIA-backed coups in the Third World – belying the fact that, as Fanon himself noted, decolonization is always a violent event.

Indeed, Wakanda's rejection of Killmonger stands in sharp contrast to his desire to reclaim his homeland. When Killmonger explains his plan to the Wakandan ruling class, they are visibly appalled by the idea of arming the poor and the oppressed. To them, Killmonger, despite having a legitimate claim to the throne, is an "outsider." After he wakes up from the beating Killmonger visited upon him, T'Challa tells the Jabari Tribe that "an enemy sits on the throne" and warns them that Killmonger will come after the Jabari next. In the first place, however, Killmonger won the throne through the procedure that Wakanda uses to elect its king. But if, by definition, Killmonger is the legitimate monarch, who is he an enemy of? In the second place, Killmonger thinks of all Black peoples as *his people*; so, why would he come after the Jabari? Even more to the point, we could ask why the Wakandans have such a strong aversive reaction to their long-lost son. Shouldn't they welcome him back? It is only at this point, considering these questions, that we can even begin to address the other difficult questions raised at the outset of this chapter. *Black Panther* is unable to answer the riddle of its own existence, however, since that would require an honest confrontation with the realities of contemporary domination.

An Impossible Return?

Is it possible to return to and recover a way of life that existed before the moment of colonization? To reclaim an identity erased by the colonial violence, genocide, and slavery that birthed the modern world? These are essential and urgent questions for anti-colonial philosophy. Making a pathological caricature of the only radical anti-colonial option it depicts in the character of Erik Killmonger, however, *Black Panther* is unable to broach them without rendering its self-presentation incoherent.

Colonialism, I have suggested elsewhere, has a way of covering over its own tracks. In *Black Panther*, Killmonger is the very site at which the terror of colonial history is sutured – the anti-heroic figure who must be depicted as a genocidal and misogynistic monster in order to dissipate the shame and the guilt he would otherwise elicit. In that sense, Killmonger is thus also a cypher, a Janus-faced synecdoche for the coloniality of power, as well as for the radical anticolonial vision which is buried beneath the stereotypes his person invokes. As we saw, that vision wielded such power as to rupture at the seams of the film – at the seams of Killmonger's character. Killmonger's character – indeed, his literal body – "scarred" by the coloniality of representation, itself provides the key that allows us to understand the extent of the horror that that representation masks. What these ruptures reveal is that *Black Panther*, despite claiming to be the most radical event of the year and despite having countless fans who think that Wakanda represents a decolonial dream, might instead be just another a sociological product reflecting what it means to inhabit a world that has been molded by centuries of white racial empire.

Notes

1. See Christopher Lebron, "'Black Panther' is not the movie we deserve," *Boston Review*, February 17, 2018, at http://bostonreview.net/race/christopher-lebron-black-panther.
2. Lebron.
3. Lebron; my emphasis.
4. Frantz Fanon, *Black Skin, White Masks*, trans. Richard Philcox (New York: Grove Press, 1967), 167.
5. Fanon, 166–167.
6. Lebron.
7. See George Michael, "David Lane and the fourteen words," *Totalitarian Movements and Political Religions* 10 (2009), 43–61. doi:10.1080/14690760903067986.
8. Tommy J. Curry, The Man-Not: Race, Class, Genre, and the Dilemmas of Black Manhood (Philadelphia, PA: Temple University Press, 2017), 2
9. William A. Smith quoted in Curry, 170.
10. Patrick Wolfe, *Settler Colonialism and the Transformation of Anthropology* (London: Cassell, 1999), 1–2.
11. Other forms of colonial domination are, of course, settler colonialism, and internal colonialism. For the former see Patrick Wolfe, "Settler colonialism and the elimination of the native," *Journal of Genocide Research* 8 (2006), 387–409. For the latter, see Stokely Carmichael and Charles V. Hamilton, *Black Power: The Politics of Liberation in America* (New York: Vintage Books, 1967) and Robert L. Allen, *Black Awakening in Capitalist America* (Trenton, NJ: Africa World Press, Inc., 1992).
12. Anibal Quijano, "Coloniality of power, eurocentrism, and Latin America," trans. Michael Ennis, *Nepantla Views from the South* 1 (2000), 533.
13. Quijano, 533.
14. Kwame Nkrumah, *Neo-Colonialism, The Last Stage of Imperialism* (London: Thomas Nelson and Sons, 1965), ix.
15. See generally Kwame Nkrumah, *Neo-Colonialism, The Last Stage of Imperialism* (London: Thomas Nelson and Sons, 1965); Walter Rodney, *How Europe Underdeveloped Africa* (Washington, DC: Howard University Press, 1982).
16. Stokely Carmichael and Charles V. Hamilton, *Black Power: The Politics of Liberation in America* (New York: Vintage Books, 1967).
17. Bobby Seale, *Seize the Time: The Story of the Black Panther Party* (Baltimore, MD: Black Classic Press, 1991), 71; my emphasis.
18. I owe this point to a discussion of the film I had with my colleague Cody Dout.

23

T'Challa's Dream and Killmonger's Means
Echoes of MLK and Malcolm X

Gerald Browning

With technology beyond the comprehension of any other country (thanks to their supply of vibranium), Wakanda has enough power to rival any nation on Earth. T'Challa oversees this power with wisdom, leading his kingdom with benevolence. Despite Wakanda's isolationism, T'Challa views outsiders positively, and ultimately he comes to see humanity as one tribe. Killmonger's perspective is different.

With his father cast out of Wakanda, Killmonger heard stories about the powerful African nation, but he never was a part of it. This, along with the murder of his father by T'Chaka, created resentment in Killmonger. When he becomes king he wants to use Wakanda's power (its vibranium weapons) to liberate Black people around the world by "killing those in power, and their children, and anyone else who takes their side." As he tells his council after taking the throne, "The world's going to start over, and this time we're on top."

Strangely, Killmonger's passion stems from a sense of pride in where he came from (he knows Wakandan traditions and he speaks the language!), creating a tension in his actions. Killmonger may be a villain, but he's a sympathetic and understandable villain, especially since his views on oppression continue to resonate in the twenty-first century.

One way to look at *Black Panther* is through the lens of the Civil Rights Movement, comparing T'Challa to Dr. Martin Luther King, Jr. and comparing Killmonger to Malcolm X. To be clear from the start, the point is not to suggest that Malcolm X was wrong, nor is it meant to say that Malcolm X acted in any way similar to Killmonger.

Black Panther and Philosophy: What Can Wakanda Offer the World?, First Edition. Edited by Edwardo Pérez and Timothy E. Brown.
© 2022 John Wiley & Sons, Inc. Published 2022 by John Wiley & Sons, Inc.

T'Challa's Dream

African Americans of the 1950s and 1960s didn't have Wakanda and vibranium technology to unite them, but they did have a home connecting them to one another, to their shared history, and to the future they dreamed of – a home that offered a peaceful refuge in an otherwise violent world. This home was the church, and its most prominent leader was Dr. King.

Like T'Challa, Dr. King was an inspirational leader, beloved by those who followed him. King wanted to build bridges and establish an open line of communication between the African American community and the Caucasian community. In his famous "I Have a Dream" speech, MLK outlines this philosophy, saying:

> We must forever conduct our struggle on the high plane of dignity and discipline. We must not allow our creative protest to degenerate into physical violence. Again and again we must rise to the majestic heights of meeting physical force with soul force. The marvelous new militancy which has engulfed the Negro community must not lead us to a distrust of all white people, for many of our white brothers, as evidenced by their presence here today, have come to realize that their destiny is tied up with our destiny. They have come to realize that their freedom is inextricably bound to our freedom. We cannot walk alone.[1]

Indeed, Dr. King's words seem prescient when we consider the George Floyd protests around the world in 2020, as people of all colors and creeds marched together. In *Black Panther*, T'Challa seemed to heed King's words. Consider his speech at the United Nations:

> Wakanda will no longer watch from the shadows. We cannot. We must not. We will work to be an example of how we as brothers and sisters on this Earth should treat each other. Now, more than ever, the illusions of division threaten our very existence. We all know the truth: more connects us than separates us. But in times of crisis the wise build bridges, while the foolish build barriers. We must find a way to look after one another as if we were one single tribe.

These words don't just reflect the sentiment of Dr. King, they also explain T'Challa's actions. He ruled with benevolence toward others (for example, sparing M'Baku's life in the challenge ritual) and was unafraid to work with outsiders.[2] For example, in *Captain America: Civil War*, T'Challa (mostly) worked with the Avengers and Agent Ross to capture Helmut Zemo. In *Black Panther*, T'Challa worked with Agent Ross to pursue Ulysses Klaue, and in *Avengers: Infinity War*, T'Challa worked with the Avengers again to stop Thanos. Indeed, T'Challa's benevolence extended to non-Wakandan individuals, too, as he used vibranium technology (and Shuri's lab) to help heal Bucky Barnes and Agent Ross. T'Challa was even willing to try to save Killmonger after their epic battle at the end of *Black Panther*. For T'Challa,

Wakanda's strength came from the secret of vibranium and the technology it inspired. Yet, to be fair, for all of T'Challa's collaboration with non-Wakandans, he wasn't always willing to share the truth about Wakanda with others.

For most of *Black Panther*, T'Challa resists the idea of sharing vibranium and helping other nations in the world. In *Civil War* (when we first meet T'Challa and the Black Panther) T'Challa wasn't necessarily supportive of Captain America's position – at least, the argument between Captain America and Iron Man didn't seem as important to T'Challa as capturing Zemo. It's notable, though, that T'Challa (as he does with M'Baku in *Black Panther*) shows mercy to Zemo, handing him over to Agent Ross rather than killing him.

T'Challa's actions at the end of *Black Panther* – where he intends to build a Wakandan International Outreach Centre – reflect Dr. King's dream of little children of different races holding hands and playing together. For T'Challa, this also includes learning together, about science and technology. It took T'Challa a while to embrace the outreach, but his change in perspective wasn't sudden. Nakia planted the seed in his mind by questioning Wakanda's global role. T'Challa thus began to consider how Wakanda could help the world, and his actions (such as saving Agent Ross in *Black Panther* and Bucky Barnes in *Civil War*) showed that T'Challa was open to helping non-Wakandans. Significantly, T'Challa questions himself in the Ancestral Plane when he speaks with his father about what he needed to do in order to be king. It's an important moment because it shows T'Challa's philosophical struggle – having to honor Wakanda and its traditions, yet feeling a moral pull in the direction of helping others. One of T'Challa's most revealing thoughts concerns his own worthiness as a king. It's a meaningful scene between father and son, with T'Chaka telling T'Challa: "You are a good man with a good heart. And it's hard for a good man to be king."

T'Challa (like his father) was focused on being the best king for Wakanda. As he says to Killmonger, "I am the king of Wakanda, not the king of the all people." T'Challa was less universal and less self-confident than Dr. King, which is why he struggled throughout the film. Of course, as Nakia tells T'Challa when he questions himself and the deeds of his ancestors, "You can't let your father's mistakes define who you are. You get to decide what kind of king you are going to be." When T'Challa finally makes this decision, he does so by embracing Dr. King's benevolent philosophy, becoming the best king for Wakanda and the best example for the world.

Killmonger's Means

Erik Killmonger's story is sympathetic and compelling. It's also tragic, especially when he enters the Ancestral Plane and talks with his father in one of the film's most heartbreaking scenes. Killmonger's pain is understandable, and so is his perspective. As T'Challa admits (and shouts during his second sojourn to the Ancestral Plane), T'Chaka was wrong to kill his own brother and especially wrong to abandon young Erik.

Much like Killmonger, Malcolm X (who was born Malcolm Little and who later adopted not just the Malcolm X moniker but also the name El-Hajj Malik El-Shabazz) experienced a tragic young life. Like Killmonger, Malcolm's father was taken away from him at an early age – and, also like Killmonger, young Malcolm turned to a life of crime. Both Malcolm X and Killmonger focused their anger at an establishment that wronged them. Both saw that they needed to stand up against authority and lash out against it. In other words, Malcolm and Erik used their pain as a weapon. Pain led Malcolm X to embrace a Black Nationalist philosophy and extremist methods to achieve freedom and equality for Blacks, arguing repeatedly in favor of speaking the language of whites, which Malcolm X defined as being a language of violence. As he stated:

> If his language is with a shotgun, get a shotgun. Yes, I said if he only under-stands the language of a rifle, get a rifle. If he only understands the language of a rope, get a rope. But don't waste time talking the wrong language to a man if you want to really communicate with him. Speak his language, there's nothing wrong with that.[3]

Or, as Killmonger says, "I know how colonizers think," observing that "where I'm from, when Black folks started revolutions they never had the firepower or the resources to fight their oppressors." Indeed, when Killmonger wrestled the throne away from T'Challa, his plan was to speak the language of colonizers directly to them by arming Blacks around the world with vibranium weapons, with the goal not just of lib-erating Blacks but of eliminating colonizers (whites). As Killmonger commands:

> We're going to send vibranium weapons to our War Dogs. They'll arm oppressed people all over the world so they can finally rise up and kill those in power, and their children, and anyone else who takes their side. It's time they know the truth about us. We're warriors. The world's gonna start over and this time, we're on top. The sun will never set on the Wakandan empire.

Much like Malcolm X, Killmonger responds aggressively to cultural oppression and racism. And much like Malcolm X, Killmonger was willing to accomplish his goal "by any means necessary," a line Malcolm X con-sidered to be not just a refrain (repeated many times during his many speeches) but also a motto.[4] Certainly, the oft-quoted phrase stands out perhaps as much as "I have a dream" does for Dr. King, encapsulating Malcolm X's perspective. Consider the following excerpts from speeches delivered on three different occasions (emphasis added):

Our objective is complete freedom, complete justice, complete equality, *by any means necessary.*[5]

I don't believe in violence – that's why I want to stop it. And you can't stop it with love [...] So, we only mean vigorous action in self-defense, and that vigorous action we feel we're justified in initiating *by any means necessary.*[6]

My reason for believing in extremism, intelligently directed extremism, extremism in defense of liberty, extremism in quest of justice, is because I firmly believe in my heart, that the day that the black man takes an uncompromising step, and realizes that he's within his rights, when his own freedom is being jeopardized, to use *any means necessary* to bring about his freedom, or put a halt to that injustice, I don't think he'll be by himself.[7]

We declare our right on this earth to be a man, to be a human being, to be respected as a human being, to be given the rights of a human being in this society, on this earth, in this day, which we intend to bring into existence *by any means necessary.*[8]

In *Black Panther*, Malcolm X's motto seems implicit in Killmonger's actions, from pulling off the Museum of Great Britain heist to facilitating Klaue's escape to executing Klaue and using his corpse to enter Wakanda to using his combat skills to best T'Challa in the challenge ceremony. Even Killmonger's knowledge of Wakanda (its traditions and language and especially the power of vibranium) equips him with means he can use to achieve his goals. Yet, for all Killmonger accomplishes, his anger towards T'Challa (and T'Chaka and other Wakandans) took him on a destructive path that ultimately led to his own demise. Perhaps it's because Killmonger, for all his similarities to Malcolm X, didn't adhere to Malcolm X's explanation that extremism must be "intelligently directed."[9] After all, it's one thing to fight back, which, at root, is what Malcolm X was suggesting, but it's another thing to completely annihilate a group of people, including children, where guns are met with guns and rope is met with rope – vibranium is cool, but does it go too far to use it in the way Killmonger wanted to use it?

Another way Killmonger differs from Malcolm X is that Killmonger never considers another perspective, remaining steadfast in his conviction, even up until his own death. For example, when T'Challa suggests that perhaps Killmonger's wound could be fixed, Killmonger asks "What for?" never considering that perhaps he and T'Challa could work together. Malcolm X, however, changed his perspective from one that not only embraced Black Nationalism but advocated for a complete separation between Blacks and whites (even suggesting that Blacks should migrate back to Africa) to one that saw people of all colors as part of a common brotherhood. The turning point for Malcolm X was his trip to Mecca, where he witnessed people of different colors and ethnicities praying together in the Muslim faith. Killmonger didn't have such faith, dismissing the religion of Wakanda (even after his visit to the Ancestral Plane), and ordering the fields of Heart-Shaped Herbs to be burned. He also viewed colonizers (and anyone who helped them) monolithically.

Ultimately, Killmonger's dedication to his master plan costs him his life. Nevertheless, much like Malcolm X, Killmonger always aimed towards freedom – for himself and for Black people worldwide. Indeed, his rejection of T'Challa's help at the end is rooted in the slave experience and the desire for freedom. As he says to T'Challa when T'Challa suggests that he could be healed: "Why? So you can lock me up? Nah. Just bury me in the ocean with my ancestors that jumped from ships 'cause they knew death was better than bondage." This is easily one of the most powerful lines spoken in the film. That it's uttered by the main antagonist gives depth to the character and to his perspective, as well as an appreciation for a villain unlike any we have seen in the many Marvel Cinematic Universe (MCU) films.[10]

Killmonger's villain status (as well as his destructive attitude) separates him from Malcolm X. Even though Malcolm X had an aggressive posture towards oppression and subjugation, he did not turn that aggression towards African Americans. Killmonger, however, was adamant in destroying anything that stood in his way. He saw Wakanda as a tool and he didn't mind using that tool to kill Wakandans who opposed him, telling W'Kabi "Man, kill this fool" when T'Challa returns, which causes Wakandans to fight against Wakandans. Or, during the challenge ritual, when he tells T'Challa: "I've lived my entire life for this moment. I trained, I lied, I killed just to get here. I killed in America, Afghanistan, Iraq … I took life from my own brothers and sisters right here on this continent! And all this death just so I could kill you." Killmonger could see the beauty of Wakanda (consider his final words and his appreciation of the Wakandan sunset), but he was all too willing to exploit Wakanda for the sake of power, which is the opposite of what Malcolm X, who sought to empower Blacks, wanted.

Adversaries for the Wakandan Throne

Dr. King and Malcolm X were not adversaries (unlike T'Challa and Killmonger), but their philosophies were diametrically opposed and, to be fair, Malcolm X was often dismissive of Dr. King, referring to him as an "Uncle Tom." However, as he grew older, Malcolm X saw the wisdom in Dr. King's methods and came to an understanding with the Civil Rights leader. In contrast, Killmonger never gave T'Challa (who wanted to atone for his father's mistakes) a chance to, well, atone. For much of *Black*

Panther, T'Challa and Killmonger act as foils of one another, just as Dr. King and Malcolm X did. Yet, at the end of *Black Panther*, Killmonger and T'Challa seem to come to an understanding, with T'Challa seemingly respecting Killmonger's decision to die and sharing Killmonger's desire for freedom and his goal of helping Blacks around the world.

Ultimately, though their methods and philosophies differed, T'Challa and Killmonger wanted the same thing – to use Wakandan technology to help others, just as Dr. King and Malcolm X both sought to help oppressed Blacks in America. T'Challa, like Dr. King, relied more on compassion to realize a dream of peace and understanding and sharing, whereas Killmonger, like Malcolm X, relied more on combative rhetoric, appealing to the aggressive nature of man to speak the language of colonizers.

Echoing Icons

To compare Martin Luther King, Jr. to T'Challa or Malcolm X to Erik Killmonger may not be entirely fair to either historical figure. To say that Malcolm X was as aggressive and militant as Killmonger misunderstands the words/philosophies of Malcolm X and his notion of Black Nationalism. To liken T'Challa's preaching of togetherness to Dr. King glosses over the fact that T'Challa held an isolationist attitude during most of *Black Panther*. However, in a world where #BlackLivesMatter continues to be a necessary hashtag, "I Can't Breathe" is a protest cry, and the injustices of the African American experience are held up for all to see, a hero such as T'Challa and a villain such as Killmonger can bring a powerful message and extend a conversation that began with Martin and Malcolm. Indeed, with themes such as colonialism, isolationism, racism, sexism, and xenophobia, *Black Panther* brings the African American experience to the MCU more effectively than any other film or television show, using the superhero genre to deal with deep-rooted social problems that have long impacted American society and continue to do so to this day.[11]

Notes

1. Martin Luther King, Jr., "I have a dream: Full text of March on Washington Speech," NAACP.org, at https://www.naacp.org/i-have-a-dream-speech-full-march-on-washington.
2. They also echo his father's words in *Captain America: Civil War*, when T'Chaka (just before he gets killed) says that Wakanda should question its legacy, that it is a country "too long in the shadows," and that Wakandans would "fight to improve the world we wish to join".
3. From a speech delivered at the Audubon Ballroom on December 20, 1964. Malcolm X. *Malcolm X Speaks*, ed., George Breitman (New York: Grove

Press, 1965), 108.

4. As Malcolm X stated in his speech at the founding of the Organization of Afro-American Unity on June 28, 1964: "That's our motto. We want freedom by any means necessary. We want justice by any means necessary. We want equality by any means necessary".

5. Breitman, 116.

6. From a speech delivered in Detroit on February 13, 1965. Breitman, 165.

7. Malcolm X, Oxford Union Debate, December 3, 1964.

8. Malcolm X, speech at the founding of the Organization of Afro-American Unity, June 28, 1964.

9. Malcolm X, Oxford Union Debate, December 3, 1964.

10. Not even Thanos had a good enough reason to snap his fingers.

11. Even *Luke Cage*, for all its depiction of Harlem's culture, arguable didn't resonate with these themes to the same degree as *Black Panther*. HBO's *Watchmen*, however, directly engages America's history with racism in a visceral way, presenting complex portraits of Black heroes through a compelling narrative. Similarly, *The Falcon and the Winter Soldier* on Disney+ dealt not just with Sam Wilson's Falcon assuming the mantel of Captain America (in a post-blip, Black Lives Matter world), it also delved into the world of Isaiah Bradley, a forgotten super solider who was effectively the first Black Captain America.

24

"It's Time They Knew the Truth about Us! We're Warriors!"

Black Panther and the Black Panther Party

Karen Joan Kohoutek

"I observed for as long as I could! All over the planet our people suffer because they don't have the tools to fight back. With vibranium weapons they could overthrow every country and Wakanda could rule them all ... the right way."

– N'Jobu

"You know, where I'm from ... when black folks started revolutions, they never had the firepower ... or the resources to fight their oppressors. Where was Wakanda?"

– Erik "Killmonger" Stevens

"What we believe in is armed revolution, permanent revolution, the creation of as many Viet Nams as are necessary to defeat U.S. racism and imperialism throughout the world."

– George Murray, Minister of Education, Black Panther Party

The origin of *Black Panther*'s charismatic villain, Killmonger, is the same as that of the historic Black Panther Party: Oakland, California. Director Ryan Coogler begins the film here, in a housing project where N'Jobu, a prince from Wakanda, has been living undercover. As Zuri tells T'Challa, "the hardships he saw there radicalized" him to the point of planning a violent resistance against oppression.

Black Panther and Philosophy: What Can Wakanda Offer the World?, First Edition. Edited by Edwardo Pérez and Timothy E. Brown.
© 2022 John Wiley & Sons, Inc. Published 2022 by John Wiley & Sons, Inc.

Years later – upon seizing the throne of Wakanda from its new king, T'Challa – N'Jobu's son Killmonger argues on behalf of the world's disenfranchised, including those, like him, who grew up Black in the United States. He plans to arm the oppressed with Wakanda's military inventions, "so they can finally rise up and kill those in power." Clearly, *Black Panther* explores complicated themes related to the use of arms: for self-defense, on behalf of an accepted authority, and against an oppressor.

In the Black Panther Party's Ten-Point Program of demands and beliefs, the first is that "we want freedom. We want power to determine the destiny of our Black Community … we believe that Black People will not be free until we are able to determine our own destiny."[1] This freedom is the difference between the citizens of the progressive, healthy nation of Wakanda and the frustrated, angry Killmonger, who experienced none of that freedom in the United States.

Considering these stances, we see very different relationships to the idea of a legitimate government, which is authorized by its citizens to use firearms in supposed defense of the nation. Wakanda's military force exists in the service of protecting its people. By contrast, the United States' military is often used against its own population, particularly against people of color, and is also used across the globe in acts of military aggression, a fact explicitly referenced by Killmonger's military career.

The often-debated Second Amendment right to bear arms has never been applied equally to Black and white Americans. Actor Wendell Pierce's tweet that "if every Black male 18–35 applied for a conceal & carry permit … there would be gun control laws in a second" has become a popular meme for a reason. Historically, the Black Panthers' program of acting upon their constitutional rights by buying and carrying guns for protection created a pivotal shift in American gun control legislation, aimed specifically at limiting the right of Black Americans to bear arms. So, Killmonger's view isn't just that of a power-hungry villain. His position resonates with the history of Black oppression and with the Black Panther Party's focus on liberation.

What We Want, What We Believe

Black Panther first appeared in Marvel Comics in the summer of 1966, a few months before the official founding of the Black Panther Party.[2] The Black liberation group borrowed the logo of the big cat from the Lowndes County Freedom Organization, an Alabama political group. In an interview, that group's chairman, John Hulett, said the symbol was chosen because "the black panther is an animal that when it is pressured it moves back until it is cornered, then it comes out fighting for life or death. We felt we had been pushed back long enough and that it was time for Negroes to come out and take over."[3] This interview with Hulett took place in June 1966, neck and neck with the Marvel comic's debut. At a Panther rally that

August, Stokely Carmichael "called on blacks to unite with people of color in Vietnam and throughout the world. He also spoke in favor of armed self-defense for blacks," saying that "a man needs a black panther on his side ... he may also need a gun."[4] Activists like Carmichael were defending themselves both from the street-level reality of police brutality and from bigger-picture institutional racism. They were "pushed back" until they were ready to fight back and "take over." Both N'Jobu and his son's respective experiences took place in the same milieu, just a few decades apart, and *Black Panther* was released in the midst of the Black Lives Matter movement.

N'Jobu's Wakanda-formed ideals of autonomy and liberation clash against the racism in the outside world, but in his desire to share the wealth with the larger group of "our people," he runs into the same problems that the Black Panther Party and the larger Black liberation movement did. Against the deep-rooted injustices N'Jobu witnesses, what strategies will lead to lasting change, and not be defeated by more powerful forces? If violence, or arming the oppressed, isn't the answer (as generations of Wakandan kings believe), then what is? Black Lives Matter has used social media to organize demonstrations, but N'Jobu didn't have Twitter in 1992. The events he likely witnessed, such as the Los Angeles Riot, largely in response to the Los Angeles Police Department's brutality against Rodney King, didn't produce positive results. Indeed, the Rodney King riots led to severe civil unrest, 64 deaths, thousands of injuries, arrests, significant economic damage, and the deployment of more than 10,000 National Guard troops, who remained for weeks after the riots ended. So, N'Jobu's options would have seemed limited, making his appeal to T'Chaka compelling, even though it was rooted in violence.

Indeed, criticisms of the Black Panthers' willingness to use violence, even in self-defense, can be found everywhere. For example, in his book on the Panthers' relationship to armed resistance, Curtis J. Austin argues "that all citizens have the right to self-defense is indisputable," but that Panther founder Huey Newton's emphasis on standing one's ground against illegal police raids "might have inadvertently brought on a lot of death and destruction."[5] It's worth noting that the right of Black Americans to self-defense was not "indisputable" in the 1960s, in 1992, or even today. This doesn't just muddy the philosophical waters; it poisons them, making it impossible to take criticisms of Black self-defense initiatives in good faith.

"Does the State Rule the People or Do the People Rule the State?"[6]

The Panthers' Ten Points embrace the rights that supposedly apply to all Americans: "The second Amendment of the Constitution of the United States gives us the right to bear arms. We therefore believe that all Black people should arm themselves for self-defense."[7] The specific need for this action is to protect "our Black community from racist police oppression and brutality."[8] Newton mentions the book *Negroes with Guns*, written by activist Robert F. Williams, as "a great influence on the kind of party we developed."[9] Williams clearly explains his position on self-defense, which brought him into conflict with both the US authorities and the branch of the Civil Rights Movement dedicated to non-violence. He states that "in civilized society the law serves as a deterrent against lawless forces that would destroy the democratic process. But where there is a breakdown in the law, the individual citizen has a right to protect his person, his family, his home and his property."[10] N'Jobu would certainly have appreciated Williams's perspective, that "the Afro-American militant ... does not *introduce* violence into a racist social system – the violence is already there and has always been there.[11] As Williams adds, "It is precisely this unchallenged violence that allows a racist social system to perpetuate itself. When people say that they are opposed to Negroes 'resorting to violence' what they really mean is that they are opposed to Negroes defending themselves and challenging the exclusive monopoly of violence practiced by white racists."[12] As N'Jobu tells his brother T'Chaka, "I observed as long as I could! Their leaders have been assassinated, communities flooded with drugs and weapons, they are overly policed and incarcerated. All over the planet our people suffer because they don't have the tools to fight back. With vibranium weapons they could overthrow every country and Wakanda could rule them all ... the right way."

Williams calls for "armed resistance to the gun-toting Klansmen."[13] There should be nothing controversial about that. The fear of Black Americans "resorting to violence" is not based on logical reasoning. When the power structure of the state grants no right to self-defense for certain people, then whatever they do to protect themselves is considered aggression; this happens time and time again, from Williams's experience down to the contemporary Black Lives Matter movement.

Black liberation groups have always faced the state in its role, defined by sociologist Max Weber, as "a relation of men dominating men" with a "*monopoly of the legitimate use of physical force* within a given territory ... considered the sole source of the 'right' to use violence."[14] This monopoly holds over all forms of violence, even self-defense, insofar as the courts determine who has the right to defend themselves, and from whom.

It is fair, though, at least in a democracy, to question the legitimacy of the state in its uses of force. A nation has an obligation to live up to its stated ideals and agreed-upon rule of law. *Black Panther* reminds us that even the most thoughtful, enlightened government and its representatives can make life-or-death decisions that go against the will of individual citizens, since even T'Challa, *Black Panther*'s hero, has a moment when he demands obedience of Zuri, screaming "I am your king now!" It's a line Killmonger repeats when he becomes king.

The idea of legitimate authority can break down completely into primitive "might makes right" justifications when a government acts against its own people – as it did in Oakland where the police were seen "as armed occupiers of the black community,"[15] creating what has been called "a colony in a nation."[16] Blacks were unable to live as citizens – unable to assume that their government would only use force in acting on the nation's best interests. In response, the Panthers claimed "their own right to organized violence" and "the constitutional right to bear arms, employing a logic of policing and the law *against* the police and the law."[17] Acting against the monopoly of the state, the Black Panthers were branded as dangerous revolutionaries for claiming their constitutional rights. And as their "strategy of armed self-defense became more and more effective … [they] attracted even greater attention among authorities, who took steps to stop them," primarily via the 1967 Mulford Act, which outlawed "the carrying of loaded firearms in public."[18]

Signed into law by Republican Ronald Reagan, then governor of California, the Mulford Act is generally accepted as a direct response to the Panthers' activities. Where Black Americans needed to defend themselves from representatives of their own government, the law stepped in to stop them. If that meant taking rights away from white gun owners, too, then so be it. Imagine if such an act were signed into law by a Democrat governor today.

"This Time, We're on Top!"

When Killmonger launches his plan for world revolution, he uses words very similar to those his father had used. "It's about two million people all over the world that looks like us," says Killmonger to the Wakandan council. "Wakanda has the tools to liberate them all." Twisted by his life experience, though, he goes beyond N'Jobu's radicalization, not only looking to overthrow governments, or even just to "kill those in power," but also to kill "their children. And anyone else who takes their side. It's time they know the truth about us! We're warriors!"

His plan, to arm the world's marginalized people, contains an exaggerated echo of the militaristic side of the Black Panthers, and certainly reflects white fears of that militancy. The widespread white belief that Black self-defense will erupt into first-strike violence gives evidence of guilt, an understanding on some level that, if the roles were reversed, white Americans would be murderously resentful of the treatment they have given to people of color.

Killmonger frames his takeover as violent altruism, in the best interests of the world's oppressed, but it is his education in the tactics of American imperialism that takes him to the point of genocide. Note that Agent Ross, an American CIA agent, identifies him as "one of ours," with targeted training and experience working directly for the CIA, using assassination and other tactics "to destabilize foreign governments," skills that Killmonger calls the tools of the "colonizers." As an American operative, Killmonger "took life from my own brothers and sisters right here on this continent," in displays of colonial power. This is reminiscent of Panther addresses to Black soldiers who were drafted into an imperialist project of war and violence, authorized by the United States government, to kill other people of color. Stokely Carmichael pointed out that "the Vietnamese are fighting the same establishment that the brothers in Oakland, Chicago and Watts are fighting."[19]

If the United States' clandestine warfare, including the kind of violence and destabilization Killmonger played a role in, is considered legitimate, then Killmonger's genocidal plan of attack against other nations would be equally legitimate on the same terms: those of a sovereign nation acting outside international law to further its own interests. There is no moral justification here, just logical equivalence.

Despite Killmonger's confidence, we have no information about how the gift of high-tech weapons would have been received by the downtrodden people of the world, or even by the Wakandan spies, whom he expected to spearhead the revolt, raised as they were with Wakandan ideals. Given that N'Jobu was "radicalized" by his observations of American oppression, one wonders how they understood and processed the racism found in the unenlightened rest of the world. Some of the resistance to violent revolution might be pragmatic. As Williams said, "The responsible Negro leadership is pacifist in so far as its one interest is that we do not fight white racists, that we do not 'provoke' or enrage them. They constantly tell us that if we resort to violent self-defense we will be exterminated."[20] Oakland member Bill Jennings described how, even in the Panthers' heyday, "by and large the majority of black people wasn't to that stage of taking up the gun."[21]

Nonetheless, earlier in *Black Panther*, T'Challa's warrior friend W'Kabi was reluctant to allow refugees into their state, but offered to help "clean up the world," not unlike the willingness of the US to use force in shaping the globe to its liking. He already sympathized with Killmonger's desire to show the world "exactly who we are," and this led him to support the idea of "waging war on other nations," even though T'Challa claimed it "has never been our way." The moral divide over whether to carry out Killmonger's plan or stop it leads the Wakandan people to open warfare. There is resistance to his plans for a genocidal military offensive, but when Killmonger becomes the King of Wakanda, legitimately placed there by its official process, he has the force of the state behind him. With his inclination to violence and selfishness, Killmonger has come to embody the kind of leadership he and his people suffered under in a racist environment, so that the people of Wakanda experience the conflicts that caused the Black Panther Party and other liberation movements to rise up against what most white Americans viewed as a legitimate power structure.

Ultimately, however, Killmonger's desire for violent revolution is shown to be a quixotic dream, thwarted by Wakandan forces which, empowered by freedom and autonomy, are the only thing that can stop his eruption of righteous, murderous anger.

"Wakanda Is Strong Enough ..."

Some aspects of Wakanda's position in the world can be seen as analogues for the United States, a metaphorical reflection and imagined alternative to failed American idealism. With its rich natural resources and enlightened, technologically advanced society, the fictional nation embodies the kind of state that the United States has described itself as in its mythology but has seldom been in practice – at least, for all its citizens. Indeed, Killmonger's grudge against Wakanda for ignoring and rejecting him is one that nearly every Black citizen could fairly hold against the United States. Certainly, in American society contemporary to the release of *Black Panther*, as the Black Lives Matter movement illustrates, systemic racism is prevalent – from the killing of Trayvon Martin that ignited the Black Lives Matter movement in 2013 to the controversy over Colin Kaepernick's kneeling in 2017 to the murder of George Floyd in 2020, which gave the movement global recognition (and caused an effect that saw widespread support for removing symbols of white supremacy throughout society, from Confederate statues to food products).

At the film's end, Wakanda abandons its traditional separatist position to follow the historical Black Panther Party's lead, pivoting from using the tools of modern warfare to protect Wakandans to channel its energy into uplifting social programs around the world, starting with the neighborhood in Oakland where the orphaned Killmonger grew up. T'Challa thus creates the first Wakandan International Outreach Centre, which will involve social outreach along with a science and information exchange.

While the popular image of the Black Panther Party focuses on its militancy and willingness to use violence, the organization long emphasized community service as well. The Party "moved with the people to implement Free Breakfast Programs to feed our hungry children, Free Health Clinics to care for the sick, Free Clothing Programs to clothe our needy, Liberation Schools to educate our youth, and Community Centers to keep the community informed."[22] These programs ran on values shared by Wakanda and the Panthers, as stated by Afreni Shakur: "you do not want us to rule you and we do not want you to rule us. We will rule ourselves, make our own progress ..."[23] One of the demands in a 1969 issue of *The Black Panther* newspaper was that "massive economic aid should be provided to rebuild the black community."[24] In *Black Panther*, this aid comes not from the negligent United States, but from Wakanda, the nation that represents an alternative history of lost potential – an African nation whose people had never been colonized or enslaved and who were able to develop without the interference and oppression they historically faced.

At first, the Wakandans wanted to deny the mistakes of their past. They wanted to ignore the Prodigal Son who pointedly blamed and challenged them, saying "Y'all sittin' up here comfortable." Ultimately, they learn from him, and while unable to undo the past, begin to make the right decisions in the present, ones that are aligned with their professed values. Claiming the right to bear arms against government tyranny, the historical Black Panther Party has given us the most constitutionally justified example of individual gun ownership that has ever been recorded: exactly what the Tea Party and white militia organizations wish they had as a justification for their stockpiles of weapons. Unlike those groups, the Black community has actually suffered from state tyranny, yet have been unable to effectively mobilize in self-defense against the state's monopoly on violence. This makes Killmonger's argument and T'Challa's solution significant.

As a role model for positive social change, and a sovereign nation that plays fair inside and outside its borders, Wakanda really does have something to offer the world and especially the contemporary United States. Indeed, T'Challa's speech to the United Nations echoes across the polarized, political divide plaguing America at the time of the film's release:

> Wakanda will no longer watch from the shadows. We cannot. We must not. We will work to be an example of how we as brothers and sisters on this Earth should treat each other. Now more than ever the illusions of division threaten our very existence. We all know the truth: more connects us than separates us. But in times of crisis the wise build bridges, while the foolish build barriers. We must find a way to look after one another as if we were one single tribe.

Of course, given all that's happened since *Black Panther*'s release – in our real world and in the Marvel Cinematic Universe's intermingled narrative – one wonders what message the sequel will advance.

Notes

1. Philip S. Foner and J. Bond, *The Black Panthers Speak: The Manifesto of the Party: The First Complete Documentary Record of the Panther's Program* (Philadelphia, PA: Lippincott, 1970), 2.
2. Maurice Mitchell, "The secret history of Black Panther by Stan Lee," The Geek Twins, 14 February, 20218, at http://www.thegeektwins.com/2018/02/the-secret-history-of-black-panther-by.html.
3. Joshua Bloom and Waldo E. Martin, *Black against Empire: The History and Politics of the Black Panther Party* (Berkeley, CA: University of California Press, 2016), 42.

4. Bloom and Martin, 43.
5. Curtis J. Austin, *Up against the Wall: Violence in the Making and Unmaking of the Black Panther Party* (Fayetteville, AR: University of Arkansas Press, 2006), 121.
6. Black Panther Party member Afreni Shakur in her "Letter from Prison," quoted in Foner and Bond, 163.
7. Foner and Bond, 3.
8. Foner and Bond, 3.
9. Robert F. Williams, *Negroes with Guns* (Detroit, MI: Wayne State University Press, 1998), 112.
10. Williams, 4.
11. Williams, 76.
12. Williams, 76.
13. Robert F. Williams, *Negroes with Guns* (Detroit, MI: Wayne State University Press, 1998).
14. Max Weber, "Politics as a Vocation," in H.H. Gerth and C. Wright Mills trans. and eds., *Max Weber: Essays in Sociology* (New York: Oxford University Press, 1946), 78. Italics in original.
15. Austin, 153.
16. Chris Hayes, *A Colony in a Nation* (New York: W.W. Norton & Company, 2017).
17. Nikhil Pal Singh, *Black Is a Country: Race and the Unfinished Struggle for Democracy* (Cambridge, MA: Harvard University Press, 2004), 201.
18. Bloom and Martin, 57.
19. Bloom and Martin, 41.
20. Williams, 75.
21. Austin, 158.
22. Foner and Bond, 13.
23. Foner and Bond, 163.
24. Foner and Bond, 178.

25

Fear of a Black Museum
Black Existentialism in *Black Panther*

Charles F. Peterson

KILLMONGER: Now, tell me about this one.
MUSEUM DIRECTOR: Also from Benin, seventh century. Fula tribe, I believe.
KILLMONGER: Nah.
MUSEUM DIRECTOR: I beg your pardon?
KILLMONGER: It was taken by British soldiers in Benin but it's from Wakanda and it's made out of vibranium. Don't trip, I'mma take it off your hands for you.
MUSEUM DIRECTOR: These items aren't for sale.
KILLMONGER: How do you think your ancestors got these? You think they paid a fair price? Or did they take it like they took everything else?
MUSEUM DIRECTOR: Sir, I'm going to have to ask you to leave.

Of course, Killmonger doesn't leave. He and Klaue steal the mining tool from the museum, along with an elaborate African mask. And yet, is it fair to say that Killmonger doesn't just take the mining tool and mask, but that he takes them back? After all, doesn't Killmonger have a point when he questions the Museum Director about how the African artifacts were obtained by British soldiers? Did Killmonger steal them or reclaim them?

Museums, or rather, curatorial spaces, are strange places, aren't they? In one sense, they house objects of historical value. Yet, in another sense, museums are fundamentally inseparable from the project of Modernity (globalization). The modern idea of a space to gather and observe a collection of objects from across the world, assembled as a distillation of the idea of a universal humanity, hinges upon the mechanics of European imperial expansion across the globe. The aggressive contact of Western European states and cultures with the Indigenous societies of Africa, the Americas, and Asia, starting in the late fifteenth century and lasting into the late twentieth century, became the ground for the establishment of

Black Panther and Philosophy: What Can Wakanda Offer the World?, First Edition. Edited by Edwardo Pérez and Timothy E. Brown.

European-based normative valuations along political, economic, social, cultural, and technological lines. These valuations created binary systems of meaning wherein the peoples, cultures, histories, and artifacts of the subjugated groups were diminished in their standing and ordered as inferior to their European and (later) American counterparts, while the aspects of Euro-American cultures were exalted and consolidated the belief of their dominance.

So, yeah, Killmonger has a point, not just about museums and the way they curate the artifacts on display, but about how these artifacts are displayed and what their display represents, especially with regard to African existence. Indeed, what does an African display really say about Africa and African identity? How does a curatorial space function as a means of power and culture? How does *Black Panther* use the museum scene to illustrate a fear of Black museums and the problems of existence observed through the philosophies of Black existentialism and Africana phenomenology?

To understand all of this, we need to first understand the history and nature of museums.

"They Tell Me You're the Expert."

The museum of the colonial moment fused the expansion of knowledge and global contact of North Atlantic powers with the aggressive nation-alist pride of their hegemonic positions, building national, cultural, and racial identity through framing.[1] This aggressive contact between North Atlantic societies and "the rest of us," was also based on brutal acts of violence, disruption, and resource exploitation, including the expropriation of minerals, crops, peoples, and artifacts.[2] The Museum Director may not have wanted to admit it, but Killmonger knew his history. Consider what Kwame Anthony Appiah says about the looting of the Asante king's palace by British commander Major Robert Stephenson Smyth Baden-Powell (later founder of the Boy Scouts organization) in 1895: "There are similar stories to be told around the world. The Belgian *Musée de l'Afrique Centrale*, at Tervuren, explored the dark side of the origins of its own collections in the brutal history of the Belgian Congo, in a 2001 show called 'ExItCongoMuseum.'"[3]

Of course, this brutal history is never really addressed in museums because museums are supposed to be refined spaces where patrons reflect on the works of humanity. It's certainly worth noting that even Killmonger, though dressed a bit loudly, wears glasses and presents himself seriously as he enquires about the African artifacts. Yet, the truth that Killmonger unmasks is that museums are whitewashed, framing the works on display through a lens that does not present the remnants of disrupted cultures and trophies of war, but rather treats "artifacts" as objects that seem to exist outside of humanity – they're priceless and, as the Museum Director notes, they're "not for sale."

The effect of this whitewashing erases the actual history of the way artifacts have been procured, de-contextualized, and mounted in an ahistorical light of aesthetic purity in, as Foucault would say, "the immediate beyond of time and space." It is a space where histories are scrubbed by the necessities of ideological and cultural imperative and the lives of entire groups positioned in an archaic amber of temporal immobility. So, while Killmonger is right to question this mode of presentation, his questioning isn't just confined to the scene with the Museum Director. Indeed, his taking of the African mask, which can be analyzed on many philosophical and psychological levels, continues the questioning throughout the film as his own identity shifts from Erik "Killmonger" Stevens to N'Jadaka, son of N'Jobu and cousin to T'Challa, to King of Wakanda.

Indeed, Killmonger's actions and questions in the museum disrupt the pristine illusion of the exhibit. His reclaiming of the artifacts is not quite the restorative violence advocated by Frantz Fanon.[4] Nonetheless Killmonger's actions – by breaking the colonial milieu, asserting the agency of African (Wakandan American) people, and disrupting the performance of dominance arranged by the museum – create space for new and different expressions of the identity, cultures, and histories of colonized people, in the museum/curatorial space.

To better understand this, let's examine what it means to curate cultural identity.

"Nah, I'm Just Feeling It."

In 2006, The Louvre Museum invited African American writer Toni Morrison (1931–2019) to curate an exhibit, which she chose to create around Théodore Géricault's painting *The Raft of the Medusa*, which she sees as articulating unspoken realities of historic and contemporary imperial conditions. Morrison states:

> When you look at it you see the raft has been cut away from the main ship and they are just left to survive or drown. And they were all lower class or enslaved people or laborers, and there's this one figure at the top [...] looks like a young black boy pointing, maybe he sees a rescue ship, maybe not, but that whole notion of misery and being cut off from the colonial ship struck me as symbolic of what the whole [exhibit] would be about.[5]

While Morrison's exhibit doesn't directly relate to *Black Panther* (though wouldn't it have been cool, in a Stan Lee cameo kind of way, if Morrison had been cast as a council elder or Wakandan poet laureate?) her observations nevertheless highlight an interesting perspective, especially in relation to Killmonger, as his arrival in Wakanda mirrors the Géricault painting. Indeed, Killmonger is like the boy in the painting, a boy cut off from his home yet also searching for his home and trying to not just find it, but reclaim it, like Killmonger does with the mask and like he does when he fights T'Challa and becomes king. Similarly, Morrison's thoughts on the exhibit enhance this perspective. As she states:

> The history of slavery in America has been mangled, cleaned up, made sanitary and polished. For me, the act of re-imagining and imagining is a kind of saying goodbye, paying my respects, putting flesh on memory, putting flesh on anonymous people, keeping them intellectually and emotionally alive, it's as though people looked away, so I thought it was time not to blink, to look at it the way it really was.[6]

Morrison's focus on migrants as a historic population – identity and migration as a condition inextricably bound to the wielding of power and bringing that discussion into the heart of "Western" material consciousness, as it were – is a form of truth-telling. By confronting the structures of Western identity (race, class, gender, sexuality) and by focusing on people marginal to those structures yet necessary to the binary nature of those artifices, it is a revelation of the hidden heart of the museum's presentation, its way of existing. The figures in *The Raft of the Medusa*, women, the poor, lowborn, and enslaved, are outsiders, those whose labor and exploitation made the museum and the narrative of the museum possible and whose lives were rarely seen as worthy of the museum's attentions.

Killmonger also engaged in truth-telling – at the museum, when he questioned the director about the history of the artifacts and how they were obtained, and in Wakanda, when he confronted the council and when he forced T'Challa to reckon with Wakanda's past (not just T'Chaka killing N'Jobu, but also Wakanda's history of isolation). In fact, T'Challa begins to question the past after he sees Killmonger wearing the mask and wearing N'Jobu's ring, which causes Zuri to admit the truth of what T'Chaka did to N'Jobu and what T'Chaka and Zuri did to Killmonger as a boy.

Killmonger's mask is largely symbolic for Killmonger – as he says, he's just "feeling it." But N'Jobu's ring functions much like the mining tool, as it represents a past that was taken and a past that was reclaimed. Killmonger himself embodies various truths – through his lip tattoo, which represents his connection to Wakanda; through the marks on his body, which represent the reality of his American military experience; through his very existence, which stands as a living reminder of T'Challa's failure as a king and Wakanda's failure as a nation.

One way to understand the significance of Killmonger's truth-telling, or truth-revealing, is to look at it through Plato's Allegory of the Cave. The allegory describes a group of people living their entire lives chained to a wall in a cave. The group faces a blank wall, watching shadows projected from objects passing in front of a fire behind them (which is what it might feel like if we watched a non-stop marathon of every Marvel Cinematic

Universe film on endless loop). Truth (and reality) is revealed when one of them breaks free and leaves the cave to discover the real world. This is the truth-telling Morrison references and it's the truth-revealing that Killmonger engages in when he confronts the Wakandan council, forcing them to see beyond their metaphorical Wakandan cave. It's also what makes Killmonger's last words so interesting when he tells T'Challa: "Bury me in the ocean with my ancestors that jumped from the ships 'cause they knew that death was better than bondage." This is another form of truth-revealing, one with at least two meanings. On one hand, there's the historical reference to the conditions of slavery and the slave trade, which is a history many often don't want to confront. On the other hand, Killmonger is yet again reminding T'Challa of the reality of Wakanda's role in the slave trade that lasted 400 years.

"The Real Question Is: What are Those?!"

Killmonger's questioning of Wakanda reveals the truth and effect of Wakanda's isolationist history. Yet, Wakanda is nevertheless shown as a representation of African history, not just in the tribal nature of Wakanda's social structure or in the clothing and physical adornments and jewelry, but also in the rituals and spirituality. Does this function like the mining tool and hammer in the Museum of Great Britain? Is the representation of "African" in *Black Panther*'s depiction of Wakanda a way to celebrate African heritage? Is the representation accurate? And how does it square with the criticism Killmonger (who observed that "y'all must be comfortable") leveled?

The very presence of Killmonger presents a dilemma for T'Challa and Wakanda. It's as if Killmonger himself is a relic, representing several levels of Wakandan and American history. First, he is the son of N'Jobu. So, as N'Jadaka, Killmonger represents Wakanda's past, from his lip tattoo and lineage to the painful reminder of N'Jobu's fate and T'Chaka's and Zuri's crime. In this sense, Killmonger is essentially an inconvenient truth that Wakanda doesn't really want to acknowledge or face. As Zuri tells T'Challa, "some truths are too much to bear." Certainly, Ramonda's reaction emphasizes Zuri's point, as she shuns Killmonger – first, by suggesting T'Challa "reject his request," then by accusing Killmonger of lying, and then by claiming that Killmonger "has no rights here."

On another level, Killmonger represents American culture, which means he's an outsider. But, he's not just an outsider, he's an American outsider influenced and trained by colonizers and colonizer methods, which are puzzling to Wakandans. Killmonger may claim to know "how colonizers think," but by showing no respect for Wakandan traditions and customs or Wakandan history and by advocating the use of Wakandan War Dogs to disseminate vibranium weapons throughout the world to enact violent uprisings, Killmonger, for all his Wakandan heritage, acts like a stereotypical American. He may rely on Wakandan tradition in order to gain the throne, but once he becomes king, his actions only benefit himself, not Wakanda, especially when he has the crop of Heart-Shaped Herbs destroyed (which essentially erases Wakandan tradition).

What we see, then, is that Killmonger's dual existence (African Wakandan and African American) resembles what W.E.B. Du Bois (1868–1963) referred to as a double-consciousness. As Du Bois writes in his essay "Strivings of the Negro People":

> After the Egyptian and Indian, the Greek and Roman, the Teuton and Mongolian, the Negro is a sort of seventh son, born with a veil, and gifted with second-sight in this American world, – a world which yields him no true self-consciousness, but only lets him see himself through the revelation of the other world. It is a peculiar sensation, this double-consciousness, this sense of always looking at one's self through the eyes of others, of measuring one's soul by the tape of a world that looks on in amused contempt and pity. One ever feels his two-ness, – an American, a Negro; two souls, two thoughts, two unreconciled strivings; two warring ideals in one dark body, whose dogged strength alone keeps it from being torn asunder.[7]

As Drucilla Cornell notes, for Du Bois, "the process of negrification allows blacks only to appear as a problem, and not as human beings carrying on in the course of their day-to-day life."[8] Again, this is how Killmonger is treated, isn't it? He is a problem that must be dealt with, and he's a problem because of his two-ness. Yet, the double-consciousness Du Bois speaks of can be applied to anyone who has experienced life outside of Wakanda.

For example, Nakia (and perhaps all Wakandan War Dogs) has experienced enough of the world that she begins to sympathize with it, as did Killmonger's father N'Jobu (and to a lesser extent, Zuri). In other words, whereas Wakandans who remain isolated might only have a single consciousness, those who leave, like Nakia, return with a double-consciousness, because they've been exposed to how the outside world, the world of the colonizer, thinks and acts in relation to Black people, perhaps in much the same way as Du Bois recounted, writing that "It dawned on me with a certain suddenness that I was different from others; or like, mayhap, in heart and life and longing, but shut out from their world by a vast veil."[9]

It's significant that, for Nakia (and for Killmonger), the problem isn't Black people, it's the oppressors and "colonizers," which is why Nakia and Killmonger want to use Wakandan technology to help those being oppressed. Even Shuri (who doesn't seem to have ever left Wakanda, but who seems to be familiar with the outside world) views colonizers in a similar way. This is what makes T'Challa's decision to open Wakanda to the outside world so interesting. If Wakanda exists in a single consciousness, why risk the double-consciousness observed by Du Bois? T'Challa may want to aid the outside world, but in doing so doesn't he put Wakandans at risk, not just of their technology being exploited or their non-interference being questioned (because, couldn't they have helped in World War I and World War II and in so many other conflicts and catastrophes throughout history?), but of their Wakandan identity being irrevocably changed?

"We Let the Fear of Our Discovery Stop Us from Doing What Is Right."

In describing Africana phenomenology and the double-consciousness observed by Du Bois, Paget Henry contrasts Du Bois with G.W.F. Hegel (1770–1831). As Henry explains, "The divided Hegelian subject moves between a desire for an 'I' that is autonomous and self-constituting, and the need for confirmation and recognition from the other."[10] But, as Henry notes, once an Africana subject is racialized, it can no longer move in a Hegelian way.[11] Rather, in the double-consciousness of Du Bois, "dualizing is not the source of the two poles between which the Africana subject oscillates. This subject moves not between a changeable 'I' and an unchangeable 'Other' but between two 'We's'."[12]

This helps explain Killmonger's double-consciousness. He's not a Wakandan or an African American, he's inseparably both. Unlike T'Chaka, who seemed to remain a Hegelian subject, oscillating between the Wakandan world and the outer world during his reign and choosing Wakanda over his brother N'Jobu (and choosing to leave young Erik behind), Killmonger is a DuBoisian subject who can't oscillate or choose. In fact, it's the recognition of his double-consciousness that seems to drive Killmonger's actions, from the museum to aiding Klaue to taking over Wakanda to even his death. Yet, consider Dwayne A. Tunstall's understanding of Africana Existentialism, according to which an Africana subject could perform an "ego displacement," not as a choice of which consciousness to embody, but rather as the ability to step outside one's consciousness. As Tunstall explains:

> One can think of "ego displacement" as what occurs once one suspends one's existential judgments about the world. In the case of racial identities, by distancing ourselves from the presuppositions of an antiblack world, we have a chance to examine how such a world is co-constituted by us. We are able to examine how we uncritically "take up" the already existing racial landscape for ourselves and for others. It places us in a position where we can acknowledge our complicity in perpetuating a world that dehumanizes people due to their racial identities.[13]

Certainly, Killmonger wants Wakanda to acknowledge its complicity through inaction, but so does T'Challa, eventually. It's why he confronts his father in the spirit realm and accuses his father and his ancestors of being wrong to "turn your backs on the rest of the world." In doing this,

T'Challa seems to transition from a Hegelian subject, who, like his father, was initially intent on keeping Wakanda isolated, into a DuBoisian one, whose goal is to open Wakanda to the world. This would indeed alter Wakanda and Wakandan identity to the point that a double-consciousness would likely emerge – but one that, as Tunstall notes, they could reflect on. Of course, we'll have to wait until *Black Panther 2* to see the full effect of T'Challa's decision.

"So, Could We All Just Wrap It Up and Go Home?"

Cornell sees Africana phenomenology as being unique in relation to European phenomenology because "the occasion for transcendental reflection is the confrontation with the searing force of racism and what Du Bois called negrification rather than in Husserl, often considered the founder of European phenomenology, the crisis of European reason."[14] Cornell goes on to explain that, from this, Black philosophies "attempt to respond to the ontological imposition that W.E.B. Du Bois often remarked was the central question for a black human being: What am I other than a problem in white society?"[15] As Cornell notes, Du Bois offers two ways for Blacks to answer this question and overcome the double-consciousness "in which the 'we' of shared cultural traditions has been shattered by negrification."[16] The first way is for Blacks to project and produce "ways of being a 'we' that goes beyond the stereotypes of black face."[17] The second is "to cultivate not a 'we' but an 'I' of first sight in which the black person can at least see himself or herself as a thinking subject."[18]

Certainly, Killmonger and T'Challa (and many characters in *Black Panther*) proceeded along the lines of cultivating an "I" and seeing themselves as thinking subjects. Yet, it seems that while T'Challa was able to project himself beyond the stereotype, Killmonger adhered to it, being unable to separate himself from the negrification imposed on him as an African American. He may be able to question the world and challenge the existence imposed on Black people by colonizers, but his declaration of knowing "how colonizers think" seems to serve more as a reinforcement of the negrification and negation of his existence rather than a liberation from it. Returning to the scene in the museum, Killmonger may have been "feeling it" with the mask, but in stealing it and in wearing it, he didn't shed his double-consciousness. Rather, he embraced it, as if he had to remind himself that his face was black. In this sense, he didn't just reclaim the mask, he also reclaimed the negrification it imposed.

Notes

1. Alesandra De Angelis, et al., "Introduction: Disruptive Encounters – Museums, Arts and Postcoloniality," in Alesandra DeAngelis, et al., eds., *The Postcolonial Museum: The Arts of Memory and the Pressures of History* (New York: Routledge, 2014), 11.
2. Chinweizu Ibekwe, *The West and the Rest of Us: White Predators, Black Slavers and the African Elite* (New York: Vintage Books, 1975).
3. Kwame Anthony Appiah, *Cosmopolitanism: Ethics in a World of Strangers* (New York: W.W. Norton and Company, 2006), 116.
4. Frantz Fanon, *The Wretched of the Earth*, trans. Richard Philcox (New York: Grove Press, 2005).
5. *The Foreigner's Home*. Dir. Rian Brown and Geoff Pingree. 2018.
6. Brown and Pingree.
7. W.E.B. Du Bois, "Strivings of the Negro people," *The Atlantic*, August 1897, at https://www.theatlantic.com/magazine/archive/1897/08/strivings-of-the-negro-people/305446.
8. Drucilla Cornell, *Moral Images of Freedom: A Future for Critical Theory* (Lanham, MD: Rowman & Littlefield, 2007), 105.
9. W.E.B. Du Bois.
10. Paget Henry, "Africana phenomenology: Its philosophical implications," *Worlds & Knowledges Otherwise*, Fall (2016), 7.
11. Which, for Henry, means that an Africana subject has been defined in relation to white. For Henry, this also means that "As a racialized subject, the Africana individual remains very much within the terms of the master-slave relationship." Henry, 7.
12. Henry, 7.
13. Dwayne A. Tunstall, "Taking Africana existential philosophy of education seriously," *Philosophical Studies in Education* 39 (2008), 48.
14. Cornell, 106.
15. Cornell, 106.
16. Cornell, 108.
17. Cornell, 108.
18. Cornell, 108.

Index

Black Panther and Philosophy: What Can Wakanda Offer the World?, First Edition. Edited by Edwardo Pérez and Timothy E. Brown.
© 2022 John Wiley & Sons, Inc. Published 2022 by John Wiley & Sons, Inc.

9 781119 635840